DESIRING *R*EVOLUTION

Columbia University Press   New York

Jane Gerhard

DESIRING REVOLUTION

SECOND-WAVE FEMINISM

AND THE REWRITING OF

AMERICAN SEXUAL THOUGHT,

1920 TO 1982

COLUMBIA UNIVERSITY PRESS

PUBLISHERS SINCE 1893

NEW YORK   CHICHESTER, WEST SUSSEX

Copyright © 2001 Columbia University Press

All rights reserved

Library of Congress Cataloging-in-Publication Data

Gerhard, Jane F.

  Desiring revolution : second-wave feminism and the
rewriting of American sexual thought, 1920 to 1982 /
Jane F. Gerhard.

       p.   cm.

  Includes bibliographical references and index.

  ISBN 0-231-11204-1 (cloth : alk. paper) —

  ISBN 0-231-11205-X (pbk. : alk. paper)

     1. Feminism—United States—History—20th century.
2. Women—United States—Sexual behavior—History—
20th century. 3. Sex (Psychology) I. Title.

  HQ1421.G47 2001

  305.42'0973'0904—dc21

                                    00-063863

Casebound editions of Columbia University Press books are
printed on permanent and durable acid-free paper.

Printed in the United States of America

c 10 9 8 7 6 5 4 3 2 1

p 10 9 8 7 6 5 4 3 2 1

CONTENTS

As I WRITE, I LOOK AT A PICTURE OF TWO GIRLS, MAYBE AGE ELEVEN, holding posters demanding girl's liberation. It's a photo taken in the late 1960s and included in the anthology *Radical Feminism* edited by Anne Koedt. I bumped into it when I began this project years ago, and it's been on the wall behind my computer ever since. On some level, I am one of those girls. Or, to put it another way, it might as well be me. I was dying to be a feminist when I was ten. Even then I knew those women on TV were on to something big. With uncanny attunement, people at church began asking if I'd burned my bra. I would if I had one, I muttered under my breath. Feminism was at the center of my midwestern mind and I had no idea what it was, beyond a vague and insistent recognition that it was about female empowerment.

And so now, twenty years plus later, I am a feminist. And I write about the history of feminism. Feminism remains at the center of my world, much more problematized, much more criticized, much more ambivalently than when I went to church in Ohio. I've seen feminism move from being on the forefront of what was possible to becoming a label with which few younger women want to be associated. Just how and why feminism matters—to me, to women I don't know, to critics, and to twentieth-century American culture—motivates my work.

I have many institutions to thank. Foremost, I want to thank the Department of American Civilization at Brown University for providing me with a professional home for many years and for financial support. The Schlesinger Library Dissertation Research Grant, Radcliffe College and the Bell Brothers Foundation at the Lilly Library, University of Indiana provided me with necessary and appreciated financial support as well. I want to thank Ann Miller and Susan Pensak at Columbia University Press for their invaluable help in bringing this volume into existence.

I want to thank the teachers who helped me become the feminist and scholar I am.

My heartfelt thanks go to Susan J. Douglas for starting it all. I never recovered from Susan's "Images of Women in Popular Culture" at Hampshire College. I am grateful as well to Susan Smulyan who offered me her friendship as well as crucial institutional and intellectual support. I want to thank Lisa Duggan who appeared at Brown just as I turned my intellectual attention to the history of sexuality. Finally, I stand in a long line of scholars who have benefited enormously from Mari Jo Buhle's sense of humor and intellectual savvy. Mari Jo pushed me constantly to write better, think with more precision, and to include more. She also provided me with ongoing conversations about feminism and psychoanalysis that have enriched my thinking. Mari Jo has always been my toughest critic, a valued teacher, and my friend.

I have been privileged to be a part of a wonderful group of feminist historians: Lucy Barber, Gail Bederman, Elizabeth Francis, Melanie McAlester, Donna Penn, Uta Poigner, and Jessica Shobow. My special thanks go to Ruth Feldstein for her friendship and support since the first day of graduate school. Ruth's friendship has always provided me with both a bridge into my work and a path back into the rest of my life, peopled by husbands, babies, mothers, and friends. I want to thank Dorothee Kocks and Linda Carter for their contributions to my thinking about feminism. Thank you a thousand times to these friends who made my project better. All mistakes and shortcomings are, of course, entirely my own.

Being a scholar on the margins, as many of us are these days, I want to thank my students at Brown University, the Massachusetts Institute of

Technology, the downtown campus of the University of Rhode Island, and Harvard Uniersity, whose questions helped me clarify my project. Their interest provided me with a professional home, even if I was without an office or a desk to call my own. On those days when I didn't know where I was or if I had the right books in my bag, they reminded me that I was a part of something larger than myself.

To Zeb Stern, six at this writing, and May Stern, two, thanks for making the heavy task of scholarship seem like a welcome haven of order in the face of your stormy, overwhelming, breathtaking love. These two made me into a mother and provided me with new appreciation for why second-wave feminism matters. To David Stern: how can I possibly thank you for everything you've done for me and meant to me? I can't. All I can say is, meet me upstairs in a half an hour.

DESIRING REVOLUTION

INTRODUCTION

Sex and the Feminist, 1970

American women are suffering, quite simply, a massive sickness of sex without self. No one has warned them that sex can never be a substitute for personal identity; that sex itself cannot give identity to a woman, any more than to a man; that there may be no sexual fulfillment at all for the woman who seeks her self in sex.
—Betty Friedan, *The Feminine Mystique*, 1963

The revolutionary woman must know her enemies, the doctors, psychiatrists, health visitors, priests, marriage counselors, police-men, magistrates and genteel reformers, all the authoritarians and dogmatists who flock about her with warning and advice.
—Germaine Greer, *The Female Eunuch*, 1970

We take the woman's side in everything.
—New York Radical Women, "Principles," 1970

We feel that we need sex, but the issue is very confused. What is it we really need? Is it orgasms? Intercourse? Intimacy with another human being? Stroking? Companionship? Human kindness? And do we "need" it physically or psychologically?
—Dana Densmore, *No More Fun and Games*, 1971

The Women's Liberation Movement caught men off guard. They thought women had already been liberated by the Sexual Revolution.
—Anselma Dell'Olio, *Ms.*, 1972

She moves her fingers to that rhythm, feeling the two inside get creamy and the clitoris get hard and red. Can you feel colors in your finger tips? This is what red feels like. The inner cave feels purple. Royal purple. As if the blood down there were blue.
—Erica Jong, *Fear of Flying*, 1973

My sexual rage was the most powerful single emotion of my life, and the feminist analysis has become for me, as I think it will for most women of my generation, as significant an intellectual tool as Marxism was for generations of radicals. But it does not answer every question.
—Sara Davidson, *Loose Change*, 1977

There was a period in the late 1960s and early 1970s when sex mattered in a whole new way. Perhaps short-lived, perhaps misguidedly, most certainly selectively, but for a moment, sex was at the center of women's impending liberation. A new generation of feminists envisioned sexual pleasure as empowering, as helping men become more human, and as a route out of patriarchal repression of the body. While pleasure did not mean the same thing to every woman, it nonetheless became synonymous, briefly, with liberation.

This moment of radical feminism sits at the center of *Desiring Revolution*. Most simply, *Desiring Revolution* is a book about why sexuality mattered to the second wave of feminism in the 1960s and 1970s. And, as it offers answers to that deceptively simple question, it get to be about many other things as well. As the above epigraphs show, sexuality meant different things to different feminists. Whereas Betty Friedan viewed sex as part of a false self women had adopted, Erica Jong saw it as the center of her authentic self. Whereas Dana Densmore questioned what it was exactly that women desired from sex, Germaine Greer pointed out how many male experts claimed that they alone knew exactly what women wanted or should want from sex.

It has become a truism to say that sexuality mattered to feminists in the late 1960s because feminist politics *was* the politics of personal life. Yet I believe this is a somewhat circular misremembering. This book argues that conflicts about sexuality for many women—about what they wanted from sex, about what they had learned about themselves (and men) by learning about sex, about what counted as "real" sex—lay the groundwork for what would become their feminism. For a specific generation, coming of age in a certain historical moment, existing in an optimistic and activist era, much of what galled women into feminism was precisely the sense of injustice forged in and through all things sexual. For radical feminists, the sexual included feminine socialization, beauty standards, sexual practices, experts' accounts of health, and the whole range of interpersonal dynamics between women and their sexual partners. In this light, sexuality mattered because feminists saw it as the raw material out of which standards of womanhood were forged. Sexuality and gender came together to create the whole continuum of female icons they rejected: the "ideal," the "normal," the "modern" and the "liberated" woman.

When I began to read and research second-wave feminism, I discovered that little had been written about what I considered to be a radical body of writing on female sexual pleasure. We had groundbreaking analyses of the connections between the women's liberation movement and the civil rights and student new left movements, accounts of the various groups of women that made up the second wave, and numerous other narrative histories of women's encounters with feminism the 1960s.[1] But nothing had been written that examined the role that sexual pleasure, or the discussion of sexual pleasure in particular, played in the creation of feminism.

There are many stories to tell about radical feminism. But the one I tell in *Desiring Revolution* is a history of how predominantly white middle-class radical feminists came to see sexuality as the primarily source of both women's oppression and their liberation. Sexual pleasure came to matter most to white middle-class feminists in the early 1970s for a number of reasons. Young, white middle-class feminists, who lay the foundation of a radical theory of women's sexual freedom, focused on sexuality because a new version of sexual expressiveness had become a key element in their generational identity. Fifties America ironically planted the seeds for what in the 1960s would flower into a new attention to sexual pleasure. In the late 1940s and 1950s anxiety about sexual behavior explicitly and implicitly influenced the situation of public discourse in the homophobic convergence of anticommunist rhetoric and popular Freudianism, in the celebration of heterosexual normalcy in the reification of home and family, and in the search by bohemians, intellectuals, young people, and cultural misfits for a more pleasurable, less rule-bound way to be. Across the cultural landscape, then, sexuality came to be linked to identity and utopian visions of a better way to live. Soon-to-be feminists, who like their male counterparts absorbed the pervasive and contradictory messages about sexuality and identity in the 1950s, desired to liberate their bodies. To do so required them to specify their relationship with sexuality as uniquely inflected in and through their experiences of girlhood and womanhood.

At the same time, only relatively privileged white middle-class women could afford, in 1969 and 1970, to see their oppression as located solely at the intersection of sexuality and gender. Radical women of color noted that minority and working women marked their identities through the overlapping simultaneous experiences of racism, classism, and homophobia, and, pointedly, that only white women could see other white women as oppressed. Black feminists, in particular, were quick to argue that the history of racism was very much bound up with sexual assault against black women and false myths about the black male rapist. Black feminists argued that white women who saw sexuality intersecting only with gender roles could not speak to the experiences of nonwhite women. Minority feminists' critiques of white feminism ascended in the 1980s with the explosion of writings about women of color that permanently changed the face of feminism, including anthologies such as *This Bridge Called My Back* (1981), *All the Women Are White, All the Women Are White, All the Blacks Are Men, But Some of Us Are Brave* (1982), and *Making Waves* (1989) and in writings by bell hooks, Audre Lorde, and Alice Walker, among others.[2]

This important revision of radical feminism has been taken up by third-wave feminists who are actively creating feminist theory that does not replicate the mistakes of their second-wave predecessors. In *Listen Up* (1995), *To Be Real* (1995), and *Third-Wave Agenda* (1997), third wavers point out that they already understand that identity is forged through *competing* identifications, and thus they embrace contradiction.[3] According to Leslie Heywood and Jennifer Drake, "The definitional moment of third wave feminism has been theorized as proceeding from critiques of the white women's movement that were initiated by women of color, as well as from the many instances of coalition work undertaken by U.S. third world feminists."[4] Coalition based on strategic alliance rather than universal categories like "woman" and "sister" characterize the political worldview of contemporary young feminists.

Yet as right as it is for third-wave feminists to begin their histories with the insights of radical women of color in the 1980s, there are also good things to be gained from remembering the insights of radical feminists in the early 1970s. The story of how "woman" became a political category, a category appropriately discarded in the late 1990s as unworkable at best and racist at worst, remains a useful one to remember. Without the politicizing of woman as a category, feminism could not have advanced. *Desiring Revolution* tells the story of how radical feminists in the late 1960s and early 1970s made woman into a political classification, highlighting both the strategic brilliance of that move and its problematic, self-defeating results. They made that move not in isolation but in dialogue and revision of what had come before them and what was taking place around them. Radical feminists participated in and transformed an ongoing discourse, by intellectuals and novelists, scientists and activists from the 1910s to the 1960s, in popular culture and academic scholarship. The explicit subject of this discourse was female sexual desire and the implicit subject, the nature of health and liberation. The conversation, if you will, whose history I've selectively reconstructed through its intersections with second-wave feminism, I refer to as twentieth-century American sexual thought.

The first half of this volume reconstructs dominant expert views of women and normal female sexuality from the 1910s to the 1960s. It was this tradition, the subject of chapter 1, that began with marriage experts in the 1910s, was added to by Freud in the 1920s, and reified into orthodoxy by American Freudians in the interwar years, second-wave feminists challenged as oppressive and misogynist. Together, marriage experts and new psychoanalytic scientists of sexuality made a significant case for how and why female sexuality was utterly and essentially unlike male sexuality. Reaching a high-water mark in the 1940s, American sex experts effectively mobilized the implicit antifeminism of Freudian psychoanalysis to argue that healthy women's sexuality was fundamentally bound up with having children.

In chapter 2 I show how and why this conception of (normal, white) female sexuality began to change in the 1950s and 1960s. The sex studies of Alfred Kinsey and Masters and Johnson dismissed much of this Freudian-dominated discourse. They claimed that their research showed women to be as sexually responsive and competent as men and, further, that reproduction had little to do with women's enjoyment of sex. When feminists in the early 1970s sought to reimagine female sexuality, they drew on and rewrote elements of both psychoanalytic and sexologic knowledge to do so. I argue that radical feminism cannot be understood without situating it in this longer trajectory of American sexual thought.

Chapters 3 and 4 focus on radical feminists' dreams of sexual freedom in the years from 1968 to 1975. As other historians have noted, radical feminism should not be seen as a coherent unified movement. Women who came together for consciousness-raising, in women's liberation groups or for "actions," rejected top-down models of leadership. They embraced, or tried to make workable, an orderly anarchy. As a group, they were tired of being silenced, eager to rewrite the rules, and contentious. Groups came together only to dissolve in six months out of frustration over their competing views of how to proceed. Groups debated each other as well. The body of sexual theory generated in this volatile moment of second-wave feminism was not, and was never intended to be, unified and consistent. Rather, it should be understood as encompassing widely divergent views of what women wanted from sex, what they wanted from men, and what they wanted from feminism.

That said, a theme nevertheless emerges when radical feminist theory is examined as a whole. That theme is the political importance of women's sexual self-determination. Feminists agreed on little else beyond the shared value of women determining for themselves what they wanted from sex. Lesbian separatists shared sexual self-determination as a value with radical heterosexual women, with feminists who saw sex and orgasm as overrated and "a male thing," and with the "militant clitorialists." Sexual freedom within second-wave feminism was about women actively determining what should happen to their bodies, about empowering women to feel entitled to their desires whatever they may be, and about transforming men—experts and boyfriends—enough for them to listen and ideally, to change.

This commitment to women's sexual self-determination shaped how feminists in the late 1960s and early 1970s saw the clitoris. Within early radical feminism, the clitoris became a distinctively feminist body part. The clitoris offered radical feminists an organ whose sole purpose was pleasure. Unlike the vagina, associated with motherhood and heterosexuality, the clitoris could stand in for a female sexuality that lay beyond or beneath sexual classifications. In feminists' sex discourse, the rhetoric of the clitoris became saturated with the values of autonomy, authenticity, and liberation. Lesbians and straight women alike could claim it as part of their sexual practice. Experts misunderstood it. Men feared it. As Anne Koedt pointed out in "The Myth of the Vaginal Orgasm," men were suspiciously aware of the clitoris during "foreplay" but "forgot" about it when "real" sex (intercourse) began. Men feared the clitoris, radical feminists argued, because they knew, deep in their hearts, that women did not require a penis to reach orgasm. Such insights led radical feminists to reinvent both heterosexuality and lesbianism as more woman-centered and less dictated by the categories and standards of men and experts.

Part of the symbolic values feminists placed on the clitoris came out of the counterculture of the 1960s, with its celebration of pleasure for pleasure's sake. "Free love" stood for sexual pleasure freed from deadening conformity, monogamy, and possessiveness. It was as much a critique of the values of capitalism that made everything into a commodity as it was about enacting a new sense of wonder about what was possible. At the same time feminists participated in the values and rituals of the counterculture, they also rejected much of it as sexist, male-centered, and oppressive to women. They absorbed and refashioned the liberated (male) body of the 1960s revolutions, with its free orgasms and unregulated pleasures, and specified it for women. Radical feminists asserted that lots of sex with lots of people did not constitute sexual freedom for women, that orgasms were overrated—particularly when men's orgasms constituted the beginning, middle, and end of any sexual encounter, that women's bodies gave them pleasure and were not simply objects for men to enjoy, that men did not necessarily know how to make love to women. Feminists proposed the existence of a realm of female sexuality that men and patriarchy had not yet discovered. This realm of female sexuality was imagined as clitoral. For some it was about touching. For others it was about masturbation. For others still, about better heterosexual sex. All the differences converged to create a moment, between 1968 and 1975, where feminists tentatively and even accidentally shared a commitment to women's sexual self-determination.

The feminist critique of expert knowledge became nearly inseparable, in this period, from an implied assertion that feminists were, in fact, far better experts on sex and on women than men could ever be. Part of becoming "expert" involved reaching more readers. This took place at a number of locations. First, through a synergy between feminists and news-hungry media, as Susan Douglas records, that seized on individual women like the beautiful Gloria Steinem, the rebel bisexual Kate Millett, and the suburban mother Betty Friedan and proceeded to stage an extended cat fight.[5] It also happened through savvy recognition by commercial publishers that feminism could sell books. From Simon and Schuster, which picked up the Boston Women's Health Collective's *Our Bodies, Our Selves* (1971) and Millett's *Sexual Politics* (1970), to Vintage Press, which published Robin Morgan's *Sisterhood Is Powerful* (1970), to Bantam, which published Shulamith Firestone's *The Dialectic of Sex* (1970) and Germaine Greer's *The Female Eunuch* (1971), these presses elevated what were mimeographs and doctoral dissertations into blockbusters.[6]

The radical feminist view of sexual freedom radiated out into the mainstream world in a number of ways. Chapter 4 examines how popular novels written by women in the early 1970s represented sexual self-determination. When histories of the 1970s are written, who will have had the greater impact? It's hard to know if that honor would fall to Kate Millett or Erica Jong. Jong's best-selling novel, *Fear of Flying*, did not translate radical feminism for a general audience. Rather, its heroine, Isadora Wing, helped make sexual freedom synonymous with feminism. Wing's escapades joined sexual self-determination to her emergent sense of self, and this was the message of radical feminist theory as well. Mainstream novels including Rita Mae Brown's *Rubyfruit Jungle* (1973), Barbara Raskin's *Loose Ends* (1973), Alix Kates Shulman's *Memoirs of an Ex-Prom Queen* (1972) and *Burning Questions* (1978), Margaret Atwood's *Surfacing* (1972), Lisa Alther's *Kinflicks* (1975), Sara Davidson's *Loose Change* (1977), Marilyn French's *The Woman's Room* (1977), and Marge Piercy's *Vida* (1979), to name only a few,[7] represented coming of age and coming into feminism as building on the same markers: menstruation, petting, first intercourse, first marriage, first divorce. Such strategies, simply put, helped to popularize feminism by making it into compelling first-person narratives.

From all these locations, women who claimed some relationship to feminism became a new breed of experts. The "feminist" provided a welcomed alternative to the male-dominated tradition of credentialed experts who had long been discussing the nature of female sexuality and healthy womanhood. With her autonomous (clitoral) sexuality, her critique of experts, and her assertion of authentic knowledge, the feminist also, and what is more important, became a third term between the heterosexual woman and the lesbian. In the liminal space between straight and gay she helped produce, the feminist offered powerful critiques of dominant notions of sexual health and normality. She was, for a brief moment, sexually unspecified and potentially subversive. Was she gay? Was she straight?

Did she hate men? At the same time, the feminist was white, university educated, and middle-class. This new expert circulated as a representative of all women, and that presumption sowed the seeds of her undoing.

The final component of my story moves forward from radical feminism to selectively explore its legacies for cultural feminism, ending with the 1982 Scholar and the Feminist Ninth Conference at Barnard College in New York City. At this historic conference, feminists publicly protested each others' views of what constituted sexual freedom for women. The lines of conflict at Barnard were complicated. On the one hand, the growing antipornography movement emphasized the radical feminist critique of sexual objectification of women and the dangerous, brutal, and often humiliating aspects of heterosexual sex for women. Antipornography feminists hoped to rid the public sphere of sexually violent images as a way to enhance women's safety. In the wake of the Barnard conference, these feminists have been mislabeled antisex feminists. On the other side, sex radicals, as they have been called, sharply disagreed with any form of censorship. They worried that censorship would backfire and be used to persecute sexual minorities. These women wanted feminism to commit to women's right to sexual expression. This group enjoyed the title of pro-sex, seeming to make them the rightful heirs of the mantle of radical feminism.

The Barnard conference and its division of the feminist world into pro- and antisex was, by all accounts, a watershed event in the history of contemporary feminism. My project takes the sex wars as its end and, in doing so, offers a necessary history of how and why this impasse around female sexuality took place. I attempt to disrupt the ways that the pro-sex/antisex divisions, bequeathed at Barnard, have been taken back in time and applied to radical feminists. Dana Densmore, member of the Boston feminist group Cell 16, for example, whose critique of the sexual revolution questioned whether (hetero) sex itself was necessary, is typically viewed as a precursor to the antisex feminism of the 1980s. No one would dispute that links between Densmore and the antipornography activist Andrea Dworkin can be made in this way. But I believe that other connections between the two periods enable us to situate Densmore and Dworkin in a longer debate over women's sexual self-determination. Situating them both in a history of feminist sexual thought specifically and twentieth-century American thought in general allows readers to appreciate differences and similarities between 1969 and 1982, and to see what was innovative and radical about both moments.

Like other humanities scholars, the work of Michel Foucault has deeply shaped my thinking about sexuality. Foremost, Foucault helped us see sex as constructed and as having a history. Foucault collapsed the distinction between ideas and experience. He called for historians to think about categories and their histories, or genealogies, and how they became embedded in bodies. For example, how did heterosexuality come to be understood as a cluster of specific body parts, desires, and identifications? How did ideas about heterosexuality regulate the body? How did heterosexual identifications shape the physiological event called "orgasm"? Like other feminists, I have absorbed and tried to apply Foucault's understanding of ideas as simultaneously inciting and "repressing" desires.

Foremost for this study, the work of Judith Butler provides a model for thinking through the paradoxical and seemingly natural stickiness between sexuality and gender. She wrote, in 1990,

> Gender ought not to be conceived merely as the cultural inscription of meaning on a pregiven sex. . . . Gender must also designate the very apparatus of production whereby the sexes themselves are established. As a result, gender is not to culture as sex is to nature; gender is also the discursive/cultural means by which "sexed nature" or "a natural sex" is produced and established as "prediscursive," prior to culture, a politically neutral surface on which culture acts.[8]

Butler's theory of gender as a regulating fiction that produces the "natural" sexed body defies the more commonly held view that the sexed body produces the terms for gender roles and identities. My work, then, applies Butler's theory of gender to the decades-long dialogue about the true nature of normal female sexuality. If we are to take genealogical methodologies to heart, this story of how experts—Freudians, sexologists, marriage counselors, and feminists—understood female sexuality is actually the story of how the female body came to be produced. It's the very unnatural story of vaginas, clitorises, orgasms, and desire itself.

Despite warnings from senior scholars, I set out to reconstruct a genealogy of the female orgasm, beginning with Anne Koedt's 1969 article, "The Myth of the Vaginal Orgasm." I started with her footnotes and went back to read those books and people. I read their footnotes and read their sources, and so on and so on, until everyone I read was speaking to each other and I could understand all the intertextual references. From a foundation in Freudianism, radical psychoanalytic theory, sexological research, popular marriage and sex guides, I reread second-wave feminism through the prism of the female orgasm. I included only writings that took up sexual pleasure and the orgasm in some way or another. I asked, for example, how Betty Friedan conceptualized sex, sexual pleasure, the orgasm. How did others, gay and straight, white and nonwhite, address the female orgasm? This is not the way to write an inclusive history of the second wave of feminism. Rather, it is a way to historicize and theorize one element of second-wave feminism. Thus the caveat at the beginning about the multiple stories one can and should tell about feminism.

My genealogical accounting of feminism ends up to be a genealogy of female heterosexuality, as it was understood in mid-twentieth-century America, among other things, as well. Methodologically, I took from gay and lesbian historians and queer theorists an enduring belief in the unnaturalness of heterosexuality. After all, who can read anything written by the popular Freudians in the 1940s, Helen Gurley Brown, editor of *Cosmo*, in the 1970s, or even "J," author of *The Sensuous Woman* (1969), and not feel that to be heterosexual was to be deeply pathological? In examining the female orgasm, then, I ended up writing a history of how so-called normal women became heterosexual, how experts came to see women as desiring first and foremost intercourse with a penis, and how experts linked that essential heterosexuality to loving housework, child rearing, and vaginal intercourse.

One last note. Like others across the humanities disciplines, I am in the process of sorting out the legacies of second-wave feminism. Born between the two waves—too young for the second and too old for the third—I feel compelled to make sense of what happened and why it still matters. I don't like the vacuum in feminism around sexual pleasure. And I certainly want to fight the crazy notion that feminists are antisex. Such a construction is breathtakingly wrong.

MODERN WOMEN AND MODERN MARRIAGE

Reinventing Female Heterosexuality

Second-wave feminists, from the liberal-minded Betty Friedan to the more radical Ti-Grace Atkinson, targeted Freud and psychoanalysis for propagating derogatory views of women. Feminists of all political philosophies agreed that male psychoanalysts had constructed accounts of women as pathological for needing more from their lives than motherhood, as frigid for not reaching sexual ecstasy through intercourse, and as masochistic for embodying the very traits of passivity and loving tolerance that Freudian experts had assigned to them. Furthermore, sex experts created a veritable industry to treat the causes of women's psychological ill health. Feminists angrily noted that, in psychoanalysis, women were the perpetual losers, damned for focusing too much on their children and damned for pursuing careers.

The answer to the question why sexuality mattered so much to second-wave feminists begins in part with the history of expert ideas about womanhood. Experts who outlined the parameters of the "normal" woman bolstered their assertions through theories about the "true" nature of female sexuality. For many experts, female sexuality served as the raw material from which a natural and healthy femininity was derived. Female sexuality promised to reveal, yet never fully delivered, the essence of womanhood, the kernel of unchanging truth about women. As historian Thomas Laqueur argues, "Almost everything one wants to say about sex—however sex is understood—already has in it a claim about gender."[1] The age-old hope that the true essence of womanhood was discoverable, a hope shared by experts and nonexperts alike, situated ideas about sexuality in the center of ongoing debates about women and womanhood. Psychologists, medical doctors, social workers, anthropologists, sociologists, and popular writers who strove to illuminate the mysteries of femininity, women's proper work, or even the most efficient way to order the social relations between the sexes, drew on narratives of sexuality to do so.

Feminists were not impervious to the lure of sexuality as a way to explain women. They too relied on visions of female sexuality to strengthen their views of a new and decidedly liberated woman. Part of the feminist project of reimagining female sexuality, then, involved revisiting and reworking American sex expert discourse and its construction of an ideal woman. Feminists were the first to point out the pernicious effects this ideal woman had had on generations of women who vainly attempted to conform to its unattainable standards of normality. In showing this ideal to be impossible and, more pointedly, a male fantasy of obedient womanhood, feminists believed they could effect real change in the social meaning of femininity. They hoped to cast off the ideal woman of expert discourse and replace her with a feminist ideal of empowered and self-actualized womanhood.

The ideal woman found in the texts of psychoanalytic theory and in the pages of marriage manuals was herself an evolving figment, an ideal that developed within a changing field of expertise itself shaped by its own unique combination of internal and external forces.[2] This changing ideal nevertheless had roots in American intellectual history that feminists felt compelled to revisit and revise. Betty Friedan, Kate Millett, and Shulamith Firestone each began their critique of oppressive views of womanhood by exploring the first modern ideas of female sexuality generated at the turn of the century, and each began with the man they loved to hate, Sigmund Freud. While, individually, feminists writing in the 1970s did not necessarily suffer directly at the hands of misogynistic postwar Freudian psychoanalysts, they, in ways different from their mothers before them, nevertheless encountered standards of womanhood that had roots in the ideas generated by Freud.

Historically minded and university trained, most second-wave feminists who attacked American sex expertise did not hold Freud alone accountable for oppressing women. They rightly understood that the damage wreaked on American womanhood was perpetrated as well by Freudians who elaborated upon the work of the master throughout the interwar and postwar period. Thus, the feminist project of reinventing female sexuality became intimately bound up with the exploration of psychoanalytic femininity, from its origins in the ideal of the vaginal orgasm in the 1920s, to its study of the dangers posed by frigidity in the 1930s, to popular Freudianism's turn to outright antifeminism in the 1940s. This trajectory of ideas about healthy female sexuality set the terms that feminists coming of age in the 1960s encountered and eventually rejected.

In the 1910s and 1920s, a new style of heterosexuality emerged in relationship to a host of social and cultural transformations sweeping the country.[3] Victorianism, with its emphasis on reproduction and sexual restraint, came under assault from two different cultural arenas. The first blow came from psychoanalysis, the new "science of self" that advocated the centrality of sexual expression to the healthy individual. The second came from the modern "revolution in morals and manners" that took is lead from working-class charity girls, Greenwich Village bohemians, and, eventually, "New Women." Both psychoanalysis and the revolution in morals and manners offered new appreciation for sexual pleasure, called for greater equality between the sexes, and presented a view of marriage as an emotional and sexual union. Both used female sexual pleasure specifically as a sign of their generation's rebellion against "stodgy" Victorianism.[4]

Self-declared moderns inherited a bifurcated view of sexuality from their Victorian forebears. On the one hand, the Victorians viewed sexuality as a form of spiritual union that elevated sexual intercourse into a form of romantic, emotional, and, ultimately, reproductive intimacy. On the other hand, Victorians also saw sexuality as a base physical appetite that was unfit for civilized discourse or civilized women and properly kept to back alleys and red light districts. Sexuality between husband and wife found its highest expression in children, an achievement that sanitized the "unseemly" business of copulation. These two coexistent views of sexuality were deeply gendered, with women cast as the spiritual sex and men as driven by their physical drive for pleasure and release.[5]

The generation of women coming of age at the turn of the century rejected their parents' sexual worldview, dismissing Victorianism as the very epitome of dullness. Commentators called these women "new" for a number of reasons, all of which centered on women's changing relationship to sexuality and to the public sphere. While many different types of women carried the banner of new womanhood, they all shared a rejection of Victorian ideas about women's proper place. The first generation of new women, who came of age in the 1870s and 1880s, challenged the Victorian gender ideology of separate spheres through their involvement with the settlement house movement and their battle for the ballot.[6] College-educated activists such as Jane Addams, Florence Kelley, and Lillian Wald moved out of their family homes to establish settlement houses in urban neighborhoods. These communities of women offered their immigrant neighbors a range of services, from education, parenting, and dietary advice to "betterment" through exposure to European art and music. At the same time, settlement house workers represented women's capacity to live independently from men. Addams and others cherished their predominantly single-sexed institutions where women set their own goals, dealt with the male-dominated city services and city government, and sustained themselves financially. Settlement house workers also relished their personal relationships, the emotional bonds that literally embodied the "sex solidarity" so central to the "woman movement."[7] Importantly, these women advocated women's singular qualifications for public and political work: as women, they were both uniquely aware of the toll industrialism took on families and children and uniquely endowed with moral and emotional vision sorely absent from early twentieth-century public culture.[8]

While often living out passionate relationships with other women in "Boston marriages," this first generation of new women did not explicitly challenge the Victorian centerpiece of sexual restraint and the code of female passionlessness. That assault came from pre–World War I working-class women who worked in factories and, to a lesser degree, in department stores and "pink-collar" jobs such as secretarial services.[9] Many of these women came into contact with settlement house workers through their mothers, sisters, and other relatives for whom their child services were targeted. Immigrant and native working-class young women gained a measure of independence from their families through wage work.[10] While these women turned over the bulk of their earnings to help maintain their families, they nevertheless enjoyed more time away from the watchful eyes of their traditional and family communities. Working women forged their own peer networks not only around work but also around leisure and the growing consumer culture.[11] These young women challenged Victorianism both by performing wage work in heterosocial settings and through their leisure activities, when they offered sexual favors to young men who "treated" them to the pleasures of dance halls, movie houses, and amusement parks.[12]

"Charity girls," working-class women who exchanged sexual favors in return for a night on the town, played a crucial part in the loosening standards of female sexual expressiveness. In dance halls, with men charity girls knew and men they had just met, they danced a slow shimmy or "pivoted," a wild spinning dance. "Tough" dances like the grizzly bear, the Charlie Chaplin wiggle, and the dip threw couples into close bodily contact and suggested sexual intercourse. Many of the social clubs charity girls attended permitted flirting, touching, and kissing games at their meetings. The music halls and cheap vaudeville shows they attended offered barely veiled sexual humor in their performances. Charity girls spent money not turned over to the family on adorning themselves to catch the eye of a male companion willing to pick up the tab for an evening's entertainment. They donned high-heeled shoes, fancy dresses, costume jewelry, makeup, and elaborate hats on their evening escapades. Young working women linked marketplace values with sexuality in a new mix through their consumption of clothes and other finery as well as through their willingness to trade sexual favors for amusements and drinks without slipping into outright prostitution. Such behaviors brought female sexuality more in line with male sexual standards.[13]

Yet, despite this working-class remodeling of sexual behavior, charity girls did not come to symbolize the era's sexual modernism. That honor fell to the "flapper," who, after World War I, came to embody the rejection of Victorian feminine restraint. Popularly, most commentators referred to any young woman with a bobbed haircut, lipstick, and a short skirt as a flapper. Flappers took inspiration both from the first generation of settlement house workers, who lived their lives outside of marriage and nuclear families, and the sexual revolution launched by the charity girls.[14] These young women were eager to distinguish themselves from suffragists and settlement house workers, whom they viewed as spinsters antagonistic toward men. Yet, like them, they rejected motherhood as women's sole purpose. Flappers, though, were decidedly apolitical. Basking in the successes of the suffrage movement, many young middle-class women of the 1920s assumed sexual equality had been achieved and set out to enjoy their newly won prerogatives. Following the earlier generation of charity girls, the middle-class modern woman enjoyed heterosociality and the numerous opportunities to enjoy the company of men in new public settings, apart from the watchful eyes of neighbors and relatives.[15] But young middle-class women who went to cabarets did not find as sexually permissive an atmosphere as working-class girls found. Cabaret owners enforced strict rules that discouraged contact between strangers. Likewise, middle-class dancers tamed the blatant sexuality of popular working-class dances into refined and more controlled movements.[16]

Between 1880 and the 1920s, modern women, be they settlement house workers, charity girls, feminists, or flappers, dismantled Victorian femininity on a number of related fronts. They proved, quite dramatically, that woman's place was no longer only in the home, running the household and raising upstanding citizens. Highly visible in the public sphere, whether shopping, working, going to amusement parks, or battling city agencies, these women literally broke free of women's domestic associations. Such challenges to the long-standing gender ideology of the Victorians changed dominant views of womanhood. As one expert explained, "By the very act of working, something has happened to her. . . . She had become in important psychological elements, a man. . . . More significantly[,] they absorb, with their jobs, the masculine attitude toward sex."[17]

While female participants in the first sexual revolution rejected the tenets of sexual restraint that had structured the lives and desires of their parents' generation, they nonetheless carried forward into their own sexual philosophies a cluster of traditional racial and class distinctions. Waves of immigration at the end of the nineteenth century, coupled with large migrations of African Americans to the cities of the North and Middle West in the early years of the twentieth century, made white middle-class Americans newly conscious of themselves as a group. Fear of new immigrants and racial others spurred many authors of marriage manuals to advocate less prudery among middle-class whites so as to combat rising numbers of frequently darker skinned immigrants—Italians, Slavs, Jews, Chinese, and Japanese—who threatened to overwhelm the dominant racial stock in the United States. The threat to white middle-class dominance lay not only in the supposed sexual potency of the foreign born but in the self-restrictive sexual morality and self-control that unnecessarily crippled their own physical and sexual vigor.[18] Defined against the effeminate elite on one side and the uncivilized masses on the other, the discourse of middle-class respectability spun together the competing values of self-control and physical vitality.[19] As changes in the structure of industrial capitalism narrowed opportunities for economic advancement for young, white, middle-class men at the turn of the century, physical strength became an important new aspect of masculinity. For women, a similarly paradoxical mix of values shaped the transition to modernity. Respectable women remained wives and mothers. Yet the new value of physical strength and sexual vitality opened up additional space for respectable women's nonreproductive sexuality.

Middle-class respectability, however, was not only a value of the white middle classes. Normality was defined against a range of other groups, from French noblemen, the Irish working class, to the black bourgeoisie.[20] The small yet established African American middle classes of the North and Middle West adopted similar terms of respectability as their own. They too defined themselves against the white immigrant masses, but added to their class identifications a rejection of the folk cultures of the black South. As the Great Migration took place in the early decades of the twentieth century, middle-class urban African Americans anxiously watched new arrivals from the rural South for behavior unbecoming to respectable people. Reformers took special interest in young women in an effort to contain the vices of prostitution, diseases, and disorganized families. Female sexuality came to represent, for these African American reformers, the threat of social degeneracy and the confirmation of a century-long representation of black women as sexually available.[21] Like whites, who saw racial others as both exotic and frightening and perpetuated the racist view of African Americans as sexually aggressive, middle-class blacks also inflected class and ethnic differences through sexuality. The folk cultures of the southern African Americans were seen as both revitalizing and as frightening.[22]

Anxiety about—and attraction to—sexual expression also shaped a new generation of sex experts in the 1910s and 1920s who offered a decidedly modern message to their readers. These experts focused on the crucial role sexual pleasure played in the creation of strong marriages and healthy adults. Experts' celebration of sexual expressiveness was matched only by their equally enthusiastic support for marriage. Gender and sexual ideologies, deeply wound together, worked in tandem to forge the new style of heterosexuality coming into vogue in the 1910s and 1920s.

By the 1920s, Sigmund Freud's startling theories of the unconscious and the childhood roots of identity had become the height of intellectual fashion. Transplanted and transformed in America, Freud's theories were popularly enlisted to help overturn the now outdated Victorian view of women as passionless and marital sex as primarily reproductive. Freud asserted that a drive for pleasure motivated not only men but also women and, scandalously, children as well. Society regulated, or attempted to regulate, the full range of individual sexual expression to ensure that people could live peaceably within families and communities.[23] Although repression was an inevitable consequence of civilization, Freud explained, too much repression led to neurosis and mental instability. Even for average people, repression and the unconscious conflict between responsibility (the ego) and pleasure (the id) generated stress and melancholy. More radically, Freud assumed that reproductive heterosexuality was a developmental achievement, not a biological inevitability.[24] Despite Freud's complexity and originality, popularizers in the United States altered his message into one that simply promoted the healthiness of sexual expression.[25]

Eager audiences also celebrated the work of another popular sex expert, British sexologist Havelock Ellis.[26] Ellis's six-volume *Studies in the Psychology of Sex*, published between 1897 and 1910, proposed that sexual indulgence did not pose a threat to health or character, but rather was "the chief and central function of life." He questioned, "Why should people be afraid of rousing passions which, after all, are the great driving forces of human life?"[27] Like Freud, Ellis included women in his account of healthy sexual expression. Unlike Freud, Ellis work on sex contained a eugenic element in that he sought to aid "evolutionary progress" by encouraging reproduction among the white middle class.[28]

White intellectuals, bohemians, and feminists, including notables like Floyd Dell, Crystal Eastman, and Emma Goldman, recognized that the new theories' "discovery" of passion in women had the potential to unleash a revolution in the organization of family life. Feminists in the 1910s and 1920s used European theories of Freud and Ellis to advocate for the sexual emancipation of women while nevertheless upholding the significance of women's procreation. These feminists did not necessarily see sexual liberation at odds with motherhood.[29] Birth control advocate Margaret Sanger, for example, saw women's emancipation as coming from a freely chosen expression of the "feminine" spirit, which included both sexual pleasure and motherhood. Emma Goldman similarly advocated free love and the free expression of women's "innate craving for motherhood."[30] These first-wave feminists believed sexual liberation was critical to women's full individual and social liberation.

By questioning long-standing notions of sexual pleasure as a male privilege, modern women of the 1910s and 1920s claimed, on a limited basis, some of the sexual expressiveness that men had long enjoyed. Marriage experts rushed to fill the void left from the collapse of women's alleged, now disproved, sexual passionlessness.[31] Most immediately, experts claimed that successful marriages depended on women's sexual pleasure as well as men's. For example, Judge Ben Lindsey's popular 1927 *Companionate Marriage* defined the features of modern marriage as intense psychological companionship and passionate sexual intimacy between partners. Lindsey explained that greater companionship between spouses was a welcome departure from the old-fashioned Victorian model of the authoritarian husband at the head of the household. Casting the Victorian wife as the antithesis of the New Woman, Lindsey wrote, "Does the husband really want a mere permanent housekeeper, a faithful drudge, an unpaid servant, or does he desire a real life companion and a friend?" In sexual matters, Lindsey urged husbands to abandon the stereotypically male Victorian sexual aggression and to embrace "sensitivity, gentleness, and a slower pace."[32]

However, while marriage experts defined modern women as liberated from Victorian restraint and repression, they nevertheless—and paradoxically—felt profound unease at the specter of unconstrained female sexual desire.[33] No matter how discredited Victorianism had become by the 1920s, its idealized vision of heterosexual stability, in which men and women took very clearly defined positions in the sexual order, remained intact and enduringly appealing. Experts thus found themselves in an ambivalent and unstable relationship to female sexuality: ideas about modernity and sexual liberation required that women partake of the fruits of sexual freedom. At the same time, experts wanted to maintain a sexual order that preserved men's sexual authority at home. Sex experts searched for a way to explain female heterosexuality as both liberated and domesticated, to celebrate female sexual expression while situating that expression in monogamous marriage. This tension between expression and containment profoundly shaped ideas about women and normal female sexuality in the early decades of the twentieth century.

The view of modern marriage produced by educators, social workers, psychologists, and physicians defined normal female heterosexuality through a cluster of related ideas and values.[34] First, marriage experts created an updated account of women's sexual dependency on men. The concern over women's sexuality brought a fresh gloss to the long-standing association between unruly, unknown, potentially disruptive sexuality and femininity.[35] In the nineteenth century, the ideologies of gender held that passionless women restrained aggressive pleasure-seeking male desire. By the 1920s, modern marriage experts and psychoanalysts taught a new gendered message: men played the role of containing and modulating female sexual desire. Husbands, marriage experts insisted, must be prepared to lead their wives through the volatile currents of sexual passion, currents with which women had little experience. At the same time, psychoanalysts constructed a view of female sexuality that required men's sympathetic handling to create mature femininity. Specifically, the companionate marriage cast husbands as teachers and wives as students in need of erotic education. While it made female sexual pleasure central to happy marriages, the companionate marriage eroticized but did not displace men's authority at home.

Second, experts attempted to naturalize a very specific form of heterosexuality for women, one that emphasized a woman's passivity, her vaginal sexuality, and her dependency on men. Psychoanalytic experts transposed Freud's drive model to theorize a natural heterosexual desire in women for intercourse and motherhood. In casting heterosexuality as a biological drive, psychoanalysts constructed a single view of sexual health, one that specified the only normal outlet for women's sexual expression to be heterosexual marriage.

Finally, and related to the project of naturalizing heterosexuality for women, the new style of heterosexuality remapped women's bodies, linking normal heterosexuality to the vagina and abnormal autonomous sexuality to the clitoris.[36] Modern sex experts diagnosed independent women—be they prostitutes, feminists, lesbians, or merely women living outside traditional family settings—as sexually disordered and fixated on their clitoris. In doing so, they defined clitoral sexuality as a dangerous aberration that threatened the stability of marriage and heterosexuality itself.[37] Doctor John F. W. Meagher, writing in 1929, spelled out the stakes of female sexual satisfaction for the health and harmony of the new age when he linked sexual dissatisfaction with misguided militant activism. "The driving force in many agitators and militant women who are always after their rights, is often an unsatisfied sex impulse, with a homosexual aim. Married women with a completely satisfied libido rarely take an active interest in militant movements."[38]

Together, these three values—women's dependence on men, women's organic heterosexuality, and the deviancy of clitoral sexuality—defined modern heterosexuality for women. While acknowledging female sexuality as central to successful marriages and, thus, to healthy femininity, sex experts also worked diligently to secure female sexual pleasure in narrow and highly specified contexts. Seen in a range of writings, from expert to popular, the discourse of modern female heterosexuality from the 1920s to the 1940s profoundly linked women's sexuality to men and, by extension, to the family. The cluster of terms that located female sexuality as dependent and vaginal gained the status of "truth" through their repetition in a number of sources. From psychoanalytic literature, to professional journals, to popular tomes, sex experts offered the public a modern view of female sexuality as important to marriages, important to women's mental health, and important to the maintenance of men's natural authority. Authored primarily by white men, the expert discourse of normal female heterosexuality took the white middle-class "woman" as its main object of study. As the "other" who resided the closest, whose influence had the potential to reach the furthest, the white woman of expert discourse carried both the white middle-class men's fears of degeneracy and their hopes for cultural dominance.[39]

The conflation between healthy sexuality and a healthy feminine identity also powerfully shaped the growing wave of antifeminism in the 1930s and 1940s. By claiming that feminists were sexually aggressive and fixated on their clitorises, antifeminists drew upon the same sex experts who defined the features of modern female heterosexuality. These related projects—defining the normal (heterosexual) and defining the abnormal (feminist)—dominated American discussions of womanhood throughout the interwar years and beyond.

Female Sexual Dependency: The Companionate Marriage

In the "revolt" against Victorian repression, New Women of the 1910s and 1920s self-consciously rejected what they referred to as the "hypocrisy" of the sexual double standard.[40] Ironically, in this moment of transition, marriage experts offered readers a picture of the modern wife as sexually innocent. The woman of the companionate marriage might be modern, but, in the texts of the companionate marriage, she remained sexually innocent despite her more public roles. Although the first wave of feminists in the 1910s rejected the sexual double standard that held male sexuality as acceptable and female sexuality as deviant, the sexologists who followed were far more ambivalent. For them, female innocence remained an important value, even as that innocence was itself sexualized.

One expert in particular, Dutch physician Theodore H. Van Der Velde, directly confronted the ambivalence at the heart of the new style of heterosexuality. He published his manual *Ideal Marriage: Its Physiology and Technique* (1926) in English in 1928.[41] It soon became America's best-selling marriage manual and went through an astonishing thirty-two reprintings by 1957. Found in bedside drawers and bookshelves across the country well into the 1960s, Van Der Velde's manual provided a crucial service to generations of readers desperate for information and advice about sex.[42] The impressive popularity of *Ideal Marriage* set Van Der Velde apart from the hordes of other marriage experts offering advice to European and American audiences. Influenced by the ancient Indian love manual, the *Kama Sutra*, *Ideal Marriage* was also the first Western marriage manual to direct its readers to the pleasures of foreplay, oral sex, and different coital positions.[43]

Along with Lindsey's *Companionate Marriage*, Van Der Velde's *Ideal Marriage* championed the new view of female sexual desire and its role in marital relations.[44] At the same time, Van Der Velde reassured his male readers that sexual equality did not have to undermine men's authority at home. Van Der Velde cleverly used the ideal of romance to combine the competing claims of men's traditional sexual authority in marriage with the new imperatives of female sexual desires. The tender, generous, and sensitive husband added to his repertoire the role of sexual educator to his naive wife.[45] Husbands, he explained, "are naturally educators and initiators of their wives in sexual matters."[46] Through romance, *Ideal Marriage* helped to ease the "passionless" woman of Victorianism into an amorous wife and, likewise, transform Victorian marriage into a "modern" union with mutual sexual pleasure at its center and the hierarchy between the sexes as its foundation. While Progressive-era doctors believed semen itself protected women from mental and physical disease, marriage experts like Van Der Velde attributed no significance to seminal fluid per se but maintained, nonetheless, the centrality of men to women's sexual development.[47]

Van Der Velde narrated sexual pleasure in the highly metaphoric language of romantic love. For example, he described "woman" as "a harp who only yields her secrets of melody to the master who knows how to handle her."[48] He referred to sexual intercourse as "communion," foreplay as "love-play," resolution as "after-glow," and orgasm as the "acme."[49] A typical passage described sexual intimacy with flowery euphemisms:

> A first shy, stolen meeting—a word—a look, given and returned; the immortal flame shoots upwards, love is born in a sense of indescrib-

able exaltation and joy. And the impulse of approach, sublimated into love, now unfolds itself. . . . It thrives and puts forth leaves and buds, and gradually the lovers attain full union and communion. In that moment, when youth and girl are fulfilled in and by one another the impulse to approach and the desire for consummation find each other and merge into a new integral emotion. Love is come of age, and is in flower.[50]

Van Der Velde's rhetoric positioned the woman as the valued object of sexual plying, one who needed coaxing, gentleness, and love from her partner to reach sexual fulfillment. In fact, the production of women as idealized objects of male protection and desire was one of the primary achievements of *Ideal Marriage*.[51] In Van Der Velde's hands, sex and love collapsed into the very function of marriage—the sustaining of the couple that would ideally provide the basis for a family. Unlike nineteenth-century marriages, which also joined sex and love, modern marriage experts described a marriage where the skillful ministrations of the (expert) husband produced a responsive and devoted wife.

Van Der Velde viewed romance as specifically erotic to women. As a sign of his modernity, he insisted that men adopt women's "superior" view of sexuality as an expression of love. Van Der Velde assumed that men already knew how to have pleasurable sex but did not necessarily know how to maintain a long-standing sexual relationship with the woman they loved. "A perfectly performed communion demands from both partners a psycho-erotic approach such as is only possible where love is. Only where love is can the sexual pleasure be at its height, the orgasm ecstatic, the relief complete."[52] Van Der Velde believed that mutually satisfying sex ultimately strengthened marriage by facilitating the "most intimate merging: [partners'] souls meet and touch as do their bodies. They become one."[53]

While asserting the decidedly modern view that sexual pleasure was the foundation of strong marriages, Van Der Velde maintained a Victorian belief in the complementary natures of men and women. Although he explained that an ideal marriage was one where each partner enjoyed "equal rights and equal joys in sexual union," he nonetheless asserted that it remained men's duty to make sure their wives found sex pleasurable.[54] Sexual fulfillment became identical with emotional and psychological compatibility between spouses. A man who asserted his sexual needs over his wife's or who simply neglected her needs violated the romantic and sexual harmony of the modern marriage contract. "The man who neglects the love-play is guilty not only of coarseness," wrote Van Der Velde, "but of positive brutality; and his omission can not only offend and disgust a woman, but also injure her on the purely physical plane. And," he added, "this sin of omission is unpardonably stupid."[55]

Advocates of modern marriage like Van Der Velde harmonized a view of male and female sexual difference through the ideal of mutuality embodied in the simultaneous orgasm. Unlike Victorian constructions of marital sexuality, where men's orgasm constituted the pinnacle of successful coitus, modern marriages strove for mutually pleasurable intercourse. Simultaneous orgasms became the tangible proof of satisfying sex. Marital sex, Van Der Velde wrote, should "aim directly or indirectly at the consummation of sexual satisfaction, and . . . concludes . . . with the nearly simultaneous culmination of sensation—or orgasm—of both partners."[56] The simultaneous orgasm integrated women's sexual liberation from Victorian passionlessness into modern, sexually animated marriage.

The companionate marriage as outlined by Van Der Velde combined the new emphasis on female pleasure with traditional gender constructions of men's authority in marriage. On the one hand, Van Der Velde's ethic of romance and mutuality demanded that his readers/husbands accurately attend to their wives' sexual signals. On the other, Van Der Velde's romantic narrative masked the ways in which men remained the dominant force in shaping marital sexuality. In this way, romance functioned in his text to elide the power dynamics of traditional heterosexuality. Rendered passive and latent, women depended on loving husbands to educate them to the world of sexual pleasure. Thus, the narrative of romantic heterosexuality operated to both enhance and circumscribe women's sexual status.

Although Van Der Velde's ideal marriage upheld male authority, fears of an uncontainable female sexuality hovered in the margins of his text. The line tethering new women to men—their sexual dependency—often felt too fragile, particularly when set against the range of independent public roles women assumed in the 1920s. Fears of female sexuality, of women who could overpower men with their sexual desires, or who would use their sexual desires to transform themselves into men, persisted alongside the view of women as fundamentally sexually dependent on men. This ambivalence was captured in the twin constructions of women as both presexual and as sexual monsters, or nymphomaniacs.[57]

Fears of uncontained feminine desire appeared in *Ideal Marriage*, despite Van Der Velde's best attempts. Throughout his manual, he struggled to erase the view of women as sexually voracious.

Some of my readers may perhaps feel that the greater feminine aptitude or tolerance of excess in coitus compared to the man's potency as just described, is hardly compatible with what has been stressed in early chapters, i.e., her less rapid and facile excitability and the frequency of feminine sexual anesthesia, "coldness," or "frigidity."[58]

Van Der Velde resolved his fears by repeatedly emphasizing women's sexual dependency on men. He explained that the newly married woman was "as a rule, more or less completely 'cold' or indifferent" to sexual intercourse. She "must be taught to love, in the complete sense." If the husband failed to impart a proper "erotic education" to his wife, she would "remain permanently frigid," unchanged from her original presexual state.[59] But, with practice and loving attention, inexperienced wives could be made into fully sexual partners. Van Der Velde explained:

Only gradually does she develop erotic maturity and experience, and when she does reach her zenith, the comparatively slight provocation which will cause ejaculation in the husband after some days of abstinence, may well be insufficient for her. . . . Her desire for sexual intercourse, in happy married life, will have become at least equal to his. And her quantitative sexual efficiency and endurance surpass his.[60]

According to Van Der Velde, women entered marriage sexually empty. The husband of a presexual woman could transform her into a sexual giant through careful teaching. The only way to keep the now abundantly sexual wife within reasonable bounds was to train her desire to match the amount of her husband's sexual potency. Van Der Velde's belief in women's limitless potential in all sexual matters was so thorough that he went as far as to warn husbands about sexually overtraining their wives. Falling back on the Victorian spermatic economy, Van Der Velde cautioned husbands "not to recklessly habituate their wives to a degree of sexual frequency and intensity, which they (the husbands) may be quite unable to keep up for any length of time."[61] While some women could make the necessary adjustments to diminishing sexual frequency, others might not be able to "modify" their desires. "Then, indeed, the husband cannot exorcise the spirits he has invoked." He faced either his wife's "chronic nerves," the result of sexual repression on the "feminine psyche" that destroys "marital peace and happiness,"[62] or chronic sexual overstrain and fatigue that would "reduce" him to "a physical weakling—a neurotic."[63]

Van Der Velde's narrative of women's erotic education at the hands of their loving husbands could not fully resolve the tension between competing views of women as nonsexual and overly sexual. He asserted that romantic love created and contained female sexuality. By his own account, however, female sexuality threatened to exceed marital containment. Van Der Velde could not definitively dismiss women's potential as sexual monsters. Despite his attempt to establish a cause-effect relationship between a husband's training and a wife's sexual responsiveness, Van Der Velde unwittingly evoked the chaos of a female sexual genie who, once released from her bottle, could never again be contained.

Van Der Velde's emphasis on husbands pleasing their wives captured the spirit of adventure and liberation of the roaring 1920s. But as that moment faded with the crippling economic crisis of the 1930s, ambivalence at modern women found new expression in a growing concern over frigidity and the frigid woman's threat to male authority. As the country faced the Depression, the emphasis on women's sexual liberation in the 1920s seemed almost subversive.[64] Women discarded the flat-chested look of the flapper and, in its place, adopted the much more reasonable and matronly little flower print dress that emphasized the bust and waistline.[65]

At the same time Americans rallied around the ideal of strong families headed by strong men, women did not abandon the heterosocial world of work and leisure in the 1930s. Working women held on to their jobs, particularly as many men lost theirs, and the number of married women in the workforce continued to grow.[66] At the same time, most commentators belied the existence of this permanent, lower-paid female workforce as they insisted, despite evidence to the contrary, that women worked only for "pin money."[67]

In this moment of national family crisis, psychoanalysis began its meteoric rise as America's premiere expert discourse on female sexuality. The psychoanalysts who produced new accounts of women's essential difference from men recast the desire for sexual liberation, the hallmark of modernism in the 1920s, into a sign of women's ill health. Women who pursued sexual pleasure too eagerly, even in the marital bed, were no longer seen as wanting sexual equality with men but rather as wanting to be men.

Organic Heterosexuality: The Vagina

In the wake of companionate marriage advocates' demand that husbands be more attentive to their wives' sexual pleasure, psychoanalysts provided new paradigms with which to interpret "normal" sexual behavior and desires. As a related discourse on sexuality, psychoanalysts shared with companionate marriage experts a fundamental ambivalence about female sexuality. Psychoanalysts, like marriage experts, worked hard to contain the specter of aggressive, undomesticated, and autonomous female sexuality through ideas about women's essential passivity, innocence, and dependence on men.

For the earlier generation of sexual moderns, psychoanalysis stood as a liberatory discourse marking a clear break from the Victorianism they despised. Psychoanalytic categories of repression, sublimation, the unconscious, and the libido seeped into popular and expert discourse on sexuality and provided new language and theories to understand the place of sexuality in the lives of ordinary people. At the same time, psychoanalysis also enabled a conservative account of men and women's enduring differences, which came to fruition, popularly, in the 1930s. Through such terms as *castration, penis envy,* and *masochism,* psychoanalysis created a theory of women's diminished sexuality. The theoretical constructs of psychoanalysis both reflected and reproduced the ambivalence at the heart of expert ideas about female heterosexuality in the 1920s and 1930s.

Between 1920 and 1930, Freud completed his major essays on femininity and female sexuality.[68] Freud concluded that, as with men, women's heterosexual desire was acquired and not inborn. He argued that girls, like boys, were originally bisexual because of their libidinal attachment to their mothers, their primary caretakers. This bisexuality in little girls had to be shaped into heterosexuality, and Freud's theories charted how that transformation took place. The Freudian tale of femininity centered on penis envy. Freud argued that women suffered from the knowledge that their anatomy was lacking and inferior. The psychic "wound" caused by the knowledge that they had no penis created a deep and unconscious propensity for masochism in women, a masochism Freud and his followers associated with mature femininity. Since women had no penis, no organ for their aggressive pleasure-seeking libido, women turned their libido inward into narcissism and masochism. This turn inward lay the groundwork for eroticizing the vagina and the mature linking of reproduction and sexual pleasure for women. Vaginal sexuality, then, defined what was essentially feminine about female sexuality.

Freud detailed women's entry into heterosexuality in *Three Essays on the Theory of Sexuality*.[69] In his third essay, "The Transformations of Puberty," Freud explained puberty as a period where the "reproductive function" first joined with and then gained ascendancy over the more infantile search for pleasure.[70] Under the influence of the reproductive imperative, the girl transferred her leading genital zone from the clitoris to the vagina. How this transfer took place appeared quite Byzantine to the uninitiated. As an infant, the girl's began a short-lived state of preoedipal, libidinal attachment to her mother, which had enduring consequences on the feminine personality. According to Freud, the girl soon realized that her inadequate clitoris could not win her mother over to be the girl's alone. She could never possess the beloved mother because she, the girl, was without a penis. At this point, the girl renounced her mother in favor of her father and a powerful wave of repression carried her into her latency period. He suggested that when the girl emerged from latency, her erotic "transfer" would have been completed and she would find her vagina fully eroticized. In this new context, the girl's (masculine) clitoris would no longer be her dominant sexual organ.

Freud acknowledged that the repression of the clitoris was never complete. Still, ideally it would come to function like "a pine shaving" to help "set a log of harder wood on fire."[71] As he explained, such a monumental transfer of erotic zones and shift in libidinal organization put women at greater risk of psychological ailments than men. If the transfer was not complete and the clitoris remained the center of a woman's sexuality, she ran the risk of suffering from such psychological problems as penis envy, hostility toward men, hysteria, and neurotic discontent. "The fact that women change their leading erotogenic zone in this way," warned Freud, "together with the wave of repression at puberty, which as it were, puts aside their childish masculinity, are the chief determinants of the greater proneness of women to neurosis and especially to hysteria."[72]

The transfer theory introduced an unstated yet pervasive problem in Freud's conception of female sexuality. As a story of development, the transfer theory created a moment where the young girl stood outside of sexual categories.[73] Within the terms of psychoanalysis, the girl, for a brief moment in latency, existed between sexual identities—she was neither purely masculine nor feminine, neither simply homosexual nor purely heterosexual, but somehow all of these at once. The outcome of such liminality, of temporarily existing between sexualities, created instability at the heart of the girl's heterosexual identity.

Freudians in the 1930s and 1940s tried to solve this problem by rooting an essential heterosexual identity in the female body.[74] Toward this end, the vaginal orgasm and its antithesis, vaginal frigidity, became two central components of Freudian femininity. Experts first assumed and then detailed, among other things, the masculine character of the clitoris and its association with infancy, the shift from clitoral to vaginal sexuality as part of a biological imperative toward reproduction, and the association between women's psychological makeup and their success or failure entry into heterosexuality. Unlike Freud, who had radically detached sexual desire from sexual object choice (who a person chose to have sex with), many of his followers argued that heterosexuality was an inevitable outcome of bodies. In doing so, they aligned bodies, sexual desire, and sexual object choice into one unified and coherent heterosexual identity. Particularly in discussions of female sexuality, major theorists in the psychology of women sought to establish a biological theory of female heterosexuality.

Two major analysts, Helene Deutsch and Karen Horney, reworked Freud's theories of femininity to emphasize the biological basis of women's heterosexual identity. Deutsch, one of Freud's favorite students, spent her professional life trying to solve the "riddle" of femininity. Deutsch's friendship with Freud, her earlier analysis with him, and her directorship at the Vienna Training Institute from its opening in 1922 until she immigrated to the U.S. in 1935, made her a key player in the psychoanalytic movement. Most important, Freud accepted and supported Deutsch's work on women, and other psychoanalysts perceived her as expanding his theories into the realm of the feminine.[75] Deutsch's work on femininity and female sexuality culminated in the two-volume *The Psychology of Women*.[76] Building on her work in the 1920s and 1930s, *The Psychology of Women* was Deutsch's most comprehensive statement on the subjects of motherhood, female masochism and narcissism, and the vicissitudes of female sexuality.[77] By the 1940s and 1950s, *The Psychology of Women* had become a classic in the psychoanalytic literature on women. Volume 2, on the psychoanalytic meaning of motherhood, was reprinted eleven times by 1960.

Like Deutsch, Karen Horney was a European-trained analyst who moved to the U.S. in the 1930s. She began her psychoanalytic training in the 1910s in Berlin under one of Freud's first and most ardent followers, Karl Abraham.[78] Throughout the 1920s, Horney's work focused on women's unique psychology. From her earliest years as an analyst, Horney had chafed under Freudian orthodoxy, which she viewed as insufficiently aware of women's essential difference from men. Under the growing threat of war, Horney immigrated to Chicago in 1932.[79] Exposure to a different culture further alerted Horney to the priority of social factors in shaping men and women's psychology.[80] In Chicago, Horney worked closely with neo-Freudians Erich Fromm and Clara Thompson, both of whom shared her interest in the cultural roots of identity.[81] With this shift, Horney left behind her focus on women specifically. In 1967, during the second wave of feminism, her articles on women were reprinted and once again gained wide readership.[82]

Deutsch and Horney shared many of Freud's basic premises about sexuality and women. Both believed that femininity was a developmental achievement whereby women gave up the dream of being "male" (having a penis) and accepted their feminine difference (their "castration"). However, unlike Freud, they situated that development in a theory of drives that lent heterosexuality an air of inevitability in their work. In basing the drive to become heterosexual in women's bodies, Horney and Deutsch attempted to root an essential feminine identity in women's experience of their bodies and not in penis envy.

Within orthodox psychoanalysis, penis envy functioned as a trope for femininity in two ways. First, it upheld the universal male body as the norm against which women were compared and measured. Psychoanalysis deemed women lacking and less psychologically intact than men because they did not have a penis and thus had no organ through which to express their aggressive libidinal desires. Second, the concept of penis envy explained how women came to repress and convert their initial "masculine" libido into mature, passive vaginal sexuality. It explained why women could not, and should not, be sexually aggressive.

Horney criticized Freud for what she saw as his masculine bias, a bias that ignored what was distinctly female in women's experience.[83] Using "Freud against Freud," Horney argued that women became heterosexual through their own experiences of their bodies and that women had a primary drive toward heterosexual femininity that was not simply a "reaction formation" against their "castration."[84] In her 1933 article, "The Denial of the Vagina," Horney argued that vaginal sensations, not castration anxiety, motivate the girl's acceptance of her femininity.[85] She cited evidence of vaginal sensations as proof that the vagina was an active organ from the beginning of a girl's consciousness and not something women "discovered" upon recognition of their so-called bodily inferiority. "From a theoretical standpoint," wrote Horney, "I think that great importance should be attached to this relatively frequent occurrence of spontaneous vaginal excitations. . . . This phenomena suggests the question whether from the beginning sexual excitations may not have expressed themselves perceptibly in vaginal sensations."[86] It was male psychoanalysts, she claimed, not "nature" that minimized the significance of the vagina to the preoedipal girl.

Horney's claim that young girls had a sexual awareness of their vaginas granted a degree of bodily productivity to women that many psychoanalysts had not. For Horney, female sexuality was expressed through the not-so-absent vagina and these experiences contributed to the creation of organic femininity. She criticized Freud for establishing the primacy of penis envy by denying the vagina. "Though Freud does not expressly state it," she wrote,

> it is nonetheless clear that if the vagina remains originally "undiscovered," this is one of the strongest arguments in favor of the assumption of a biologically determined, primary penis envy in the little girls or of their original phallic organization. . . . If, on the other hand, as I conjecture, a little girl experiences from the very beginning vaginal sensations and corresponding impulses, she must from the outset have a lively sense of this specific character of her own sexual role, and a primary penis envy of the strength postulated by Freud would be hard to account for.[87]

By claiming that Freud's understanding of the vagina was riddled with his own denial, Horney stepped out of the Freudian mainstream.[88] She was one of few analysts in the late 1920s to identify the role social values played in psychoanalytic theory and the place of culture in the creation of women's subjectivity.[89] By casting doubt on the objectivity of psychoanalytic accounts of women, Horney opened up possibilities for distinguishing what she viewed as an authentic female experience from the masculine norms of psychoanalysis and society at large.[90]

Like Horney, Deutsch also reworked Freud's concept of penis envy in ways that allowed a greater and more productive role for women's bodies.

She too located the original moment of femininity not in the girl's first sight of the literal penis but in girls' experiences of their bodies. Deutsch argued that girls' femininity came from their own bodily sensations. Asserting that women were not "little men," she instead argued that women had unique female instincts.[91] In the preface to *The Psychology of Women*, Deutsch introduced those instincts as a "feminine core," an essence she claimed existed within all women. "While we recognize the importance of social factors, we assume that certain feminine psychic manifestations are constant and are subject to cultural influences only to the extent that now one and now another of their aspects is intensified. . . . The facade may change, but the feminine core remains unchanged throughout all storms."[92]

Discounting the cultural influences Horney emphasized, Deutsch nonetheless did not fully reject Freud's concept of penis envy. Rather, she replaced it with what she referred to as women's sense of "organlessness" as the primary, fundamental experience of femininity. Deutsch claimed that a girl suffered "genital trauma" when she realized that her clitoris was an "inadequate outlet" for her "active-aggressive instincts." Without a penis, the marker of aggressive sexuality, the girl felt that she had no organ for her active sexuality. This sense of physiological limitation induced her to give up what had been her primary sexual organ, the clitoris. "Thus the inadequacy of the organ [clitoris] can be considered a biologic and physiologic cause of the psychologic sex differences."[93]

Deutsch's theory shared most psychoanalysts' coding of the clitoris as harboring an aggressive sexuality out of step with mature femininity. She insisted that women could not bear the burden of the aggressive (male) libido and it was this biological limitation on aggression (the inadequacy of the clitoris) that was the original moment of femininity. "We believe that the development toward femininity proceeds by virtue of a constitutional impulse. . . . Genital trauma . . is a biologically predetermined inhibition of development that paves the way to femininity."[94] In short, Deutsch explained that the female body (not the sight of the penis) produced masochistic femininity and a rejection of the clitoris as inadequate.

In their recuperation of the female body as unique, Horney and Deutsch helped to produce a new style of heterosexuality that valued women's sexuality. Yet, their work also shared the widespread ambivalence about active, aggressive female sexuality found in the discourse of the companionate marriage. Along with Van Der Velde, Horney and Deutsch had to resolve the tension between the new importance granted to female sexual pleasure and the fears set off by the specter of uncontainable female sexuality. They did so through the related ideals of female sexual dependency, vaginal sexuality, and essential masochism.

Deutsch based her theories of female psychosexual development on what she viewed as women's innate heterosexuality. Such a drive explained why women embraced men and renounced the clitoris. Symbolically, the vagina brought together women's reproductive and sexual identities, two aspects of women's psychology that Deutsch sought to harmonize under the rubric of innate heterosexuality. However, the clitoris, cast as the discarded lover in the sexual drama of Freudian womanhood, continued to disrupt the psychoanalytic narrative of women's pleasurable dependency on men and the penis. The girl's original libidinal relationship with her mother and her earliest assumptions that she was identical to her brother, both represented as clitoral sexuality, hovered throughout psychoanalytic discourse as a threat to the girl's entry into mature heterosexuality, defined as purely vaginal. Psychoanalysts had the difficult task of explaining how and why the girl renounced her mother and her clitoris and entered the heterosexual world. Deutsch accounted for the shift by charting the slow and painful process by which the vagina became eroticized.

Deutsch offered her account of women's path into heterosexuality by using the passive vagina as a synecdoche for mature femininity. She explained that the mentally healthy and sexually mature woman found joy in her roles as sexual partner and obedient wife to her husband. "Feminine women," wrote Deutsch in *The Psychology of Women*,

> adapt themselves to their companions and understand them. They are the loveliest and most unaggressive of helpmates and they want to remain in that role; they do not insist on their own rights—quite the contrary. They are easy to handle in every way—if one only loves them. Sexually they are easily excited and rarely frigid; . . . They demand love and ardent desire, finding in these a satisfying compensation for the renunciation of their own active tendencies.[95]

Deutsch's feminine woman shared the conservative features of the ideal woman of the companionate marriage: a passive female sexuality nurtured within a marriage marked by clearly defined role and identity differentiation between husband and wife. While Deutsch's feminine woman conceded control over the outside world, she was not powerless. Rather, Deutsch reaffirmed the authority bestowed on women through their domestic roles by arguing that women's mastery of the realm of emo-

tions gave them power and authority in families and the world of relationships. According to Deutsch, healthy women successfully turned their
libido, or activity, inward to the world of emotions and intimacy. "If we
replace the expression 'turn toward passivity' by 'activity directed inward,'" wrote Deutsch, "the term 'feminine passivity' acquires a more
vital content and the ideas of inactivity, emptiness and immobility are
eliminated from its connotation."[96]

Deutsch's account of women's journey into femininity bound it intimately to their bodies. The female body, with its uniquely doubled genitals, embodied the conflict girls faced as they matured. Deutsch encoded
the conflict between sexual pleasure and motherhood in her analysis of the
clitoris and the vagina. She optimistically offered a biological "plan" reconciling these opposing forces.

> It's as though the biologic architect had planned two different organs for
> the two functions—the clitoris for sexuality, the vagina for reproduc-
> tion—but later found it safer to attach the vagina also to the more self-
> ish aim of sexual pleasure. Thus, in the new plan, the clitoris with its in-
> fantile sexuality, useless for reproduction, was to resign, and the vagina
> was to take up its services only when sexual maturity and readiness for
> reproduction were attained.[97]

According to Deutsch, the young girl's body propelled her into a period of latency from which she emerged as a mature, vaginal, heterosexual
woman with her sexual desire and her need to mother successfully
merged. But, as Deutsch admitted, this "plan" was not completely successful, as the clitoris was "unwilling to cede its function smoothly," and the
vagina, for its part, "did not prove completely willing to take over both
functions, reproduction and sexual pleasure."[98] Women's journey to mature heterosexuality, the joining of reproduction and orgasm in the vagina,
was not easy, nor did it come without help from a man.

Bolstering the ideal of female sexual dependence, Deutsch argued that
women's entry into heterosexuality—i.e., their ability to sexualize their
vagina—required the penis. The penis and the first experience of vaginal
penetration brought women out of latency. "The 'undiscovered' vagina,"
she wrote "is—in normal, favorable instances—eroticized by an act of
rape. . . . This process manifests itself in man's aggressive penetration on
the one hand and in the 'overpowering' of the vagina and its transformation into an erogenous sexual zone on the other." Deutsch's view of

women's sexual innocence shaped her understanding of rape not as a violent assault but as "only a mobilization of [women's] latent readiness."[99] The pain of the virgin's initial heterosexual intercourse also served as proof of women's fundamental masochism. Female sexuality, Deutsch concluded, created in women "some measure of constitutional readiness . . . something we may call a masochistic reflex mechanism."[100]

Deutsch's understanding of women's dependence on the penis meant that marital rape was the only way that women could overcome their sexual innocence. Since a virginal woman did not know her "true" sexual nature (the sexual role of her vagina), and had not yet assumed her full heterosexual identity, a man had to overcome her "natural" resistance to intercourse. Thus, the man not only led his wife into the joys of heterosexual intercourse but into full consciousness of her heterosexuality. Like the vagina, which lay silently awaiting penetration, the woman's full heterosexual identity also lay fallow, awaiting its consolidation through vaginal penetration.

Deutsch's strenuous and violent account of women's sexual development compromised her attempt to establish an organic heterosexual drive in women. Rather than women's heterosexual desire expressing itself through the vagina, she argued that women's desire for penetration came well after the act, implying there was little that was "natural" in women's transition into heterosexual pleasure. While Deutsch disagreed with Freud's reduction of femininity to failed masculinity, her attempt to reshape Freudian terms and categories to fit women's bodies did not add up to the heterosexual vaginal drive she hoped to secure.

Horney took issue with Deutsch's assumption that women were essentially masochistic. Horney interpreted such "feminine" traits as passivity and masochism to be characteristics assigned to women by a society that valued men. Horney explained that Western societies fostered women's emotional dependence through a system of economic dependence. Societies that restricted women to "spheres of life that are built chiefly upon emotional bonds," she wrote, created ideas about women's "natures" as innately weak, emotional, dependent, and limited.[101] "It is fairly obvious that these ideologies function not only to reconcile women to their subordinate role by presenting it as an unalterable one, but also to plant the belief that it represents a fulfillment they crave, or an ideal for which it is commendable and desirable to strive."[102]

Horney also dismissed Deutsch's notion of heterosexuality as rape.[103] She explained that women had an innate desire for men and for penetration by the penis.[104] Women, be they virgins or girls, knew of the sexual nature of their vaginas before their first encounter with the penis because they experienced vaginal sensations that gave them a sense of their uniquely female sexuality.[105] The vaginal sensations Horney identified thus granted women a degree of sexual autonomy from men that Deutsch's theory did not. Since these vaginal sensations occurred at the same time a girl's sexuality was (theoretically) organized around the clitoris, they were not associated with the penis. Such vaginal sensations, she implied, proved that heterosexuality in women was a natural drive, a drive that women followed rather than being coerced or raped into. Horney's view of female (hetero)sexuality, then, was that it existed independently of men.

While Horney also attempted to theorize an organic heterosexual drive in women, her cultural or anthropological perspective made the dream of organic heterosexuality as elusive for her as for Deutsch. On the one hand, Horney criticized the social construction of women as passive and masochistic. On the other hand, the organic heterosexuality Horney claimed for women tightly bound female sexuality to men's activity. Despite her cultural turn, Horney never fully renounced her belief that part of women's passivity was a product of their biology.[106]

For example, in "Inhibited Femininity: Psychoanalytic Contribution to the Problem of Frigidity," Horney analyzed women's frigidity as caused by men's behavior, behaviors that interfered with women's sexual dependence on their husbands.[107] She explained that women became frigid when men divided their sexuality into "sensual and romantic components," a situation in which men expressed themselves sexually with prostitutes while adoring their wives romantically. This gap men suffered between sex and love was the very same one that Van Der Velde and other modern marriage experts had hoped to bridge by encouraging husbands to view wives as lovers. Horney followed suit. She wrote that the split between sex and love "seems to be about as frequent in educated men as frigidity is in women." Yet, as Horney pointed out, psychoanalysts did not view men's separation of sex and love as dysfunctional. Horney did. Men's separation of sex and love, she argued, had the effect of actually diminishing women's sexual pleasure." She wrote in "Inhibited Femininity" that "the effect on women is clear. It can very easily lead to frigidity, even if the inhibitions [the wife] has brought with her from her own development are not insurmountable."[108] According to Horney, the "peculiarity of contemporary male eroticism" interfered with the emotional and sexual bonds between husband and wife. Like companionate marriage experts, Horny claimed that women, above all, needed love and sex, romance and pleasure to be inseparable in order to find orgasmic satisfaction.

Horney's attempt to shift women's so-called sexual dysfunction onto social relations between men and women was an important break from most psychoanalytic experts. At the same time, Horney continued the impulse in expert discourse to view women's sexual pleasure as dependent on men's willingness to view their wives as sexual. Without the proper gaze from her partner, a woman's desire remained unrealized at best and frustrated at worst. For the wives of men who turned to prostitutes to fulfill their sexual needs, a husband's splitting of eroticism and love inhibited the wife's discovery of her full heterosexuality. "Since in women the emotional life is, as a rule, much more closely and uniformly connected with sexuality," wrote Horney, "she cannot give herself completely when she does not love or is not loved."[109] While less violent than Deutsch's account, Horney's theory of female sexuality similarly cast women as dependent on men to awaken their sexual desires, thus reaffirming female sexual passivity.

By scripting the sexual drama of modern womanhood around female sexual dependency, psychoanalysts like Deutsch and Horney reworked heterosexuality and its ambivalence about female sexuality for the modern age. They offered important new theories of female pleasure, yet tied that pleasure to the penis. They constructed a femininity that tied women's identity to their sexuality, yet tethered women's sexuality to men to ensure its "healthy" development and expression. The ideal woman of psychoanalysis bore striking similarities to the ideal woman of Van Der Velde's *Ideal Marriage*. Van Der Velde's expressed his ambivalence about women's sexual desires in his use of romance, which he mobilized as a way to contain women's growing sexual autonomy. Psychoanalytic accounts of female sexuality were equally ambivalent about female desire. Yet because of its scientific and medical affiliations, psychoanalysis did not rely on romance as a way to contain the threat of female sexual anarchy. Rather, it attempted to establish the parameters of normal female sexuality and to explain all other unacceptable female behavior as illness. Within Freudianism, disordered sexuality functioned as a crucial foil to female mental and sexual health, helping to clarify and strengthen ideas about heterosexual normality.

Abnormal Femininity: Frigidity and the Clitoris

Few doctors worked harder to define frigidity and the pathology of the clitoris than psychoanalysts Edward Hitschmann and Edmund Bergler in the 1930s and 1940s. Both Hitschmann and Bergler had psychoanalytic training in Europe, near Freud and his circle of analysts, and both emigrated to the United States in the late 1930s. Their most important work on the topic of frigidity was the 1936 monograph *Frigidity in Women: Its Characteristics and Treatment* in which they attempted to clarify the diagnostic criteria by which a woman could be called frigid.[110] The authors defined frigidity as

> the incapacity of woman to have a *vaginal orgasm*. . . . It is of no matter whether the woman is aroused during coitus or remains cold, whether the excitement is weak or strong, whether it breaks off at the beginning or the end, slowly or suddenly, whether it is dissipated in preliminary acts, or has been lacking from the beginning. The sole criterion of frigidity is the absence of the vaginal orgasm.[111]

In *Frigidity in Women*, Hitschmann and Bergler consolidated the existing psychoanalytic literature on frigidity and were the first to outline the role of the clitoris in heterosexual women's neurosis. Bergler, for instance, published a short version of *Frigidity in Women* in the first volume of *Marriage Hygiene* in 1947, a journal directed at marriage counselors, doctors, and social workers.[112] While Hitschmann and Bergler's monograph broke no new ground in psychoanalytical theory, it nonetheless succeeded in drawing attention to the problem of female frigidity. The authors drew heavily on Deutsch's discussion of the pain associated with femininity, women's initial, if metaphoric, rape, and the pain of childbirth for their understanding of female sexuality as vaginal, masochistic, and dependent.

The psychoanalytic diagnosis of frigidity embodied, quite literally, a profound ambivalence about female sexual expression. Technically, psychoanalysts labeled a woman frigid if she was unable to reach orgasm through intercourse. But, as a diagnosis, frigidity also contained other related concerns about what constituted normal female sexuality. For instance, a woman who was deemed "neurotically undersexed" or who simply cared nothing for sexual pleasure was viewed as frigid. At the same time, if a woman was too sexual or too aggressive she was also labeled frigid. Frigidity thus became a label and diagnosis that defined how much sexual desire a woman must have to be healthy. Rather than identifying a specific problem, frigidity became a highly productive, loosely associated set of ideas that helped define the normal and the abnormal woman.

Hitschmann and Bergler's definition of frigidity rested on their view of the clitoris as the site of an aggressive and neurotic form of female sexuality and the vagina as a site of passive and healthy female sexuality. Psychoanalysts of the 1930s and 1940s no longer saw the clitoris and its pleasures as merely a remnant of an early state of libidinal attachment to the mother as did Freud but, thanks in no small part to Hitschmann and Bergler, increasingly saw it as causing feminine neurosis and ill health. For the authors, clitoral sexuality embodied women's refusal to accept their feminine roles. It represented the chaos of women behaving like men, of women overpowering men, and of women rejecting their passive and maternal destinies. Women who desired clitoral stimulation represented gender and sexual anarchy and, in doing so, threatened social demise. "The sense of inferiority in the impotent wife, the lesser value set upon her by her husband. . [who] having before his marriage known women capable of fulfillment, . . . easily [draw the husband] to become unfaithful. . . . Adultery, discord, divorce threaten from both sides. The frigid woman only too easily becomes lonely, neglected, betrayed, neurotic, dejected, and ill."[113] The authors warned that the social cost of frigidity was nothing short of family destruction. Unlike the marriage experts of the 1920s, who claimed good sex made for happier marriages, psychoanalysts like Hitchmann and Bergler claimed that "disordered" sex between husband and wife put marriage and family at risk.

The authors likened frigidity's danger to the family to the dangers posed by feminism. Implicitly, feminists, like lesbians, were women who could not sexually "surrender" to men. Associating frigidity and feminism as related crises, the author promised that as psychoanalysis cured sexually dissatisfied women, "ridiculous manifestations of the woman's movement would [also] disappear."[114] "Here we deal with women who suffer, unconsciously, from the fact that they are women and not men. The essential context of this wish . . . to be a man, is "I want a penis myself." This fantasy is repressed. Only rationalizations are conscious; for example, recriminations regarding the restricted sexual, economic and social freedom of women."[115]

The link between gender disorders such as feminism and sexual disorders such as frigidity structured Hitschmann and Bergler's monograph. The authors explained that women could discover their sexual pleasure only in loving heterosexual unions, since they could not separate love and sexuality. By threatening the love between a man and a woman, feminism, like frigidity, threatened family and marriage. Like Van Der Velde,

Hitschmann and Bergler insisted that "to be feminine in bed, in the sexual act, [brings out] the feeling of community in marriage . . . the sense of "we" and "each for the other."[116]

For Hitschmann and Bergler, the vaginal orgasm functioned as both the sign of a feminine woman and the process by which the feminine woman was created. The authors endowed the vaginal orgasm with the power to transform a girl, reluctant to have sex, into a wife who found submission to her husband erotic.[117] They explored one case of successful treatment in "Case Study A," in which they explained how psychoanalysis helped one woman discover her femininity. In treatment, the woman "learned to understand her envy and hate. . . . Born with a female body, she should have found her destiny in passive surrender, receptive, wide open, not in a false identification with the 'stronger sex.'" Thanks to psychoanalysis, the woman "straightened out her disordered development. . . . Femininity, identification with her mother, maternity, housewifeliness, come to the fore. . . . [The woman,] freed from vaginal frigidity, has become a different and socially valuable person."[118]

Hitschmann and Bergler explained that heterosexual intercourse with a loving husband consolidated a normal woman's heterosexual identity, an identity that "lay fallow" until penetration. Anything that blocked a woman's acceptance of her dependence on men, be it feminism or frigidity, thus also blocked her from becoming fully heterosexual. "The necessary shift, leading to normalcy, from activity (clitoris) to passivity (vagina) has not been inaugurated in these sick women by defloration. . . . . Defloration (organically and psychologically) frees woman's leading zone in the vagina."[119]

Like Horney and Deutsch, Hitschmann and Bergler struggled to account for women's entry into heterosexuality. Fearful of the social disruption caused by "pathological" heterosexual women, the authors' railed against the dangers of clitoral pleasures in a way that was unique in psychoanalytic annals. The clitoris, like the sexually overtrained wife of Van Der Velde's *Ideal Marriage*, became a point of rupture within Hitschmann and Bergler's narrative where the sexually aggressive, uncontainable woman lurked. Women who could not or would not find sexual satisfaction through the vagina could only be understood as outside heterosexuality.

Psychoanalytic accounts of frigidity like Hitschmann and Bergler's framed sexual dysfunction as a problem of gender.[120] The frigid woman, who denied her femininity, and the innocent woman, who celebrated her femininity, structured psychoanalytic accounts of women's development. Sexually, the innocent woman depended on her husband and her feelings of love to render sexual intercourse pleasurable. The frigid women, on the other hand, battled with her husband for control and power. She did not find sexual intercourse pleasurable because she longed for clitoral stimulation to maintain the neurotic fiction of her similarity with men. The vaginal orgasm encapsulated the ideal of feminine woman who knew her place in bed and in the family.

Hitschmann and Bergler's monograph helped to define normal femininity by categorizing female psychosexual pathology. In this way, frigidity and the vaginal orgasm functioned as parameters for identifying normal women. Women for whom sexual intercourse with a man did not result in orgasm, or women who appeared overly aggressive, too career oriented, or not maternal enough, were newly legible as dysfunctional through the psychoanalytic diagnosis of frigidity. By linking gender traits to sexuality, whether for healthy women who had vaginal orgasms or dysfunctional women who did not, psychoanalysis continued to conflate femininity and female sexuality. In so doing, it perpetuated the myth that for healthy, well-adjusted women erotic dependence on men and their identities as wives and mothers were normal outgrowths of their female bodies.

In the 1920s, psychoanalysis and companionate marriage had worked hand in hand to establish the importance of female sexual pleasure. By the 1940s, the climate that encouraged female sexuality as a sign of modernity was fully transformed into one that viewed mothering as the most important feature of women's lives. Freudian psychoanalysis proved useful as commentators in the 1940s retooled its analysis of female development to emphasize the importance of mothering to women's psychological and sexual well-being. The same language used to describe the normal healthy woman was also used to create her opposite, the unhealthy or abnormal woman. Antifeminists utilized the link between a woman's mental health and her "proper" sexual demeanor to explain unacceptable behavior as sexual ill health.

From Sexual Pleasure to Sexualized Maternity: The Pathology of Modern Women

Throughout the interwar period, sex experts reconstituted heterosexuality over and against a number of potential threats. In the 1920s, companionate marriage represented the expansion of femininity to accommodate a greater degree of female pleasure and acknowledgment of female desire. Against the backdrop of sexual modernity, women's sexual pleasure was the mark that distinguished Victorian from companionate marriages. The 1930s and 1940s witnessed a backlash against sexual modernity and feminism. As the country weathered its worst economic crisis and a second world war, Americans valued a model of traditional family life with its attendant definitions of masculine men and feminine women as symbols of social stability. Concern over proper female sexuality, deemed exclusively vaginal, replaced the concern over women's sexual pleasure in marriage. Heterosexual gender identities, organized in new ways around pleasure in the 1920s, were reoriented in the 1940s toward reproduction and family relationships.

Psychoanalytic theories that located problematic gender behaviors in sexual pathology lent scientific credibility to the spirit of antifeminism in the post–World War II period. Antifeminism had been growing in America since the Depression and reached a high point during and after the Second World War.[121] Many critics singled out feminism as a root cause of many of the country's social problems. They viewed the feminist language of equal rights as an effort to dismantle the "natural" differences between men and women. Simply put, antifeminists saw feminists as women who neglected their children and scorned domestic and care-taking roles; feminists were women who longed to be men. One reader of the *Washington Star* complained, "Whenever I see these smug pictures of women who have abdicated their normal functions and entered the field of politics and the like I instinctively say failure and slacker. Such women have flunked at their own jobs and yet pretend to tell men what they should do in their normal field."[122] A writer for the *Atlantic Monthly* explained that many Americans perceived feminism as seeking to eradicate the distinction between masculinity and femininity.[123] Popular and expert commentators deemed feminism radical at worst or misguided at best.

This construction of feminists as angry, sexually failed women had a long history. From its beginnings in the nineteenth century, critics viewed the woman's movement as a threat to harmonious relations between the sexes. As such, many accused feminism of fostering gender chaos. As early as 1897, the *New York Times* published Reverend Charles Pankhurst's attack on "andromania," a sickness in women causing a "passionate aping" of men.[124] In 1913, biologist J. Lionel Taylor argued that the "campaign for woman suffrage was an effort of certain women" to make women a "female man."[125] That same year, scientist Walter Heape argued that "the present woman's movement has its origins in sex antagonism" and the desire to "alter the laws which regulate the relations and therefore the relative powers of the sexes."[126] By the 1930s and 1940s, critics seized upon newly popular psychoanalytic literature that dismissed feminism as a form of sexual deviance and used it to dismiss any woman who did not embrace motherhood as neurotic.

Ferdinand Lundberg, a journalist and historian, and Freudian psychiatrist Marynia Farnham published their best-seller, *Modern Woman: The Lost Sex*, in 1947. Their text stands as a testimony to their close association between psychoanalytic ideas about normal womanhood and the antifeminism that reached a high-water mark in the immediate postwar period.[127] As one historian of American psychoanalysis explained, a sizable number of analysts shared the authors' view that "the flight from manhood and the crisis of femininity" were related disorders.[128] Popularizing Freudian psychoanalysis, particularly the work of Deutsch and Hitschmann and Bergler, *Modern Woman* fully articulated the attack on feminism as a gender disorder rooted in sexual dysfunction. The impact of *Modern Woman* was far-reaching. A study of the feminist movement written in 1950 described psychiatrist Marynia Farnham as "possibly the most frequently quoted writer on the modern woman."[129] Historian Mary Beard was so troubled by the book's possible influence that in 1947 she wrote to the president of Radcliffe College who shared Beard's concern over "what seems to be a rising wave of 'antifeminism' of which *Modern Woman: The Lost Sex* is symptomatic."[130]

Farnham and Lundberg were not alone in their enthusiastic embrace of psychoanalytic theory. Hollywood had utilized psychoanalytic characters and plot structure to explore the illness of careerism in women. The popular film *Lady in the Dark*, which opened in 1944, explored the psychic toll enacted on the heroine for abandoning her reproductive destiny for a high-powered editorial post. Film directors used analysts as characters, for example, Alfred Hitchcock in his 1946 *Spellbound*, where Ingrid Bergman played a psychoanalyst. Novelists and playwrights like Tennessee Williams, Eugene O'Neill, and Lillian Hellman drew on psychoanalysis for inspiration. *Time* and *Life* magazines covered the popularity of psychoanalysis, as did women's magazines like *Good Housekeeping* and *Cosmopolitan*. Such coverage helped to familiarize thousands of readers with Freudian terms and theories. For example, one *Life* magazine article illustrated Freud's triadic structure of the id, ego, and superego. The superego ("decides moral issues") bore uncanny similarity to Freud with his small round glasses and distinctive beard, the id ("produces primitive impulses") to an early homo sapien, and the ego ("turns thought into action") to a midlevel manager, complete with suit, tie, and desk. "The normal mind," the article explained, "has sound balance between impulses, practical judgement, [and] conscience."[131] Luminaries like Erich Fromm, Karen Horney, Rollo May, and Karl Menninger regularly published articles in the *Atlantic Monthly* and *Scientific American* that kept readers up-to-date on trends in the field. Menninger became a household name through a monthly column for the *Ladies Home Journal*. Widely popular it-happened-to-me accounts such as John Knight's *The Story of My Psychoanalysis* (1950), Harold Greenwald's *Great Cases in Psychoanalysis* (1959), and Dr. Robert Linder's *The Fifty Minute Hour* (1956) walked readers through fictional analyses, offering them an imaginative way into the cryptic work of a psychoanalysis.[132]

Such widespread coverage of Freudian theory lent its antifeminist leanings great credibility. Readers who were already familiar with psychoanalytic concepts, who had come across them in magazines and in popular films, whose husbands or sons encountered psychoanalysts and their tests during the mobilization for the war, and whose marriage and child-rearing manuals were infused with its terms heard in accounts like *Modern Woman* messages they had gleaned elsewhere.

While *Modern Woman* ostensibly explored the social, historical, and psychological origins of women's status, Farnham and Lundberg were predominantly concerned with tracing the relationship between feminism, sexuality, and pathological femininity. Feminism occupied a privileged place in their text as a psychological disorder that had the power to strike at the nation's center: women at home, women mothering children, women making love with their husbands. The authors represented feminism as a disease that threatened to infect unsuspecting women. "Feminism . . . was at its core a deep illness,"[133] they wrote, an "intellectual construction" that grew out of "deep emotional maladjustment and bewilderment."[134]

Like other postwar commentators, Farnham and Lundberg believed the crisis of the Depression and Second World War had masculinized women. As a result, the country now suffered from an unprecedented outbreak of neurosis, with only one-third of its citizens free of contaminating emotional distress.[135] The authors, along with other social critics, pointed to feminism as a pathological manifestation of the country's poor mental health. They explained that the goals of feminism had little to do with attaining political rights for women. Rather, it was a device to symbolically castrate men. "One can readily demonstrate, even on the surface, that the social and political programs of feminism were the least of the objectives sought." Their goal, translated the authors, was to be men. Belittling the most significant political accomplishment of the nineteenth-century woman's movement, the authors explained that the franchise was little more than an "ego-prop" for feminists who only wanted the empty symbolism of being able to say that they were the "equal of men" in the political sphere. "Most of the social and political program of feminism . . . was an ego-prop, sought by the most articulate and emotionally deprived women as a way of restoring their self-esteem and self-confidence."[136]

Like other Freudian experts, Farnham and Lundberg's anxiety about women's autonomy from the home, reduced to and encapsulated in the term *feminism,* led them to see women's work as a rejection of their "biological" destinies as mothers. The authors could associate mental illness and feminism precisely because they viewed feminism, or women's autonomy, as a product of women's sexual dissatisfaction. Feminism's threat to the sexual order tangibly shaped their text: "Underneath all their talk about the reform of woman's sphere (which referred most directly to her ego sphere), the feminists were unconsciously chiefly concerned with reform of her libidinal sphere, her sexual life."[137] According to the authors, feminists "were out after nothing other than sexual gratification and to throw off male sexual restraints on women."[138] Thanks to the misguided sexual revolution of the 1920s, women longed to be freed from the limits their biology placed on their sexuality. Women who suffered from a masculinity complex strove for "orgiastic equality" with men. Such women sought to experience sexual pleasure as men did: unencumbered by love, dependency, or reproduction. Simplifying Deutsch for a popular audience, the authors insisted that women required an acceptance of their feminine role to find sexual satisfaction. "It is precisely in development of femininity that capacity for female sexual gratification lies." In a passage striking for its conflation of gender and sexuality, of mothering and sexual pleasure, Farnham and Lundberg explained that the erotics of female sexual pleasure lay in pregnancy.

> For the sexual act to be fully satisfactory to a woman she must, in the depths of her mind, desire, deeply and utterly, to be a mother. If she does not so desire, if she regards the sex act as ending with orgasm, it will be sensually unsatisfactory in various ways, and will often fail to result in orgasm. . . . The rule therefore is: The less a woman's desire to have children and the greater her desire to emulate the male . . . the less will be her enjoyment of the sex act.[139]

According to the authors, modern women's rejection of motherhood left them frigid. Repeating Deutsch's celebration of the feminine woman,

Farnham and Lundberg characterized normal femininity as "receptivity and passiveness, a willingness to accept dependence without fear or resentment, with a deep inwardness and readiness for the final goal of sexual life—impregnation. It doesn't admit of wishes to control or master, to rival or dominate."[140] Healthy women found pleasure in vaginal sexuality, where reproduction and pleasure, sexuality and gender, came together. "Satisfactory sexuality . . . is linked for a woman with wanting and having children. As a general rule, the fewer children a woman has . . . the more disordered is her sexual life apt to be in terms of satisfaction to herself. . . . For the sex act is primarily concerned with having children. Women cannot make its immediate pleasure an end in itself without inducing a decline in the pleasure."[141] By casting motherhood as an expression of women's fundamental, essential sexuality, Farnham and Lundberg extended the view of the vagina as women's only normal sexual organ and motherhood as women's only normal social role.

Modern Woman ended its hand-wringing account of American culture by setting out a program for healing the mental illness besieging modern women. Toward that end, the authors recommended that the federal government subsidize psychoanalysis for feminists and give cash grants to mothers. Only by revaluing motherhood, they insisted, could modern women cease their emotional, and ultimately dysfunctional, search for meaning and return home where they belonged.

Farnham and Lundberg articulated the links between sexuality and gender stability that had guided discussions of female sexuality from the companionate marriage of the 1920s to the vaginal orgasm of the late 1940s. Women who did not mother, who prioritized careers over motherhood, or who simply rejected the submissive ideal of the sexually innocent woman were increasingly pathologized to have disordered sexual identities. Frigidity, feminism, and lesbianism constituted the dangerous behaviors that threatened the stability of the family and protected the ideal of the innocent and maternal woman.

The long-standing conflation of female sexuality and women's social identities by sex experts essentialized a specific set of traits for women that by the 1940s tightly associated women with motherhood, sexual dependency, and men. Psychoanalysis helped to articulate the bounds of normal and implicitly white and middle-class femininity with its reading of feminism as a form of gender pathology rooted in frigidity. Thus, the psychoanalytic ideal of the vaginal orgasm was ripe for antifeminist picking. Antifeminists based their logic on a set of ever widening assumptions, moving outward from the opposition between the clitoris and the vagina, between feminine women and masculine women, between mothers and feminists, and ultimately between sexual order and gender chaos. Female sexuality bore the freight of social order or social breakdown. While Farnham and Lundberg offered extreme views about the dangers posed by feminism, they were by no means lone voices in the wilderness. Rather, they joined an illustrious crew of experts who used psychoanalysis as a theory of women's essential difference.

The women who, in the 1960s began to argue for women's equality had a tougher row to hoe than had Karen Horney and Helene Deutsch. Rejecting the older paradigm of female passivity and motherhood as women's highest calling, women in the 1960s had to struggle against ideas of women's dependence that by now had become thoroughly encrusted with assumptions about women's sexual normality.

At the same time, the ideal of the normal heterosexual woman articulated in the interwar years that so galvanized white feminists in the 1960s and 1970s also contained within it layers of troubling assumptions. While feminists rejected the Freudian ideal woman, they absorbed many of its categories and beliefs. Like psychoanalysts, white second-wave feminists from Friedan to Firestone privileged the role sexuality played in identity, specifically, gender identity. They elevated the nuclear family as a microcosm of society that possessed the potential for both liberation and oppression. They tended to see the unconscious as a universal category independent of class, race, and nation. These fundamental beliefs that second-wave feminists took from psychoanalytic experts inadvertently helped to seal feminism into an unconsciously white perspective, one that adopted standards of normality premised on the so-called universal experiences of white middle-class women. The unmarked category of "woman" that second-wave radical feminists adopted to do the historic work of politicizing women's experience also contained within it the seeds of the second wave's undoing. By the 1980s, feminists of color no longer accepted the white psychoanalytically inspired underpinnings of either radical or cultural feminism nor the second wave's foundational premise, based on psychoanalytic assumption, that sexuality was the universal source of women's oppression.

BETWEEN FREUDIANISM AND FEMINISM

Sexology's Postwar Challenge

*W*hen radical feminist Anne Koedt issued her historic denunciation of the vaginal orgasm as a misogynist myth in 1969, she rejected a paradigm that had offered psychoanalysts in the 1920s a way to theorize women's social role and sexual behavior as a coherent, organic whole. Ironically, unbeknownst to Koedt, female psychoanalysts in the 1920s had embraced the idea of vaginal sexuality as an innovative alternative to Freud's male-derived models of psychosexual development, which had all centered on women's envy of the penis.[1] Yet as more analysts and experts embraced the view of women's organic heterosexuality, the vaginal orgasm ceased to be an alternative to Freudian penis envy and became part of orthodox Freudian psychoanalytic theory. By the 1940s, the vaginal orgasm became a standard through which women's sexual impulses were deemed healthy or pathological. It was through this set of overlapping psychoanalytic terms and associations that the view of feminism as a sexual disorder emerged and gained credence. The antifeminism implicit in

American Freudianism compelled second-wave feminists to revisit a painful history of ideas that continued to fester in the 1960s culture of sexual liberation.

However, feminists in the 1960s were not the first to raise doubts as to the so-called truth of Freudian femininity. The new experts of sex, the postwar sexologists Alfred Kinsey and his heirs, William Masters and Virginia Johnson, offered women in the 1960s an intellectual bridge out of Freudianism and into feminism. But before feminists could utilize sexological knowledge, they had to sift through a legion of popularizers who attempted to translate the arcane language of sexology into a new lexicon of sexual freedom.

In 1953, six years after Farnham and Lundberg reaffirmed in *Modern Woman: The Lost Sex* that female sexuality was fundamentally maternal, dependent, and deeply anchored in love and monogamy, Alfred Kinsey published *Sexual Behavior in the Human Female (SBHF)*.[2] The second of his groundbreaking reports on American sexual behavior at mid-century, Kinsey's report on women offered a new language in which to discuss female sexuality, one that used "science" to prove that men and women were similar, if not identical, sexual citizens. The following year, in 1954, William Masters began his twelve-year project on human sexuality, which also sought to use science to unlock the mysteries of sex. His and partner Virginia Johnson's research, published in 1966 as *Human Sexual Response*, completed what Kinsey had begun: to "modernize" Americans' understanding about sex and to affirm its centrality to both men's and women's identities.[3] Neither spoke of female sexuality in terms of mothering, but, in the spirit of liberalism so prominent in the postwar era, viewed women as individuals with desires upon which they acted. Such conceptual shifts put male and female sexuality on a common, in the sexologists' words, "human" measurement scale and constituted a major transformation in expert discourse on female sexuality.[4]

The research of Kinsey and Masters and Johnson participated in the remaking of female heterosexuality in the postwar years on a number of levels. In terms of American sexual thought, their work posed a significant challenge to the psychoanalytic view of women that had dominated expert and popular accounts since the 1930s. Both Kinsey and Masters and Johnson viewed Freudian psychoanalysis as having obscured female sexuality through misinformation and false assumptions about what women wanted and desired sexually. While postwar psychoanalysts prided themselves on their scientific rigor and theoretical sophistication, the sex researchers argued that Freudianism had bred ignorance and fear in many men and in most women about the nature of female sexuality. They claimed that neither in terms of behavior (Kinsey) nor physiology (Masters and Johnson) could they find any grounds for the Freudian link between the clitoris and "neurotic" behaviors such as frigidity, lesbianism, and envy of men. In contrast to the psychoanalytic view of women as passive, dependent, and less sexual than men, sexology discovered a responsive, sexually capable and potentially autonomous female body underneath social and expert myths of feminine passivity. The sexologists hoped to use this responsive female body toward their goal of establishing sexual similarity between women and men.

Kinsey and Masters and Johnson also acknowledged a greater degree of "healthy" female sexual desire than the twentieth-century sex experts that had come before them. Rather than viewing women as primarily mothers or mothers-to-be, sexologists saw women as having the same right to sexual pleasure as men. Using a range of new methodologies, Kinsey and Masters and Johnson offered Americans a modern view of heterosexuality organized around mutual pleasure between sexually similar partners. The postwar sex researchers and the generation of sexologists who followed in their wake reworked the companionate marriage for a new age that once again prioritized sexual expressiveness as a route to strong marriages.

By challenging the dominant role ascribed to the vagina and, by extension, to intercourse and reproduction in ideas about normal female heterosexuality, sexology provided a crucial bridge between Freudianism and radical feminism.[5] Second-wave feminists in the late 1960s and 1970s drew selectively on postwar sexology to construct a new liberated woman, one who based all her sexual encounters on self-determination rather than on what experts deemed normal.[6] By doing so, feminists offered not just a modern but a revolutionary view of female sexuality.

The Kinsey Report on Women

In many ways, the 1953 Kinsey report on women reflected the logic of American cold war society, a society that promised individuals the right to "the pursuit of pleasure" at the same time it anxiously constricted such freedoms in the name of family stability. As many historians have noted, the tension between the growing public visibility of sexuality and the conservative turn to a "new traditionalism," defined through rigid, complementary gender roles and family "togetherness," constituted a central paradox of the postwar period.[7] The new traditionalism enshrined the home as a haven from the stress and impersonality of corporate America, a place where men could assert both their authority and their personalities and where women could nurture families. Alienated "occupational men" retreated home to reconnect themselves to emotions and relationships in a world that stood in stark contrast to the competitive work-a-day one in which they measured themselves. If men's sense of self was rhetorically situated in work, women's sense of self was deeply embedded in the multiple activities that made up the home and the family.[8]

Generated by and produced for white middle-class Americans, the view of the family that gained prominence in the postwar world concerned itself with what many commentators, experts, and policy makers viewed as the "average" and the "normal."[9] Experts and popularizers applied standards of what constituted family health and normality to all Americans and judged African Americans and working-class families as potentially lacking in strong fathers, forceful discipline, and a firm commitment to the work ethic.[10] Yet as many people wrapped themselves in what they referred to as traditional family life, they were, in fact, engaged in the invention of a new kind of family life. The new traditionalism rested on a host of developments such as uncharacteristic affluence, the growth of suburbs, and a rapid and steady expansion of the national economy. Both black and white families enjoyed the growth of economic opportunity, even as it remained structured by race. Ironically, despite the importance attributed to homemaking and mothering, working women constituting one of the fastest growing sectors of the labor force during the post-1945 years.[11] The home, headed by a husband and tended to by a full-time, stay-at-home wife, was, at least rhetorically, the productive center for the national celebration of dichotomous, biologically based gender roles, "togetherness," and, as it was termed by magazine publisher Henry Luce, "the American century."

Postwar sociologists, most notably Talcott Parsons, offered new theories about the distinct roles women and men fulfilled in modern society.[12] In positive terms, Parsons explained that the modern (and implicitly white) nuclear family was highly specialized in its functions and this division of labor was itself a sign of civilization.[13] For Parsons, clearly defined masculine and feminine roles functioned not only as the cornerstone of the family but of a stable, healthy society. Psychoanalysts repeated Parson's view of the essential health of men and women's dichotomous tasks, many speaking out against what they viewed as the dangerous blurring of sex roles in American homes. At a conference held in 1957, psychiatrists wondered how "a boy can learn what it means to be a man . . . when mother and father in so many homes carry out identical tasks."[14] The *New York Times Magazine* in April of the same year quoted Dr. Irene Josselyn of the Chicago Institute of Psychoanalysis as warning that the country was "drifting toward a social structure made up of he-women and she-men."[15] Psychoanalysts looked down on such gender ambiguity and role flexibility as disordered and pathological and worried about their effects on the next generation. For experts like Parsons, dichotomous gender roles and the very division of the world into masculine and feminine arenas enhanced sexual pleasure: "A mature woman can love, sexually, only a man who takes his full place in the masculine world. Conversely, a mature man can only love a woman who is . . . a full wife to him and mother to his children."—[16] The harnessing of sexuality to marriage and families became a primary formulation of the postwar period's vision of mental and sexual health.

No expert group did more to establish the reigning guidelines for understanding sexual health and normality than did Freudian psychoanalysts. Like Parsons and other postwar experts, psychoanalysts conflated sexual health with dichotomous gender roles. Psychoanalysis reached a mass audience during and after World War II through the burgeoning field of psychiatry, which had incorporated Freudianism as its theoretical structure. Empowered during the war by the thousands of psychological tests given to American soldiers, psychiatry directed part of its considerable cultural authority to normalizing heterosexuality as the only healthy form of sexual behavior and to explaining male homosexuality as either a sign of immaturity or the result of failed gender roles at home such as a domineering mother or weak father.[17] For example, psychoanalyst Edmund Bergler argued that homosexuality was a serious regression to the oral stage of development and, as such, represented a pathological sexual orientation. He warned that older homosexuals were using the 1948 Kinsey report on male sexuality to "recruit" younger men to their lifestyle.[18] Freudian psychoanalysts helped to cultivate fear in many average American men that any sign of gender nonconformity indicated their repressed or latent homosexuality. The same conflation psychiatrists made between men's gender nonconformity and deviant sexuality, or, conversely, gender conformity and sexual health, operated for women. It was this psychoanalytic understanding of female sexuality that Kinsey's report on women most directly challenged.

Kinsey's report on American women's sexual behavior at mid-century severed the ties between mental pathology and sexual behavior so central to Freudianism and instead advocated for a democratic acceptance of all sexual practices and behaviors. Yet, while Kinsey attempted to move beyond the psychoanalytic belief in men and women's healthy and fundamental difference, he also created new terms for understanding sexual difference. Ironically, Kinsey reached conclusions about women that bore striking similarity to those reached by Freudians.

Kinsey first became interested in sex research when he taught a class on marriage at the University of Indiana in 1938.[19] Amazed at the paucity of sources, Kinsey began a massive study of human sexual behavior that, by its end, involved interviews with 17,500 women and men. Kinsey worked alone in the first years of his new project and personally recorded 7,000 of the first 12,000 sex histories that comprised his data base—an average of fourteen interviews a week for ten years.[20] He was soon joined by Drs. Pomeroy, Gebhard, and Martin and formed Indiana University's Institute for Sex Research, known simply as the Kinsey Institute. In 1941 Kinsey applied for and received funds from the Rockefeller-sponsored Committee for Research in Problems of Sex. After a small initial grant, the committee increased funding for Kinsey's research each year until 1947, when the Institute for Sex Research received half of the committee's $75,000 annual budget.[21]

Kinsey and his team of researchers traveled the country interviewing volunteers about their sexual histories and behavior patterns. The standard one- to two-hour interview addressed a range of behaviors, asking how often the subject had reached orgasm from the following six practices—nocturnal sex dreams, masturbation, heterosexual petting, heterosexual intercourse, homosexual intercourse, and contacts with animals. Kinsey also asked for information about social and economic status, marital histories, sex education, and physical and physiological health as well as histories of sexual contacts.[22] The researchers then coded the interviews on index cards that they entered into their IBM computer to compile their sex statistics.[23]

Like other postwar experts, Kinsey participated in the construction of American womanhood as white and middle-class.[24] Far more than his report on men, his report on women rested on a universal subject. Whereas his report on male sexuality explained that his research into African American sexual behavior was numerically insufficient to include, Kinsey offered no such explanation for the absence of racial specificity in *SBHF*.

In fact, racial minorities were not even listed among those for whom the data might not be accurate.[25] Similarly, Kinsey did not situate his female respondents in economic class to the same extent he had in his report on men. Instead, he organized his data on women primarily through date of birth. Kinsey discovered that the decade when a woman was born proved to be the most striking forecaster of women's "total sexual outlets," with women born after the turn of the century experiencing almost twice as many orgasms as those born in the late nineteenth-century.[26]

Unlike Freudians, who emphasized sexuality as an impulse rooted in the unconscious, Kinsey viewed sexuality as primarily biological. Being an empiricist, he understood orgasm as constituting the most direct measure of sexual excitability and frequency of orgasm, the best indicator of sexual potency. "The use of such a unit," Kinsey wrote in his introduction to *SBHF*, "is justified by the fact that all orgasms, whether derived from masturbation, petting, marital coitus, or any other source, may provide a physiologic release from sexual arousal. . . . There seems . . . to be no better unit for measuring the incidence and frequencies of sexual activity."[27] Unlike psychoanalysts, Kinsey made no surface/depth, conscious/unconscious distinctions between behavior and impulse. As with his report on male sexuality, Kinsey viewed female sexuality as merely an impulse that sought pleasurable release. He neither linked female pleasure to pregnancy nor pathologized women's nonreproductive sexual behavior. Rather, Kinsey legitimated female sexual pleasure, or orgasm, as a physiological event in and of itself.

One of Kinsey's most radical assumptions was his view that heterosexual intercourse existed on a continuum of outlets, none of which he viewed as inherently "healthy" or "pathological."[28] Using an analogy with animals, he argued that humans had the innate capacity to respond to a range of sexual stimulation but society limited that capacity in an effort to uphold its own norm of reproductive heterosexuality. The reality that society defined some behaviors as "deviant" and others as "normal" had no bearing on the pleasure individuals took from sexual release. Kinsey stated that "unless it has been conditioned by previous experience, an animal should respond identically to identical stimuli, whether they emanate from some part of its own body, from another individual of the same sex or from an individual of the opposite sex."[29] Yet while many took his report as long-awaited confirmation of the normalcy of homosexuality, Kinsey himself did not explicitly challenge the dominance of heterosexuality. Rather, he questioned the limits of any sexual identity. Not asking why individuals became homosexual, Kinsey turned the question on its head and wondered instead why "each and every individual is not involved in every type of sexual activity."[30]

One of Kinsey's most important accomplishments was his rejection of the Freudian map of the sexual female body. Specifically, he questioned the belief that the vagina gave women orgasms and the clitoris led them into psychological degeneracy. Beginning with Freud and elaborated upon by Freudian analysts in the 1930s and 1940s, psychoanalysts viewed the clitoris as a masculine organ because they associated it with aggression, pleasure, and envy for the penis. Kinsey dismissed these associations. Far from masculine, he argued that the clitoris was a nerve center of female orgasm. Similarly, using illustrations and diagrams, Kinsey explained that the vagina simply did not have the endowment of nerves to make it the center of female sexual response. Rather than the seat of "mature" female sexuality as psychoanalysis claimed, the vagina, Kinsey wrote with typical understatement, was "relatively unimportant as a center of erotic stimulation."[31]

> It is difficult in light of our present understanding of the anatomy and physiology of sexual response, to understand what can be meant by "vaginal orgasm." The literature usually implies that the vagina itself should be the center of sensory stimulation, and this, as we have seen, is a physical and physiologic impossibility for nearly all females.[32]

With this, Kinsey cast doubt not only on the existence of the vaginal orgasm but the centrality of the vagina in heterosexual practice. Clitoral stimulation, he argued, led women neither to lesbianism nor pathological envy of men but merely to orgasm.

Kinsey implied quite directly that it was men and experts, not women, who had made the vagina so central to female sexuality. He argued that Freudianism's rigid hierarchy of pleasure and health, with the vagina and intercourse ranked as most healthy and the clitoris and its stimulation deviant, led women into a morass of confusion and ignorance. Clinicians, psychoanalysts, and marriage counselors, he wrote, expended "considerable effort attempting to teach their patients to "transfer 'clitoral responses' into 'vaginal responses.' Some hundreds of the women in our own study and many thousands of the patients of certain clinicians have consequently been much disturbed by their failure to accomplish this biologic impossibility."[33] He concluded—much to the horror of Freudians who later reviewed his report—that the vagina was "of minimum importance in contributing to the erotic responses of the female" and "may even contribute more to the sexual arousal of the male than it does to the arousal of the female."[34]

Kinsey's challenge to the Freudian map of women's sexual body figured prominently in his efforts to modernize female sexuality. Whereas Freudians insisted that sexual difference was a sign of mental and social health, Kinsey insisted that sexual similarity was more scientifically accurate and thus more healthy than sexual difference. Kinsey established sexual similarity in two ways. First, he emphasized women's innate desire for and capacity to reach orgasm. He claimed that the desire for sexual release led women, like men, to engage in a variety of behaviors such as masturbation, adultery, and homosexuality. Second, Kinsey established sexual similarity through an implicit analogy between the penis and the clitoris, which he supported by his claim that the vagina was incapable of generating sufficient stimulation for the woman to reach orgasm. By displacing Freudianism's normalizing of the unreachable vaginal orgasm, Kinsey hoped to free women to more fully engage in pleasurable (because more accurate) sex.

Yet, at the same time Kinsey attempted to establish sexual similarity, contradictions in his methodology repeatedly reaffirmed sexual differences between men and women. Most of the report's contradictions about sexual difference can be traced back to the chapter titled "Marital Coitus." In this chapter, Kinsey's empiricism—his belief that sexuality can be measured by orgasm and sexual desire by frequency of orgasm—collapsed as he tried to account for a major discrepancy he found between women's and men's rate of orgasm.

In support of women's sexual capacity, Kinsey recorded that twenty-five percent of women in his survey recalled experiencing orgasm by the age of fifteen, more than half by the age of twenty, and more than three-quarters by the age of twenty-five. Not specifying the behaviors through which women attained orgasms, Kinsey utilized these statistics in his case for women's sexual competency. When he situated orgasm in marriage, Kinsey reported that in the first year of marriage 63 percent of women reached orgasm and that by the fifteenth year of marriage the percentage of women reaching orgasm rose to 81 percent.[35] It would seem that most women found marriage, or grew to find marriage, sexually satisfying.

Yet, when examined closely, a troubling portrait of female sexuality emerged from the very same data. It would appear that marital coitus did not satisfy women as much or as regularly as it did men. Of Kinsey's female respondents, a full third—between 36 and 44 percent—reached orgasm inconsistently. Another third reached orgasm "infrequently."[36] Thus, while 70 percent of wives experienced orgasm in marital coitus in the course of marriage, far fewer did so with any consistency. During the first year of marriage, one wife in four failed to experience an orgasm in coitus. Education did not seem to help: in the twentieth year of marriage fifteen percent of marital coitus still failed to end in female orgasm.[37]

Kinsey's discovery of the sexual inequality in marriage as measured by men's and women's different rates of orgasm constituted a serious problem for his belief in sexual similarity. To account for the difference, Kinsey contradicted his earlier statements about the orgasm as constituting the best measurement of human sexuality. "It cannot be emphasized too often," he wrote, "that orgasm cannot be taken as the sole criterion for determining the degree of satisfaction which a female may derive from sexual activity." Kinsey explained that, unlike men, women gained "considerable pleasure" from sexual activity that "does not proceed to the point of orgasm" yet comprised part of what he referred to as "the social aspects of a sexual relationship."[38] He wrote that, even if coitus did not end with an orgasm, "many a female finds satisfaction in knowing that her husband or other sexual partner has enjoyed the contact and in realizing that she has contributed to the male's pleasure." In a startling break from his rhetoric of equality, Kinsey announced that "this is much more true for the female than it would be for the male. It is inconceivable that males who were not reaching orgasm would continue their marital coitus for any length of time."[39] With this conception of the nonorgasmic pleasures women gained from sexual contact and, likewise, its intolerability to men, Kinsey reverted to a narrative of women's essential difference, a view that at other points in his report he challenged. Women, it would seem, found love to be erotic in a way that orgasm could not measure and in a way completely different from men's experience of either love or sex.

This "social aspect" of female sexual pleasure, along with women's lower rates of orgasm, introduced an important contradiction into Kinsey's report. On the one hand, Kinsey had a commitment to sexual similarity. He repeatedly asserted throughout his report that women and men shared an innate physiological capacity to reach orgasm in response to proper stimulation. On the other hand, Kinsey was equally committed to the empiricism that set him against the major sex research studies that had come before him. In "Marital Coitus," however, his empirical methodology came into direct conflict with his desire to establish similarity. His empiricism coded sexual response as orgasm and his research showed that women had fewer orgasms than did men. Thus, by Kinsey's own logic, women were "less sexual" than men. Convoluting matters further, within Kinsey's methodology—which viewed impulse and behavior, orgasm and desire, as identical—it was conceptually impossible to determine whether women's lower rate of orgasms could be attributed to biology or to social limits placed on women. Did women have fewer orgasms because they were simply "less sexual" than men, or because society had alienated women, more than men, from expressing their full capacity? The conflict between Kinsey's empiricism and his commitment to similarity in the female report became the point of slippage in his analysis between sexual behavior and gender. It too became the point at which Kinsey's assertions of sexual equality collapsed.

Kinsey's slippage between biological and cultural influences on sexuality structured the final section of *SBHF* where he sought to resolve questions raised in "Marital Coitus" about women's lower rates of orgasm and the role of love in women's sexual lives. In part 3, entitled "Comparisons of Female and Male," Kinsey reviewed the literature on human sexual response. Comprised of five chapters that covered the psychology, anatomy, physiology, hormones, and neurology of sexual response, this section captured in microcosm the difficulty of locating the origin of sexual difference. It would appear from the conclusions drawn in this final section that Kinsey had set out to prove sexual similarity. In four of the five chapters, Kinsey explained that females and males "do not differ in any regard" to the basic elements of sexual response.

While such a survey of anatomy and physiology revealed no cause for why women had fewer orgasms than men did, Kinsey found one arena through which he accounted for the different rates of orgasm between men and women. In "Psychologic Factors in Sexual Response," Kinsey explained that men and women reacted differently to what he called "psychosexual stimuli."[40] Kinsey defined "psychosexual stimuli" as thirty-three erotic or sexually motivated activities including pictures of nudes, "erotic fine art," reading erotic stories, observing genitalia, burlesque shows, sexual action of others, animals in coitus, peeping and voyeurism, and sexual graffiti on walls.[41] He found that men reacted far more to such visual stimulation than did women. From this he concluded that men were more sexually suggestible or "conditionable," and, consequently, "more sexual" than women, since the world for them was filled with more potentially erotic stimulation. Not questioning whether his selection of erotic materials might be at fault, Kinsey concluded that women's lower frequencies of orgasm resulted from the fact that women had fewer sources of erotic stimulation. Ironically, Kinsey did not consider love or "the social aspects of a sexual relationship" to fit within the category of "psychosexual stimulation." Rather, love existed in a category he applied only to women.

Kinsey interpreted women's and men's different levels of response to visually stimulating images and to love as indicative of inherent and irrefutable sexual difference.[42] Nothing in his report helped him to generate an alternative interpretation that could reach beyond empirical differences in male and female behavior. He could only explain these differences in behavior by referring back to sexual difference itself—the difference that he set out to demystify. After searching the bodily systems related to sexual response for the origins of sexual difference, Kinsey concluded that more research was needed.[43] The biological roots of the undeniable differences between men and women—which manifested itself in different rates of orgasm—was there waiting for science to decode. Ironically, as part 3 illustrated, this difference could not be seen when examining the discrete aspects of human physiology and anatomy. This difference was more apparent in the organism as a whole, an organism in culture, rather than in its physical systems. Sexual difference, the most obvious difference of all, kept the secrets of its origins hidden from the scientific gaze.

Kinsey's category of "psychosexual stimulation" and women's response to love became, in short, the loopholes that returned him to the mystery of sexual difference his study attempted to solve. Despite his efforts to separate female sexuality from ideas about morality and social custom, Kinsey tacitly reasserted the connection that Freudians and other experts had made between emotion and female sexuality. Since women did not respond as much as men did to the thirty-five forms of psychosexual stimulation Kinsey documented, they were thus less sexually responsive than men. Yet, at the same time, Kinsey left room for emotion, love, and romance as erotic stimulation for women—forms of stimulation he did not acknowledge for men.

Ironically, while Kinsey asserted a common "human" sexuality based on orgasm, he also reconstructed women's essential difference from men. Despite his rejection of earlier sex experts who for generations had deemed healthy women less interested in sex than love, Kinsey's final chapter used "science" to explain that women were essentially less sexual than men and found love erotic. The significance of Kinsey's report on women, however, was not simply that he failed to establish sexual similarity between women and men or that he reconstructed a view of women's essential difference. Rather, its significance lies in how the report established sexual difference. Through methodologies that shared little if anything with those of psychoanalysts or marriage experts, Kinsey nevertheless reached a similar conclusion.

Reactions to Kinsey's report on women came swiftly for the Kinsey Institute. Dr. Pomeroy, one of Kinsey's closest associates, explained that the responses to *SBHF* were much more "irrational and emotional" than to the male report. Most national magazines emphasized the sensational news about women's infidelity and rates of premarital sex. For example, *Cosmopolitan* passionately denounced Kinsey's report as slanted against chastity and toward free love. Nevertheless, the editors at *Cosmopolitan* chose to illustrate their coverage of *SBHF* with two nude women. The *New York Times* refused to print any advertising for the book and then delayed reviewing it, despite its high standing in their best-sellers lists. Others openly ridiculed Kinsey. In the wake of the *Female* report, the comic strip "Abbie 'n' Slats" of Capp Enterprises introduced a character named "Dr. Pinsey" whose transformation from mild mannered scientist to sexual leach proved popular. The offended Kinsey threatened legal action if the character was not dropped.[44]

Popular perception held that Kinsey had been resoundingly condemned and discredited. The institute countered by pointing to the fact that more clergy and more scientists supported his research than criticized it. Despite evidence to the contrary, many laymen continued to insist that Kinsey had "trampled" upon the honor of American women. Such negative public response gave many the impression that *SBHF* was a financial disaster. Yet, despite public denouncements, the book proved to be a commercial success. After two years, it had reached 75 percent of the total sales achieved by the *Male* volume in six years. Internationally it also sold well. It was translated into Hebrew, French, Portuguese, German, Spanish, Norwegian, Finnish, Italian, and Dutch.[45]

Much of the public's perception of *SBHF* came from experts who launched scathing criticisms of the volume. Margaret Mead, one of America's most popular and respected sex experts, proclaimed that the book should not be permitted to become a best-seller because "the sudden removal of a previously guaranteed reticence has left many young people singularly defenseless in just those areas where their desire to conform was protected by a lack of knowledge of the extent of nonconformity." Whereas the most serious attacks on the *Male* volume centered on interviewing techniques and statistical interpretation, attacks on the *Female* volume focused on morality.

Critical clergy denounced Kinsey from pulpits across the country. In Indiana, the Provincial Council of Catholic Women brought pressure to bear on the president of the university to sever its relationship to the Institute for Sex Research. "If you do not recognize how dangerous it is to popularize incendiary suggestions like these," wrote the council, "we tremble at what may happen to our sons and daughters entrusted to the care of Indiana University." Such concerns were aired on a national level by religious leaders and theoreticians Billy Graham and Reinhold Niebuhr.[46]

Psychoanalysts were among Kinsey's harshest critics. Karl Menninger, who had supported Kinsey's male report, attacked the female report for "forcing human sexuality into a zoological frame of reference" that neglected human psychology and for defining normality as "that which is natural in the sense that is it what is practiced by animals." Dr. William S. Kroger and Dr. Edmund Bergler criticized Kinsey not only for separating sex and love but also for mistaking "what is widespread for what is normal," and for encouraging women to discount the importance of the vaginal orgasm to women's mental health.[47] According to the authors, Kinsey's crime against womanhood was his reduction of sex to a matter of orgasm alone, a conception they claimed permitted ill health to flourish under the label of "normal." Women, they stated, could not and should not separate love and sex. "A normal woman invariably refuses sexual performance without love. Only neurotic women, incapable of tender love, adhere to the practice of sex for the sake of 'releasing tension.' "[48] Kroger went so far as to accuse Kinsey of equating a good husband with a stud animal.[49]

In 1954, at the height of the public outcry against *SBHF*, Dean Rusk, the new head of the Rockefeller Foundation, cut all funding for Kinsey's research. Fearful of a congressional investigation, the foundation made public its decision to end its support for Kinsey at the same press conference in which it announced its grant of $525,000 to Union Theological Seminary, one of Kinsey's primary critics. It was the largest single grant the foundation had ever made. The university took over what it could of financing the institute and Kinsey's research. But his research on Americans' sexual behavior ground to a halt as the institute struggled to regain its footing in the wake of its notoriety and Kinsey's failing health.[50]

To the Laboratory: Masters and Johnson's Human Sexual Response

William Masters, a medical doctor specializing in obstetrics and gynecology, and Virginia Johnson, a divorced mother of two with no advanced degree, began their study of human sexual response in Washington University in St. Louis in 1954, the same year the Kinsey Institute lost its funding. His mentor at the Rochester School of Medicine and Dentistry, Dr. George Washington Corner, had warned Masters that studying human sexuality was "professional suicide," but Masters remained determined. Following Corner's advice, Masters nonetheless waited until he had become well-respected in his field, affiliated with a major research institution, and passed the age of forty before he began to work on his long-standing interest in the physiology of sexual response.

Masters and Johnson moved away from the sociological, question-and-answer format used by Kinsey. In the Reproductive Biology Research Foundation, established in 1955, the researchers invited their subjects into a lab where researchers' measured their heart rates, temperatures, and other physiological responses as they engaged in a variety of sexual behaviors. Such research methodologies remained pornographic to most Americans. Kinsey himself had secretly observed and filmed a handful of hetero- and homosexual couples having sex and masturbating but believed the practice to be so professionally dangerous that he stopped.[51] Nothing like this had ever been done before on such a scale, and Masters and Johnson did their best to keep their research safe from public scrutiny. After observing over ten thousand orgasms experienced by men and women, in pairs and masturbating, Masters and Johnson constructed a composite portrait of what they called the "human sexual response cycle." This became the basis for their physiological analysis of human sexual response.

Like Kinsey's reports, Masters and Johnson's 1966 *Human Sexual Response* became an overnight sensation when it was published. Its first printing of fifteen thousand sold out the day it went on sale and it spent six months on the *New York Times* best-sellers list. More than three hundred thousand copies of *HSR* sold in hardback and five hundred thousand in paperback.[52] *HSR* was translated into nine languages and sold internationally. Their Reproductive Biology Research Foundation in St. Louis became world-renowned almost overnight. Self-help books popularized their techniques to mainstream readers and helped to extend Masters and Johnson's influence on American understandings of sexuality and sex.[53]

Masters and Johnson drew their research population for *HSR* from the medical and academic community around Washington University in St. Louis. Of the 694 participants, over half were married couples. Of the single participants, all but 44 had previously been married. While most were highly educated, with more than 200 attending graduate school, another 200 had not gone to college and some had not finished high school.[54] Eleven of the 276 married couples who participated in the research were black. Thirty-four couples were over the age of fifty. One female participant was born without a vagina.[55] The single criterion that all participants met was the capacity to reach orgasms under the gaze of the cameras and the researchers.[56]

Like Kinsey before them, Masters and Johnson further contributed to the construction of paradigms for understanding human sexuality that ignored race as a category of difference. As racial liberals, Masters and Johnson conflated "human" with "white." Their belief in the sexed body unmarked by racial difference, along with their concern with identifying the characteristics of "human" sexuality, led them to believe that the overwhelming whiteness of their research pool made no significant difference on their research findings. While eleven African American couples participated in their research, race did not figure in the organization of their findings or their conclusions. As with many liberals in the 1960s, Masters and Johnson understood their "color-blind" research to be inclusive of all humans who engaged in sexual behavior, no matter their race, country of origin, class background, culture, or religion.

Masters and Johnson's approach to sex was itself a monument to their belief that science could be used by educated practitioners to enhance and improve everyday life. Stressing the medical nature of their research, the authors downplayed the rather unprecedented events taking place in their laboratories. The basic sexual activities Masters and Johnson asked their male and female participants to perform included masturbation with the hand or fingers, masturbation (rarely) with a mechanical vibrator, sexual intercourse with the woman on her back, intercourse with the man on his back, and stimulation of the breasts alone, without genital contact. Most famously, Masters and Johnson developed what they called "artificial coition": vaginal penetration with a transparent probe named Ulysses. With a camera and light built into the probe, they were the first to document what took place within a woman's vagina during orgasm. Through direct observation of the participants, Masters and Johnson recorded, filmed, and documented the physiological changes involved in the sexual response of men and women.

From direct observations of these sexual activities, Masters and Johnson developed what they called the "human sexual response cycle," which for women centered on the clitoris. For men, this cycle centered on the penis. Masters and Johnson structured into sexology an important new parallel between the clitoris and the penis. Whereas Kinsey used frequency of orgasm and types of sexual behavior to place men and women on the same measurement scale, Masters and Johnson used the four-phase cycle to establish the common features of "human" sexual response. As Masters and Johnson explained, the four-phase cycle allowed them to identify "direct parallels in human sexual responses that exist to a degree never previously appreciated."[57]

Commentators, however, focused not on the new role of the clitoris but rather on the four-phase cycle as groundbreaking. Some heralded it as one of the most important accomplishments of *HSR*, claiming that it represented proof that science could unlock the mystery of sexuality. As one enthusiastic supporter described it, "Just as there exists a stereotyped sequence of events which comprises the normal digestive cycle, and a stereotyped normal cardiovascular cycle, so there exists in ordinary men and women a normal cycle of physiological events in response to erotic stimulation."[58] Critics argued that no such uniform response cycle existed and that the changes Masters and Johnson assigned to the individual phases were prevalent in every phase of sexual excitement.[59] Such criticism was lost on most readers.

Like Kinsey, Masters and Johnson established their "modern" approach to sexuality by claiming men and women to be sexually similar. Yet, to a degree that far exceeded Kinsey, their model of similarity relied heavily on the explicit analogy between the clitoris and the penis.[60] Whereas the analogy of the clitoris as a "little penis" had been made by Freud to highlight the deficiencies of the clitoris, Masters and Johnson used theirs to bolster the clitoris's significance. As the researchers explained, a man would not expect to reach orgasm without having his penis stimulated, and neither should women allow their "little penis" to be ignored or passed over.

However, despite such analogies, differences between male and female response once again undermined any sexual similarity the authors claimed. In fact, their data overflowed with rich details that documented the uniqueness, or dissimilarity, of male and female sexual response. The contradiction between their desire to establish a modern form of heterosexuality based on sexual similarity and their data, which regularly disproved sexual similarity, constituted a major tension running through *HSR*.

When faced with a plethora of major and minor differences in male and female sexuality, ranging from ejaculation to postorgasmic blood levels, Masters and Johnson insisted on sexual similarity. Their belief relied on two kinds of evidence: women's and men's physiological changes leading up to orgasm and their common trajectory across the four-phase sexual response cycle. Physiologically, both women and men experienced a rise in heart rate and temperature and changes in skin tone and color, specifically, muscles tightened and skin blushed red. Both engaged in rapid breathing as they neared orgasm. Both also had a .08 rate of contraction during orgasm. In addition, men and women also shared a progression through the sexual response cycle, from excitement, to plateau, to orgasm, and, finally, to resolution.[61] According to the authors, men and women might experience differences within each response phase, but these differences did not matter as much as the "fact" that they both moved through each phase. Based on this information, Masters and Johnson wrote that "the parallels in reaction to effective sexual stimulation emphasize the physiologic similarities in male and female response rather than the differences. Aside from obvious anatomic variants, men and women are homogeneous in the physiologic responses to sexual stimuli."[62]

Many elements of *HSR* flagrantly contradicted Masters and Johnson's belief in sexual similarity, but none more than their findings on the clitoris. The clitoris occupied the epicenter of a sexual difference that unsettled the researchers' conviction about men and women's shared "human" sexuality. *HSR* offered the most frankly positive account of the clitoris found in twentieth-century sex expert discourse. Their account extended Kinsey's challenge to psychoanalytic understandings of femininity and the geography of desire Freudians had imposed on the female body. Unlike Kinsey, who based his finding that the clitoris was the center of female sexual response on an examination of the medical literature on anatomy, Masters and Johnson proved the importance of the clitoris by direct observation. They wrote that the clitoris "is a unique organ in the total of human anatomy," yet its role in female sexual pleasure has "created a literature that is a potpourri of behavioral concepts unsupported by biologic fact . . . [and] uninformed by female subjective expression."[63] In other words, experts had based their "facts" about the clitoris neither on women's "subjective expression" nor on accurate physiological information. This combination left many women sexually ignorant and unfulfilled.

By all measures, the clitoris played the role of the newly discovered "starlet" in *HSR*'s sections on female sexuality. Aided by the glass phallus Ulysses and their "cinematographic techniques," Masters and Johnson recorded that women's most intense orgasms came not through intercourse with a man but through masturbation where the woman herself could control the kind and intensity of the stimulation. Unlike Kinsey, who shocked his readers when he claimed that women masturbated, Masters and Johnson shocked theirs by claiming that masturbation provided women with a far more intense level of stimulation than heterosexual intercourse. "The maximum physiologic intensity of orgasmic response subjectively reported or objectively recorded [in the laboratory] has been achieved by self-regulated mechanical or automanipulative techniques . . . and the lowest intensity of target-organ response was achieved during coition."[64] Masters and Johnson concluded that clitoral stimulation was by far the most pleasurable sexual technique for women and the one that offered the most consistent level of orgasm. Like Kinsey before them, their research threw into question the prominent role of intercourse in heterosexual practice and raised the possibility that the very organization of heterosexual practice did not enable women's full sexual satisfaction.

As Masters and Johnson remapped the erogenous zones of the female body, they inadvertently discovered a major difference between men and women's capacity for orgasm, a difference that once again centered on the clitoris. Masters and Johnson were the first to document that, with proper stimulation of the clitoris, women had the capacity for multiple orgasms. Unique to themselves, women did not return to lower levels of arousal once they reached orgasm but remained at near orgasmic levels for a much longer period than did men. This enabled properly stimulated women to have multiple orgasms in a relatively short amount of time. Masters and Johnson cautioned their readers that one orgasm may not be enough for some women. "The human female," they explained, "frequently is not content with one orgasmic experience during episodes of automanipulation involving the clitoral body. If there is no psychosocial distraction to repress sexual tension, many well-adjusted women enjoy a minimum of three or four orgasmic experiences before they reach apparent satiation." The authors concluded that "physical exhaustion alone terminates such an active masturbatory session."[65] The authors employed no such language to describe male sexual response. If Kinsey made the case for men's greater degree of sexuality through their responsiveness to psychosexual stimulation, Masters and Johnson made the opposite case with their account of women's capacity for multiple orgasms.

Masters and Johnson's remapping of the responsive female body involved the vagina as well. Unlike Freudian accounts of the utter passivity of the vagina and Kinsey's view of its deficient nerve endowment, Masters and Johnson documented the active responsiveness of the vagina to simulation.[66] Their discussion showed the vagina as a sensitive organ actively changing in response to sexual arousal. Far from the "log of harder wood" as Freud claimed, Masters and Johnson constructed a view of the vagina as responsive both to the phallus (or penis) and to stimulation centered on the clitoris. At the same time, Masters and Johnson also discounted the existence of the vaginal orgasm. Whereas Kinsey dismissed the vaginal orgasm by arguing that the vagina lacked the nerves to make it sexually responsive, Masters and Johnson dismissed it by showing the interdependence of the clitoris and vagina.[67] Rather than separate entities, a network of nerves and musculature connected the clitoris and the vagina, and that together constituted female sexual response. Armed with the artificial phallus, Masters and Johnson were the first to monitor that the retraction of the clitoris drew the hood over the gland during vaginal penetration, which frequently created sufficient stimulation of the clitoris to produce orgasm.[68] This, they explained, created the mistaken view in psychoanalysis that such a thing as a vaginal orgasm existed.

Masters and Johnson's construction of the interdependent, responsive vagina and the sexually precocious clitoris leveled a serious blow to Freudian ideas of female sexuality. The researchers disproved, through science, the existence of the vaginal orgasm, cast serious doubt on the psychoanalytic belief that achieving orgasm through phallic penetration alone constituted psychosexual "maturity" for women, and challenged the construction of the clitoris as a pathological, immature, and ultimately dangerous source of sexual pleasure. Most important, Masters and Johnson constructed a portrait of the clitoris and vagina working together in a coherent unit that fed stimulation back and forth across both organs. This sexological female body defied any Freudian division between vaginal and clitoral sexuality, between intercourse and clitoral stimulation, and ultimately between healthy and unhealthy sexual behavior.

While Masters and Johnson did much to rework the meaning of female sexuality within the terms of American sexual thought, they did not challenge the organization of sexual knowledge or attempt to think about female sexuality outside the heterosexual parameters of what had gone before them. Thus, at the same time they affirmed women's sexual competency through their capacity for multiple orgasms, Masters and Johnson continued to tie human sexuality to a relatively narrow understanding of genitality. Despite all the data they gathered about the numerous changes that took place across the entire body during sexual arousal, Masters and Johnson crowned women men's sexual equals/superiors through orgasm alone. Ultimately, within *HSR*, sexual responsiveness itself was not valued as much as orgasm.

The researchers also did not address lesbianism or any sexual identity besides heterosexuality. While their findings on the clitoris could have led them to see lesbianism as a "natural" form of female sexuality, their commitment to monogamous marriage kept them from doing so. Like Kinsey, Masters and Johnson upheld the view that women needed love, or a "lasting relationship," to fully develop their sexuality. In a 1970 interview, Masters and Johnson explained that "because of prevailing social attitudes . . . a woman with sexual dysfunction is apt to require a deeper, more lasting relationship with a partner than would a man in order to receive good treatment results."[69] Ironically, such clinical applications of their research were in flagrant contradiction to their laboratory techniques, where women proved again and again that they were as capable as, or more capable than, men in reaching orgasm in nonmarital and far from romantic settings. Like most twentieth-century sex experts, Masters and Johnson believed without question that improving women's enjoyment of sex resulted in stronger marriages.

Masters and Johnson's ranking of female sexual pleasure, with masturbation as the most intense and coitus as the least stimulating, along with their findings about women's capacity for multiple orgasms, would prove to be among the most explosive assertions in *HSR*. Their study had shown women to be orgasmic in a way men could not match, and yet the researchers concluded that their scientific data proved men and women's sexual similarity. Like Kinsey, who had intended to prove sexual similarity but "proved" men's sexual superiority in terms of frequency of orgasm, Masters and Johnson set out to establish sexual similarity and proved instead women's sexual superiority in terms of the clitoris. Both teams of researchers based their sexual modernism on sexual similarity, yet both inadvertently provided new grounds that upheld sexual difference.

Masters and Johnson helped secure the white-coated scientist of sex as a welcomed alternative to the Freudian psychiatrist in the popular imagination. As *Newsweek* explained in 1968, Masters and Johnson's treatment for sexual dysfunction left behind many of the standard principles of the older "talking cure." In pointing out the differences between sexology and psychoanalysis, they unofficially marked the end of popular Freudianism's reign over American ideas about sexuality. Reported *Newsweek*,

Masters and Johnson reject the traditional psychoanalytic probing into the patient's past to determine the hidden cause of impotence or frigidity. . . . Emphasis on the treatment of symptoms, rather than the deep-rooted causes, may account for the popularity of the Masters and Johnson method. "People don't want to wait and find out that their problem is that they want to sleep with their mother," explains a therapist familiar with the therapy.[70]

Sexologists had arrived as legitimate experts on human sexuality.

Sexology's most significant twentieth-century practitioners, Kinsey and Masters and Johnson relied on sexual similarity and mutual pleasure as the foundation for their vision of "modern" heterosexuality. Yet both teams of researchers found that their ideological commitment to sexual similarity based on a shared "human" sexual responsiveness frequently contradicted the materials they marshaled as evidence. Ironically, while both Kinsey and Masters and Johnson set out to prove sexual difference was an outdated moral code (rather than a scientific reality), they proved over and over again the disjunction between men and women's sexuality. Their use of "human" as a category marked them as liberals—in this case sexual liberals—committed to applying science to all arenas of life. Encapsulated in the term *human* lay the researchers' hope of moving beyond difference into a realm of equality based on equivalency. Such ideological stakes also became the measurement by which their failure to prove sexual equivalency was measured. Ultimately, difference could not be dismissed. "Human" as a transcendent category, it would seem, could not finally triumph over "female" and "male," despite the researchers' diligent efforts.

As a discipline, sexology in the postwar period rewrote sex experts' knowledge by both challenging and affirming traditional ideas about female sexuality. Kinsey challenged the view that women were uninterested in sex by documenting the range of sexual behavior in which they engaged. He affirmed sexual difference by locating it in the realm of the psychosexual, a concept that emphasized the psychological difference between male and female sexuality. The same text that shocked the country by announcing that women engaged in homosexual, premarital, and extramarital sex also concluded that women found the need for love as erotically satisfying as orgasm and that women found the world less stimulating than men. Kinsey's radical intervention into psychoanalytic femininity, forged by counting orgasms, was held in check by his account of women's essential and psychological orientation toward love.

Masters and Johnson challenged sex expert knowledge by using physiological data to prove the super-responsiveness of the clitoris and women's unique capacity for multiple orgasms. Rather than less responsive, they found women to be more responsive for longer periods of time than men. However, the researchers contained their new portrait of abundant female sexuality in a rigid narrative of sexual similarity organized around equivalency between women and men. At key moments, Masters and Johnson's narrative of equivalency threatened to overshadow their more radical findings, for example that women's most intense orgasms came from masturbation and not heterosexual intercourse. Instead of challenging the organization of heterosexuality, they assumed heterosexual marriage to be the norm and encouraged women to teach men how better to arouse them sexually. Masters and Johnson generated an account of the female body that had the potential to explode the construction of gender in sex expert's knowledge. Yet, despite the stirrings of social and sexual revolutions around them, they lodged unmovingly that super-responsive, clitoral, and potentially autonomous female solely in monogamy and marriage.

The historical importance of sexological inconsistencies, their simultaneous fanning of sexual revolutions and rewriting of gender logics, is not that they failed to prove sexual similarity. Rather, their value lies in the ways in which they blended their challenges to and revisions of normative female heterosexuality. The multivocality of their texts is the source of their historical significance. Both Kinsey and Masters and Johnson enabled men and women to question the postwar organization of sexuality while simultaneously making them feel "normal." They introduced new information into sex experts' discourse that critics of sexual freedom could neither dismiss nor contain. This blend of challenge and affirmation was key to the unstable and shifting contribution of sexology in postwar America.

Popular Sexology

Sexologists, particularly Masters and Johnson, found themselves at the center of shifting ideas about sexual liberation in the mid-1960s. The world had changed between 1954, the year the Kinsey lost his Rockefeller Foundation funds, and 1966, when *Human Sexual Response* became an overnight sensation.[71] Most centrally, the consensus about keeping adult sexuality a marital affair had all but eroded. The postwar containment of sexuality in early marriages and through taboos against pre- and extramarital sex, which had been in place since the 1940s, no longer seemed unshakable as a generation of teenagers and young adults questioned the sexual categories of their parents.[72] Masters and Johnson's view of women as sexual athletes capable of multiple orgasms suddenly harmonized with the spirit of sexual freedom or, more accurately, sexual experimentation sweeping the country.[73] These popular sex experts helped sustain the new and unprecedented attention being paid to the importance of sexual pleasure in the 1960s. They also made sexual practice an issue without questioning the sexual politics of heterosexuality. In doing so, popular sexologists, with their reaffirmation of women's sexual dependence on men, nearly ensured that second-wave feminists would have to take up the issue of women's orgasm.

The notoriety of the postwar sex studies drew hundreds of would-be practitioners to sexology. The fledgling discipline mushroomed in the wake of *HSR* as did the publication of sex manuals, including David Reuben's very popular *Everything You Always Wanted to Know About Sex** (*But Were Afraid to Ask*) (1969), J's *The Sensuous Woman* (1969) and Alex Comfort's *The Joy of Sex* (1972).[74] These paradigmatic texts of popular sexology communicated the blend of sexual liberation and gender conservatism that characterized the reports by Kinsey and Masters and Johnson. Appealing to a wide assortment of readers, these popular sex manuals schooled would-be sexual revolutionaries on the ins and outs of modern sexual response without overturning enduring beliefs about the nature of male and female sexuality. Popular sex manuals thus served an important function. They introduced and domesticated a set of behaviors such as partner swapping and "swinging" for the married set and "free love" for those in the counterculture, behaviors once seen as degenerate, pathological, and obscene.[75] Each took a frank and novel approach to teaching the improved techniques discovered by the postwar sex studies while, at the same time, each paid special attention to the expression of female sexuality in the marriage bed.

An eerily familiar message to women appeared in these new marriage manuals: this generation of sex experts once again reminded their readers that sexual dependency remained the hallmark of healthy female sexual response. In speaking to women about how to give men what they wanted from sex, these manuals, like the reports by Kinsey and Masters and Johnson from which they drew, offered a telling example of how much sex expertise had changed in the wake of sexology's postwar challenge and how much it had stayed the same. In manuals written in the era of sexual freedom, vaginal sexuality continued to bear the symbolic freight of proper womanhood. Now armed with vibrators and techniques gleaned from the infamous St. Louis laboratory, popular sex authors told women that good, marriage-producing sex remained essentially unchanged from the 1910s—mutual orgasm occurring through intercourse.

"In virtually every patient," wrote Doctor David Reuben, "I see a person living in the Space Age who has left his (or her) sexual organs in the Stone Age." Continuing the analogy of the popular NASA space program, he explained that most Americans "are in the uncomfortable position of knowing more about what occurs 238,000 miles away on the surface of the moon than what happens six inches below our own navels."[76] A down-to-earth combination of common sense and the latest research into human sexuality, Reuben's book addressed a range of issues associated with sex organs, sexual response, and orgasm. He covered, for example, whether or not penis size mattered to women's orgasm ("In sexual intercourse, as in every artistic endeavor, it is quality not quantity that counts."),[77] the new hormonal research on the common origins of male and female sex ("the testicles are nothing more than female ovaries which have found a new home in the scrotum"),[78] whether the intact hymen is a reliable indictor of virginity ("It's possible for a woman to have sexual intercourse twenty times a day, give birth to a dozen children and still have that flag of virtue, the hymen, waving at the vaginal portal."),[79] as well as more sensational topics like aphrodisiacs, venereal disease, and sexual perversions ("Anyone who isn't interested in the penis-vagina version of sex is often considered a pervert and shunned by normal people.").[80]

Reuben's lengthy account of frigidity in women, though, vividly captured the impact of sexological research on popular understandings of sexuality. Reuben reminded his readers that sexual dysfunctions like impotence and frigidity were not physical but emotional impairments. While, certainly, such reassurances helped relieved suffering men and women from unnecessary fear, his approach to treatment was deeply gendered. Women's healing of sexual dysfunction came by way of a loving male partner. As told through a case study of Ellen, who could not reach orgasm despite her husband Jack's studious and up-to-date sexual techniques, Reuben wrote, "In sexual intercourse, real human emotions can make up for any lapses from perfect form. Even if the technique lacks perfection, love and tenderness can fill in the gaps."[81] Infused with the language of both Freud and Masters and Johnson, Reuben reminded his readers that at one point in her life every woman has "strong sexual impulses with almost certain orgasmic capability." Squashed by mother or by a bad boyfriend, "victims" of frigidity required "the help of an understanding and sympathetic man" to "revive" her "latent" sexual responsiveness.[82] Reuben encouraged women like Ellen to practice orgasm by using a vibrator again "until orgasm is no longer a sometime thing but occurs regularly like clockwork." He wrote, "It is essential for a woman to realize that orgasm is not magic—it is an easily attainable neurovascular reflex." However, despite prescribing the vibrator as a cure for frigidity, Reuben could only imagine healthy female orgasm as coming from intercourse with a man. The once-frigid woman must now transfer the newly established "reflex mechanism" (orgasm) to sexual intercourse, the true pinnacle of sexuality.

For men who suffered impotence, however, Reuben did not offer the same "practice makes perfect" advice that he gave women. For them, premature ejaculation and an inability to achieve or sustain erection signaled deep hostility toward their wives, their problems symptomatic of a desire to punish their partners for crimes real or imagined. Reuben advised impotent men to seek psychiatric help to resolve their ambivalence toward women and never suggested that love or romance could help men overcome the "gap" between impulse and performance.[83] Like most twentieth-century sex experts, Reuben closely associated female sexuality with romantic love.

If Reuben's manual was intended to answer questions curious people felt too embarrassed to ask, *The Sensuous Woman*, published the same year, set out to teach women how to achieve the perfect blend of sexual expressiveness and sexual dependency that men found erotic. Philosophically, J's 1969 *The Sensuous Woman* was close to Helen Gurly Brown's *Sex and the Single Girl*, published seven years earlier, which offered young single women a manifesto on the "joys of singleness" and instructions for how to manufacture big city glamour and popularity.[84] J's offering was both more circumscribed and more ambitious. J conceived of *The Sensual Woman* as the single girl's step-by-step guide to sexual liberation. Sexual liberation in this case translated quite literally into liberation from misguided ideas about proper sexual technique and acceptable behavior. J's message was simple: any woman can become a "sensual woman."

J sustinctly translated the archane research of Kinsey and Masters and Johnson into a simple message: modern women, unlike their mothers and grandmothers, admitted that they enjoyed sex. Yet J saw a chasm between new sexological information and women's sexual behavior. She stepped into the breach, using herself as case study number one. "For years my response pattern was so low you couldn't have picked it up on the most sensitive seismograph. . . . My instinct kept telling me I could be a Sensuous Woman; there really was a torrent of passion pent up inside me waiting to be freed."[85] J invented a treatment plan for herself, and soon began having "great sex." She discovered that having "great sex" made her popular and sought after by hordes of eligible men. Doing some ad hoc market research, J tested her treatment on friends, who too found themselves transformed into Sensual Women. "The Sensual Woman worked for me, a number of my friends and some of their friends. I think it will work for you too," she cooed to her readers.[86]

Part of the success of J's manual lay in its disarming tone. J spoke directly to the reader, casting herself as the woman on the street who could unlock the mysteries of the sexual revolution for the average and sexually insecure woman. J's was one of the first manuals to offer readers explicit directions on how to masturbate and how to perform fellatio. Yet, J did not rest with such preliminaries. She went on to explain to her reader how to behave at an orgy, when and how to fake orgasm ("To become a fabulous fake, study again every contortion, muscle spasm and body response . . . and rehearse the process privately until you can duplicate it"),[87] and how to talk dirty during intercourse.

J stubbornly held a vision of the early 1960s as a sexual utopia for women. Now that sexologists had blown open the conspiracy to make women believe they did not like sex, a view propagated by Freudians, women could ride a wave of sexual self-involvement. "Techniques varied, but the rules were clear. Women were sexually responsive and it was up to the men to arouse and satisfy women, no matter how much effort was involved. . . . That old, old rule that woman was designed to give pleasure to man went down the drain."[88] According to J's unique understanding of history, men began strenuously trying to make women reach orgasm. Such pressured competition drove both parties to the brink of exhaustion and alienation. For women, such an emphasis on their own orgasm led them to deny their true instinct: to please the man they loved.

> We were so busy in bed getting "satisfied" that we forgot our responsibilities as women. We were greedy, selfish and dumb. We forgot that there were two of us in that bed and that it was just as important to give the man a wonderful experience sexually as it was to receive it. We forgot what females have been taught since time began: that as women we should be ardent conservationists of our most important natural resource—man—instead of heedlessly using him up.[89]

J's manual both counseled women that they had already enjoyed a sexual revolution and warned them that their own sexual liberation put them at odds with their gendered destiny of romantic devotion to a man. Such a combination prepared readers for J's overarching goal, which was to fully integrate women's now infamously responsive sexuality into an updated model of sexual dependency and romantic love. One of her primary methods for doing so was to teach women how to become more sexually responsive and then to direct their enhanced sexual responsiveness to their partners. "Remember," she wrote, trotting out a familiar threadbare promise, "the more wonderful you are to him in bed, the more wonderful he will be to you."[90]

Despite the attention J paid to masturbation, she, like Reuben, upheld the distinctions between foreplay (clitoral stimulation) and intercourse (sex).[91] Masters and Johnson's tentative attempts to break down the age-old belief that intercourse equaled sex were lost on J. She integrated the importance of the clitoris in a way that never challenged the significance of vaginal intercourse. J nevertheless threw in tidbits of advice telling women how to get more clitoral stimulation without directly asking for it. "Your increased flexibility allows you to tilt your pelvis to get maximum clitoral stimulation and we both know the positive results of that!"[92] For J, direct clitoral stimulation was beside the point. She counseled her readers that cunnilingus, while "distasteful," should be engaged in out of good manners and with practice can be enjoyed since men find it erotic.[93]

But perhaps the most important service J provided her readers came at the end of *The Sensuous Woman*. In the chapter entitled "Love, Love, Glorious Love," J offered her readers a way to interpret male indifference outside of the bedroom and, in this way, provided an answer to the crucial problem women faced as more and more sexuality took place outside of marriage.[94] Men, with whom Sensuous Women have sex, admitted J, do not necessarily think about them or romantically commit themselves to women even after fabulous sex. "It's not unnatural for him to forget all about you for hours at a time, even though he loves you dearly. But it is natural for you to be unable to erase him from your mind and body, no matter how hard you try. . . . To a man love and life are a thing apart. To a woman, love is life itself."[95] J recast male indifference as indicative of the essential differences between men and women, not as something to worry needlessly about. J advised modern women to look beyond such potentially hurtful behavior on their partner's part and to focus instead on the satisfaction women took from having a man in their lives. "Since he is unable to love you one hundred percent of the time, should you retaliate in kind? Absolutely not!" J answered adamantly. "You would be insane to go against your nature and cheat yourself of many tender, sweet, entirely female moments . . . that give you so much satisfaction. Women were born to love and only when we love to capacity are we happy."[96]

Popular sex authors, who translated both the new sexual techniques offered by sexology and new sexual behaviors like orgies, swinging, and heterosexual promiscuity for the uninitiated also, at the same time, upheld marriage as the ultimate form of sex. Alex Comfort, author of *The Joy of Sex*, did so by incorporating formerly sexually deviant practices into the familiar language of food: sexual desire was akin to the desire for delicious food, sexual practices to meals or menus. As with Epicureans who might balk at being served too many chicken dishes in one week, modern men and women similarly needed to enliven their sex lives through a vary of sexual practices. His cookbook-styled manual enabled readers to easily locate areas of concern with entries such as "frigidity," "impotence," and "vasectomy" as well as areas of curiosity such as "g-string," "Indian style," "swings," "anal intercourse," and "leather." Like J, who for all her sexual frolicking held on to marriage as the most important achievement of a woman's life, Comfort's familiar tone set out to help married couples incorporate the "new sexual freedom" into their own lives.

Like all other postwar sexologists, Comfort clearly held on to intercourse as the pinnacle of adult sexuality. Despite his democratic presentation of all things sexual, he reassured his reader that "the piece de resistance is the good old face-to-face matrimonial, the finishing-off position, with mutual orgasm and starting with a full day or night of ordinary tenderness."[97] Comfort offered his readers a way to enjoy the fruits of the sexual revolution without taking any of the risks, which, while they might lead to excitement, might also lead to disappointment and divorce. To "spice" up marital sex, he refurbished the romance of female sexual dependency, now set against the backdrop of modern sexual freedom. In the entry titled "Women (by her for him)," Comfort explained that women have the unique, and undoubtedly convenient, capacity to teach themselves to respond to what their partner finds erotic. Speaking as a woman, Comfort wrote "we seem to be less heavily programmed than you for specific turn-ons (like nudity, erotica) but once we see one of these working on a man we care about, we soon program it into our own response."[98] Veering uncomfortably close to seeing women as an empty vessel, quite literally someone who gained character only through what (literally) filled her, Comfort continued: "A woman's lovemaking will only be good with a good lover and, more important, she will resent any man who is unexciting, not only because it is unexciting but also because she will know she had been unexciting too."[99] Employing the metaphor of woman as an instrument, found both in *The Joy of Sex* and Van Der Velde's *Ideal Marriage*, Comfort stood in a long line of marriage experts who enshrined and eroticized women's sexual dependency. Ironically, in "Men (by him for her)," Comfort offered his readers the opposite advice. Here, he encouraged women to take more initiative, to "start the plays, tak[e] hold of the penis, giv[e] genital kisses before asked," in short, to be "an initiator, a user of your stimulatory equipment."[100] The mixed messages in *The Joy of Sex*, as in J's *The Sensuous Woman*, counseled women to be both assertive and receptive, not to take control but not to be passive, to be willing to try new things and also to enjoy the missionary position, all in the name of modern monogamy and better sex.

Popular sex manuals like those of Reuben, J, and Comfort offered a portrait of the sexually liberated woman that bore an uncanny resemblance to the ideal woman of the companionate marriage. The ideal woman of the 1960s engaged in more extended foreplay, oral sex, and extensive clitoral stimulation than her predecessor. She (ideally) had orgasms as frequently as did her partner. And this ideal woman shared a desire for satisfying sex that was equivalent to any man's. These were historic revisions of Victorian womanhood.

At the same time, this female figment of the popular sexological imagination was devoted to pleasing her man. She was told to use feelings of romantic love to overcome any deficiencies in sexual technique that left her unsatisfied. She heard, once again, that the highest expression of her sexual self lay in vaginal intercourse that resulted in simultaneous orgasms. Such a portrait of "liberated" womanhood, while certainly more sexually expressive, continued to embody the tortured and convoluted ways in which ideas about sexuality worked in tandem with views of gender.

Once again, new standards of womanhood—woman as sexually expressive, devoted to a dyadic relationship with a man, eager to please, not too passive or too aggressive—were articulated in and through sexual prescriptions. Such discussions of the nature of female desire and of liberation made it almost inevitable that radical women in the late 1960s would take up the issue of sexual pleasure, marriage, and, even more centrally, the organization of heterosexuality itself.

Three POLITICIZING PLEASURE

Radical Feminist Sexual Theory, 1968–1975

Thanks to the convergence of a burgeoning market for anything related to sex and the language of sexual freedom circulating in the mass media, women of the 1960s were beset by a menu of fashionable sexual practices and new information about sexual response. The birth control pill, available in 1960, further separated sex from reproduction. By 1965 almost six million women used it daily.[1] Both the pill and the rhetoric of sexual liberation put in women's hands the possibility of approaching sex in a way that was comparable to men's. By 1970, however, mixed messages and flagrant contradictions in the discussion of female heterosexuality led a new generation of experts, or anti-experts, to critique the male biases they saw in both popular and expert standards of liberated womanhood. Much of this critique came from radical women and women learning to call themselves feminists. Radical women saw a horrible similarity between the way Freudians in the 1930s had defined healthy femininity and the way sexual liberationists in the 1960s defined a healthy "modern" woman. Sixties counterculturalists, who no longer saw women as mothers or potential mothers as Freudians had, nevertheless infused female sexuality with the symbolism of ideal womanhood. In this discourse, the female orgasm signified women's liberation from monogamy. It stood in for both the healing potential of unfettered pleasure and the skills of the man who could make his partner have as many orgasms as the women from Masters and Johnson's infamous laboratory. Yet, as new feminists complained, the symbolic meaning of the female orgasm remained troublingly detached from women's personal agency. Female sexuality and, by extension, women, remained tethered to male standards of behavior, standards that feminists began to protest in the late 1960s.[2] Feminists reclaimed the orgasm from experts and male lovers and reinfused it with new symbolic meaning. Within second-wave feminism, the female orgasm came to represent women's self-determination, making "the great orgasm debate" central, not incidental, to the project of women's liberation.

But recasting the symbolism attached to the female orgasm required both a revisiting and a rewriting of existing sexual thought. Discussion by experts about human nature and sexuality itself was undergoing significant change in the late 1950s and 1960s. Radical psychoanalysts and human potential psychologists emphasized the human capacity to change and grow. Feminists Betty Friedan, Kate Millett, and Shulamith Firestone absorbed and synthesized this new psychology and used it to theorize three foundational concepts of second-wave feminism: the social construction of femininity, the psychological origins of patriarchy, and the political nature of sexuality. Together, Friedan, Millett, and Firestone refurbished psychoanalytic terms for feminism. But the project of reworking the symbolic meaning of the female orgasm did not require only a refurbished psychoanalysis. Feminists Anne Koedt, Ti-Grace Atkinson, and Dana Densmore, among others, drew on and radicalized the sexological insights of Kinsey and Masters and Johnson. Combining psychoanalysis and sexology in new ways, radical feminists across the spectrum elaborated on the sexual basis of women's liberation, from an authentic and pro-active heterosexual agency to a cuddly lesbian identity in which the entire female body, not just the genitals, polymorphously expressed desire.

Symbolic Pleasures: Psychoanalysis, the Counterculture, and the Sexual Revolution

The new symbolism attached to the female orgasm had roots in radical psychoanalysis and in the counterculture of the mid- and late 1960s.

Radical psychoanalysts like Herbert Marcuse and Norman Brown linked sexuality to politics in a way that enabled students and intellectuals to re-think the cold war containment of sexuality.[3] Marcuse and Brown claimed that mass culture had made the distinction between culture and politics obsolete and, further, linked the desexualized or genitally organized body to social repression.

In the preface to his 1955 *Eros and Civilization*, Marcuse announced that psychological categories had become political categories. "The tradi-tional borderlines between psychology on the one side and political and social philosophy on the other have been made obsolete by the condition of man in the present era." In an age of abundance, when Western socie-ty depended on advertising, mass culture, and an ethos of personal satis-faction as vehicles of social control, "psychological problems . . . turn into political problems." Privacy had been eroded and, with it, the individual that "could be for himself."[4] Likewise, Brown, in his 1959 *Life Against Death*, also analyzed the political role of pleasure in the maintenance of civilization. Civilization's repression of the primary "polymorphous" pleasures of bodies created culture, and culture, in turn, drew on re-pressed and sublimated sexuality for its continuation. Returning to Freud's conception of the inherent conflict between the dialectical forces of the pleasure and reality principles, Brown, too, offered a political anal-ysis of repression and the power of unbounded pleasure as resources to transform society.[5]

The link Brown and Marcuse made between authentic selfhood and polymorphous sexuality became an important element in the growing counterculture of the 1960s and early 1970s. As Theodore Roszak ex-plained his 1968 *The Making of a Counter Culture*, Marcuse and Brown were "major social theorists among the disaffiliated young of Western Eu-rope and America."[6] With their analysis of society's repression of pleasure, Brown and Marcuse helped purge psychoanalysis of the "vulgar Freudi-anism" that had dominated postwar American culture.

Classical Freudianism, however, also faced challenges from a new gen-eration of psychologists who, unlike Marcuse and Brown, dismantled rather than embraced the metapsychology of Freud's theories. The human potential movement, led by Abraham Maslow and Carl Rogers in the 1950s and early 1960s, viewed itself as the "third force" between doctri-naire Freudian psychoanalysts and mechanistic behaviorists.[7] The "new psychology," which also influenced the counterculture, saw humans as en-gaged in growth across a "life cycle." It asserted the goodness of human in-stincts, the potential for limitless creativity, and a view of life as an opportunity and adventure rather than a tragedy. In contrast to Freud, human potential psychologists focused on healthy people and their resiliency. The emphasis on health in the new psychology promised "self-actualization" through psychological growth. As Rogers wrote, the individual "has within himself the capacity, latent if not evident, to understand those aspects of himself and of his life which are causing him dissatisfaction, anxiety, or pain" as well as "the tendency to reorganize himself and his life in the direction of self-actualization and maturity."[8] An important aspect of the new psychology was its tolerance of multiple routes to self-actualization.[9]

Critics who found Maslow's ideas of "normality" too oriented to adjustment and conformity could turn to other illuminaries in the movement. Psychologist Frederick Perls became famous for the mantra "Do your own thing." Perls had impressive Freudian credentials: he had trained under Helene Deutsch in Vienna and had been analyzed by Wilhelm Reich. Yet, in the 1950s, Perls found himself drifting toward the emergent bohemian world. Perls's 1951 *Gestalt Therapy*, coauthored with Ralph Hefferline and Paul Goodman, complained that society created illness and pathology by turning "spontaneous discharges into symptoms."[10] Joining a critique of social control with a celebration of spontaneity, the authors called for a society that would allow the body to be unregulated. Psychologists George Bach and Herb Goldberg warned that growth could be thwarted by a repressed spouse or by existing commitments to children, jobs, and bills.[11] Rather than one finding oneself in and through the roles one willingly adopted, new psychologists prioritized the search for authentic selfhood. The journeys to selfhood justified what in earlier generations marked one as "immature." New psychologists no longer saw divorce as a failed marriage, for example, but rather as a difficult passage successfully navigated.[12]

The values of the new psychology dovetailed with the growing counterculture and political subcultures of the mid-1960s. The tenets of the human potential movement—that the self constituted the highest authority, that humans needed to feel good about themselves, the importance of experiencing emotions directly, and an emphasis on growth, spontaneity, and change—found an eager audience in the sixties.[13] The counterculture embraced key words of the new psychology, such as *self-actualization* and *peak experiences* in their rituals of be-ins, hallucinogenic drugs, and communal living arrangements. Cultural rebels upheld the belief that emotional health and growth had important political effects. Linking sexuality, politics, and the new society, Abbie Hoffman, a former student of

Maslow's, wrote in 1968, "Look, you want to have more fun, you want to get laid more, you want to turn on with your friends, you want an outlet for your creativity, then get out of school, quit your job. Come out and build and defend the society you want."[14] The human potential movement thus contributed to the new emphasis on personal freedom in the 1960s by outlining the importance of self-expression to empowered social agents. The counterculture and other sixties activists took these links to new political heights when they asserted that empowered social agents could change society. For those in the counterculture who were not interested in changing society, the human potential movement provided a way to critique standards of success, productivity, and responsibility.

In contrast to the Freudians, for whom sexuality marked the unconscious conflict between pleasure and reality, sixties rebels infused sexuality with the values of autonomy, wholeness, and selfhood. The countercultural emphasis on authenticity led to a powerful celebration of the body as the highest expression of an unsullied nature. This body came to symbolize the new citizen of the sixties revolutions: it was a body freed from the effects of racism, classism, technology, and sexual repression. The utopianism of the moment held that the joining of authentic bodies in freedom and in pleasure would provide the glue for the beloved community.[15]

Other communities embraced sexuality as a cornerstone of a healthy, self-actualized existence. The "singles scene" functioned as a mainstream counterpart to the political and bohemian subcultures of the 1960s. Whereas young white hippies claimed Haight-Ashbury and San Francisco as their Mecca, Manhattan led the way in servicing upwardly mobile young white swingers. Singles flocked to such clubs as Maxwell's Plum, P.J. Clarke's, and TGI Friday in the mid-1960s, making them hot new spots to meet potential partners. Neighborhoods like Chicago's Near North Side and Old Town, Boston's Beacon Hill and Back Bay, and New York's Upper East Side became ghettos for middle-class singles where bars and clubs further commodified a singles culture and identity.[16] Magazines like Hugh Hefner's *Playboy*, founded in 1953, and Helen Gurley Brown's revamped *Cosmopolitan*, in 1964, brought a "singles' identity" to a national audience. They contributed to the new ethos of sexual expressiveness with their antiwife, antimarriage, pro-pleasure philosophies. *Playboy* and *Cosmo* replaced the traditional husband-wife dyad with a new pairing: the bachelor and the liberated single woman.[17] Both Hefner and Brown, as well as the icons they helped launch, became beacons of sexual expressiveness and symbols of the joys of singlehood.

The mainstream singles scene also introduced words that resonated with the themes of the human potential movement, such as *relationship* to indicate one's involvement in a marriage or an affair and *lifestyle* to accommodate a range of living arrangements. Singles who grew disillusioned with scripted pickups, one-night stands, and the "meat market" atmosphere of the bars could met dates in therapy and encounter groups. Barbara Ehrenreich described these therapy-singles as "look[ing] for psychological 'growth' in their sexual encounters."[18] This predominantly white upper-middle-class generation of sixties youth remained relatively untouched by the political movements of their activist counterparts and stayed conservative in all ways except sexual.

New emphasis on sexual expressiveness found unlikely support from the Supreme Court. Legal changes in the definition of obscenity allowed for a dramatic increase in the amount of sexual imagery in the public sphere. Between 1957 and 1967, the Supreme Court responded to a series of cases that changed the legal meaning of obscenity.[19] Liberalization of obscenity laws had immediate effects on the status of pornography in terms of mainstream acceptance. In 1967, at the urgin of President Lyndon Johnson, the Commission on Obscenity and Pornography investigated the effects of pornography on American youths and adults, and its report, published in 1970, concluded that "interest in sex is normal, healthy [and] good." The *Report of the President's Commission on Obscenity and Pornography* described obscenity legislation as a menace to freedom of expression. Rather than being harmful, it argued that exposure to sexually explicit material had positive effects in that it made people more tolerant. In short, pornography "liberalize[d]" peoples' understanding of sexuality as a healthy, normal part of identity. Changes wrought through the courts and government had an immediate impact on businesses involved in selling sexually explicit materials. Pornographic books, magazines and films rapidly poured into an ever growing market.[20] In the late 1960s, pornographic films *The Devil and Mrs. Jones* and *Deep Throat* became enormously popular and profitable and were viewed widely.[21] Hefner faced competition from new publications like *Hustler* and *Penthouse* and more marginal hard-core magazines *Finger* and *Screw*. A burgeoning market for sex novels offered eager readers explicit sexual scenes in Marco Vassi's popular *Mind Blower* and *Stoned Apocalypse*, among others.[22]

Younger women faced more and more images of themselves as sexual commodities, a situation many found disturbing. Particularly galling to activist women in the New Left was the outbreak of "dildo journalism" in the underground press. Protected by the Supreme Court's restrictions on legal definitions of obscenity, new papers such as the *New York Review of Sex*, *Pleasure*, *Kiss*, and more established countercultural papers like *Rat*, introduced sexually explicit language and images into the alternative press. By 1969, personals' sections, bearing titles such as "Tomcats, Alley Cats and Pussycats," overwhelmed the political coverage of some papers. These ads became flash points between male and female staffers. Sex ads were enormously profitable for these small operations and brought in thousands of dollars each week to their shoestring budgets. Male editors defended their practice by claiming their treatment of sex shattered stodgy notions of sexuality.[23]

Part of the revolutionary aspect of the "sexual revolution" of the 1960s was the greater acceptance of women as agents with sexual desires. Yet many women found their ability to be full sexual agents severely compromised by limits on reproductive control. The singles culture encouraged both men and women to celebrate spontaneous sex and bodily pleasures. The birth control pill contributed to women feeling more free, yet, by the late 1960s, even the pill no longer seemed so safe. Thanks to Barbara Seaman's *The Doctor's Case Against the Pill*, women discovered the dangers associated with regular hormone use. And even a relatively sexually autonomous woman still found herself in trouble if she became pregnant. Illegal abortions could be costly and dangerous.

Sexual liberation as it was conceived by both mainstream and alternative subcultures—in practice and in rhetoric—became a dilemma for radical and nonactivist women alike. Opportunities for more sex with more partners did not necessarily translate into sexual liberation for women. Many women rejected accounts of their "liberation" that viewed them as Playboy bunnies. Women learning to call themselves feminists found themselves having to reconstruct the concept of a "sexual revolution" to include women's sexual, political, and social agency. They did so by borrowing and reworking the symbolic associations between autonomy, selfhood, and sexuality from the counterculture and the social significance of private life from radical and Freudian psychoanalysis.

The Freudian Mystique: Betty Friedan

The feminine mystique derived its power from Freudian thought. . . . It is a Freudian idea, hardened into apparent fact, that has trapped so many American women today.[24]

In her best-seller *The Feminine Mystique* (1963), Betty Friedan set out the first pillar of second-wave feminism—that femininity was a cultural construct permeated with social values that had little basis in biology or genuine female experience. Identifying what she termed a "malaise" afflicting white middle-class American women at mid-century, Friedan argued that this malaise was caused by the social denial of women's "human potential" in the name of femininity.[25] Throughout all levels of society, from advertisements to experts, women were taught to channel their energies and creativity into domestic and maternal activities or, as she referred to it, into the female "sex role." Women's single-minded focus on the home, on children, and on being perfect wives had cost them their "identity." In short, American middle-class white women (or "women," as Friedan referred to them), had lost their sense of self and individuality thanks to the ideology of "the feminine mystique."

Friedan's criticism of the "feminine mystique" self-consciously invoked and challenged the liberal promise of individualism. While Friedan did not challenge the implicit racial underpinning of liberalism, she subversively transposed its implicit masculine bias into more gender-inclusive terms. She argued that middle-class women had been denied their status as equal citizens not by legal restrictions but by organized cultural messages that denigrated women's nondomestic capacities. Thanks to the media, to experts like sociologists, psychologists, and doctors, and to educators, women had renounced their individuality and creative engagement in public society for the world of the home. Friedan claimed that all women had become too identified, both personally and in the collective mind of society, with their sex role as mother and wife. Instead of working in the arts or the professions, these women stayed at home and became obsessed with sex—what Friedan called "the only frontier open to women." In the last fifteen years, she wrote, "the sexual frontier has been forced to expand perhaps beyond the limits of possibility, to fill the time available, to fill the vacuum created by denial of larger goals and purposes for American women."[26] According to Friedan, sexual performance had taken the place of women's personal self-development and political engagement.[27]

Friedan's analysis of the oppression women felt by being only mothers and their desires to shed the domestic world for a life of productive work in the professions rested on specific racial and class assumptions. For many African American women, for example, the home and the labor associated with maintaining it was often far more fulfilling than the marginal labor available to them in the hostile, racist American workplace.

Rather than oppressive, the home was a source of control and nurturance, and women's roles prioritized as preserving traditions and communities.[28] For many working-class women, wage work was not a source of empowerment and identity but a tedious, often dehumanizing way to survive. Both Friedan's vision of the home and of work, then, replicated and reproduced the presumptions of "normality" found in the white professional middle class.

Friedan, like many liberal humanists of the 1960s, believed that Americans of all races and classes shared common desires for security and self-hood. Friedan's contribution to this discourse was to specify its gendered implications. Friedan's account of middle-class white America in the postwar period operated from two sets of paired terms: femininity versus human growth and sex versus self. She attributed these oppositions to Freudianism, which she blamed for providing the feminine mystique with its intellectual foundation. Freudianism, she claimed, replaced women's "human potential" with sex and an overly sexualized view of femininity. Drawing on Abraham Maslow's humanist psychology and Erik Erickson's emphasis on identity, Friedan argued that the drive to reach one's full potential were essential "human" needs that sex could not meet.[29]

> It is my thesis that the core of the problem of women today is not sexual but a problem of identity—a stunting or evasion of growth that is perpetuated by the feminine mystique. It is my thesis that as the Victorian culture did not permit women to accept or gratify their basic sexual needs, our culture does not permit women to accept or gratify their basic need to grow and fulfill their potentialities as human beings, a need which is not solely defined by their sexual role.[30]

Friedan's major criticism of the Freudianism "that settled everywhere like fine volcanic ash" was its association of femininity with sexuality.[31] Whereas Victorian women were denied their rights to a full "basic" sexuality, American women at mid-century could not escape their sexuality. Society denied women their rights to be nonsexual, to be "humans" capable of growth. The Freudian mystique bombarded women at an early age: "Girls who grew up playing baseball, baby-sitting, mastering geometry—almost independent enough, almost resourceful enough, to meet the problems of the fission-fusion era—," wrote Friedan, "were told by the most advanced thinkers of our time to . . . live their lives like Nora, restricted to the doll house by Victorian prejudice."[32] Socialized to give up interests in sports, school, and work for the single pursuit of finding a husband, women looked for fulfillment from a small range of sex-related activities. This search, asserted Friedan, was bound to fail because women, like their brothers and husbands, required more of life than these roles could give.

Friedan also criticized Freudianism's domestic preoccupations. She situated the stunning popularity of Freud's oedipal drama in the social upheaval of the Depression and the Second World War. "After the depression, after the war," explained Friedan,

> Freudian psychology became much more than a science of human behavior, a therapy for the suffering. It became an all-embracing American ideology, a new religion. It filled the vacuum of thought and purpose that existed for many for whom God, or flag, or bank account were no longer sufficient—and yet who were tired of feeling responsible for lynching and concentration camps and the starving children of India and Africa. . . It gave us permission to suppress the troubling questions of the larger world and pursue our own personal pleasures.[33]

For Friedan, then, Freudianism mirrored the retreat from politics and social engagement in the postwar period. Looking for the "sexual roots in man's behavior" replaced looking critically at society and, most important, acting to change society. "We lowered our eyes from the horizon, and steadily contemplated our own navels." It was "easier to think about love and sex," mused Friedan, "than about communism, McCarthy, and the uncontrolled bomb."[34] Critical of its single-motive theory of culture, she complained that Freudianism mistook the desire for creativity and social engagement as merely another expression of sublimated sexuality, and thus rendered it apolitical. Unfortunately, the search for the origins of politics in the individual or in the collective unconscious of society held women, as the "guardians" of the domestic world, unduly accountable for society's ailments.[35]

Friedan turned to the liberal promise of individuality to help women break out of the Freudian mystique. She argued that women must shed their association with the home and the female sex role through nondomestic work, be that work artistic or economic. Only by moving into the public sphere could women break free of femininity and attain equal status as humans. She believed that individual merit could overcome any obstacles to public success, despite her detailed account of how women individually suffered from a prejudice based on their membership in a social group.[36] Friedan did not question the line that demarcated private from public, sexuality from politics, but rather called for women to enjoy the same distance from sexuality as did men. She assumed that the experiences of gender, organized primarily around sexuality, were the main obstacles to "women's" self-actualization.

Hugely popular, Friedan's analysis of the social construction of femininity catapulted her to celebrity. However, Friedan's was not the only voice raised against Freudianism. Another group of feminists in the late 1960s attacked it for its fundamental misunderstanding of female sexuality through its constructions of female sexual pleasure.[37] Defining themselves as "radical," these women placed the politics of sexual practice front and center in their brand of feminism. While Friedan herself had had strong connections to radical politics, particularly the labor unions in the 1940s, her critique of Freud ultimately preserved the line between sexuality and politics.[38] Other intellectuals would take up the critique of Freud pioneered by Friedan, but theirs would be a different task: to dismantle the line between sex and politics in order to make sexuality itself political.

Following Marcuse and Brown, radical feminists and others in the counterculture turned to Freud for a theory of culture and history as well as for a theory of the unconscious. However, unlike other radicals in the counterculture, radical feminists had to first account for the male bias in Freudian theory before they could utilize psychoanalysis for their own theory of culture. Specifically, radical feminists like Kate Millettt had to overturn the Freudian paradigms of femininity before they could use psychoanalysis to theorize the patriarchal roots of society.

From The Feminine Mystique *to* Sexual Politics*: Kate Millett*

Although generally accepted as a prototype of the liberal urge towards sexual freedom . . . the effect of Freud's work, that of his followers, and still more that of his popularizers, was to rationalize the invidious relationship between the sexes, to ratify traditional roles, and to validate temperamental differences.[39]

Kate Millett's 1969 best-seller, *Sexual Politics*, put patriarchy on the political map. In it, Millett offered a critique of Freudianism that shared important features with the one offered by Friedan six years earlier. Both saw Freudian psychoanalysis as playing a central role in the backlash against women of the 1940s and 1950s. Like Friedan, who complained that Freudianism provided "the ideological bulwark of the sexual counter-revolution" or the "feminine mystique" of postwar America, Millett too referred to Freudian theory as laying down the intellectual foundations for what she called the "counterrevolution" against sexual liberation in the twentieth century.[40] Both Friedan and Millett noted the material and psychological effects on women of the widespread popularization of Freudian theory. Women were both pathologized if they stepped out of the narrow sexualized realm of "normal" feminine behavior and, at the same time, ridiculed for their narrow lives. For both Friedan and Millett, Freudian theory, popularized and simplified into Freudianism, had profoundly shaped the meaning of modern femininity.

Despite their similarities, however, Millett and Friedan stood on opposite sides of both a generational and a political divide that deeply shaped their feminisms. Millett, first as a graduate student at Columbia University and later as a prominent radical feminist in the Women's Liberation Movement, spoke for a younger, university-based generation of women. Friedan represented herself as women's voice from the white suburbs, a generation of women who attended college to get their "Mrs." and who avoided appearing too intellectual. *Sexual Politics* was Millett's doctoral dissertation, whereas the nucleus of *The Feminine Mystique* was a Smith College alumnae survey.[41] Likewise, Millett and Friedan stood on different ends of the left-leaning political spectrum. By 1970, Friedan was one of the dominant voices in liberal feminism through her leadership of the National Organization for Women (NOW);[42] Millett, on the other hand, was a self-declared radical whose bisexuality gained her national notoriety when she appeared on the cover of *Time* magazine's August 31, 1970, issue.[43]

If Friedan gained fame through her discovery of "the problem with no name," Millett earned hers by naming the condition Friedan so vividly detailed. The name she offered for women's problem was *patriarchy*.[44] Whereas Friedan discussed the feminine mystique and popular Freudianism as a pervasive and damaging cultural message about women, a problem primarily of socialization, Millett understood patriarchy as a profound organizational principle that affected all of culture and society. "Our society, like all other historical civilizations," wrote Millett, "is a patriarchy."

What goes largely unexamined, often even unacknowledged (yet is institutionalized nonetheless) in our social order, is the birthright priority whereby males rule females. Through this system a most ingenious form of "interior colonization" has been achieved. It is one which tends moreover to be sturdier than any form of segregation, and more rigorous than class stratification. . . . However muted its present appearance may be, sexual dominion [is] . . . the most pervasive ideology of our culture and provides its most fundamental concept of power.[45]

Millett's analysis of patriarchy as a form of "interior colonization" was the first to conceptualize the relationship between men and women as a form of political domination. She explained that patriarchy provided all societies, including modern American society, with a fundamental power structure based on the difference between the sexes. For patriarchy to exist, sexual difference had to be maintained and continuously elaborated upon. The elaboration of sexual difference, Millett theorized, was gender. Rather than an account of "real" (innate) differences between men and women, gender was the social and cultural production of sexual difference. Millet explained that patriarchy created and enforced the "myth" of femininity to justify male dominance.

Like Friedan before her, Millett held Freudian psychoanalysis accountable as a key discourse in the narrow and belittling definition of femininity. But Millett moved beyond Friedan to elaborate what would become the second pillar of feminist thought in this period: the psychological origins of patriarchy. Millett analyzed Freudian theory and its influence on modern femininity through a history of what she called the "sexual revolution" in Western society, specifically in twentieth-century America. Millett's history, however, did not simply record Freud's influence on American women but rather explored the usefulness of Freudian thought to the patriarchal social order.

Millett began her history of the sexual revolution in the 1830s, which she said was a period of expanding sexual freedoms. This initial period of sexual liberation lasted until 1930 when a backlash swept the West. Freud and his followers participated in what she called the "counterrevolution" against the sexual revolution.[46] By "an irony near tragic," wrote Millett, Freud's theories, with their liberatory potential, had been used by his followers and popularizers to sponsor a campaign of sexual repression. This campaign profoundly limited women's efforts to achieve social and sexual freedom. In terms of "the sexual revolution's goal of liberating female humanity from its traditional subordination," wrote Millett, "the Freudian position came to be pressed into the service of a strongly counterrevolutionary attitude."[47]

Millett's understanding of sexuality as the central feature of American gender relations proved to be an extremely productive conception for second-wave feminists. Unlike Friedan, who complained that sexuality was a diversion from politics, Millett viewed sexuality as politics. She saw the intersection of sexuality and gender as the most important feature of women's identities and thus their oppression. Millett's analysis of patriarchy as a social, historical system enabled feminists to challenge a number of enduring representations of sexuality and women: the construction of sexuality as natural and unchanging, the classifying of men and women's relationships as private and thus nonpolitical, and an understanding of women as "naturally" subordinate to men. At the same time, Millett's analysis of patriarchy, like Friedan's of liberalism, minimized the role race played in the social relations between men and women and among women.

Millett's view of patriarchy self-consciously and strategically adopted psychoanalytic theory. Her theory of sexual politics required the psychoanalytic categories of repression and the unconscious. Millett explained that the first sexual revolution failed because it was unable to change the "psychic structure" of patriarchal society. The second sexual revolution, in which Millet saw herself participating, must not repeat the mistake of the first by emphasizing the "superstructure of patriarchal policy," its legal and educational abuses, to the neglect of the psychological realm of individual socialization. "Basic attitudes, values, emotions—all that constitute the psychic structure several millennia of patriarchal society had built up—remained insufficiently affected, if not completely untouched."[48] Drawing on Marxism but inverting its logic, Millett argued that sexuality provided the "base" upon which culture, or the "superstructure" of patriarchy, rested.

> Patriarchy could, as indeed it did, remain in force as a thoroughly efficient political system, a method of social governance, without any visible superstructure beyond the family, simply because it lived on in the mind and heart where it had first rooted itself in the conditioning of its subjects, and from which a few reforms were hardly likely to evict it.[49]

With her focus on "the mind and heart," Millett sounded a crucial theme in radical feminism, the political nature of subjectivity. With her emphasis on the process by which individuals came into social consciousness, Millett identified the origins of society in individual subjectivity as much as in the "superstructure" of formal politics and laws. Millett's account of patriarchy, then, placed the family and the identities it nurtured at the center of the formation of political consciousness. A feminist sexual revolution, she proposed, must reach deep into individuals' psyches to root out patriarchy.

While both Friedan and Millett criticized the role Freud and psychoanalysis played in the evolution of modern femininity, their analyses differed in important ways that reflected larger divides between liberal and radical views of the relationship between culture and politics. Radical feminists like Millett challenged the very distinction between culture and politics. Private life, with its web of intimate relations, did not exist apart from "real" politics, nor was the domestic world the "problem" from which women needed to escape, as Friedan argued. Radical feminists like Millett argued instead that the political significance of sexuality lay in the fact that sexuality defined the boundaries between public and private life.

Organized around the politics of sexuality, Millett's *Sexual Politics* did away with the distinction between private (domestic) and public (political) life. She understood sexuality as a key site in the establishment of male power. Millett explained that Freudianism "solved" the problem of women's discontent by sexualizing it, reducing it to "penis envy," a matter of women's individual and sexual pathology, and, in so doing, diffused any potential threats to existing "sexual politics." Friedan, on the other hand, understood women's conflation with sexuality as the result of, not the origin of, women's secondary situation.[50] She envisioned women's social equality following their departure from the private world of the home and their entry into the public world of work, and not in the refiguring the very categories of private/public. Whereas Friedan understood women's "obsession" with sex as a diversion for those on the margins of power, Millett understood the conflation of women and sexuality as the site wherein men established and sustained their social dominance over women. Both also inadvertently racialized the foundations of feminist theory as "white." Without more nuanced accounts of how race shaped gender and sexuality, white middle-class women's experiences came to stand in for all women's experiences.

Despite the damning discourse about femininity generated by orthodox and popular Freudianism, psychoanalysis continued to harbor many feminists' hopes for uprooting the oppression of women. Shulamith Firestone, a Marxist and radical feminist, used psychoanalysis to explain the internal structures of identity that perpetuated patriarchal authority and women's sexual oppression. In doing so, she did what many feminists found unimaginable: she used Freud to dismantle patriarchy.

Patriarchal Heterosexuality: Shulamith Firestone

Freudianism is so charged, so impossible to repudiate because
Freud grasped the crucial problem of modern life: Sexuality.[51]

The final concept on which the second wave of feminists based their
political analysis of sexuality came from Shulamith Firestone, whose
analysis of heterosexuality completed the foundational triad of feminist
theories of sexuality. Whereas Friedan analyzed the social construction of
femininity, Millett the psychological structure of patriarchy, in *The Dialectic of Sex*, Firestone theorized heterosexuality as an identity rooted in the
unequal relations between men and women. By theorizing heterosexuality as a sexual and social identity produced historically, over time, Firestone
integrated Friedan's analysis of femininity with Millett's view of the political nature of sexuality.

As with Friedan and Millett, Firestone both questioned and relied
upon the categories of psychoanalysis for her theory of women's liberation.
At the same time, she used psychoanalysis in a way that neither Friedan
nor Millett did. Unlike other feminists, Firestone viewed patriarchy as a
natural result of biology. According to her, Freud did not produce patriarchy but only reflected what was already in existence. She thus recast
Freud's theories as a useful map of patriarchy rather than as an oppressive
ideology that itself required overturning. Firestone used Freud's narrative
of the oedipal complex quite literally as a text of the inner workings of the
nuclear family. That is, rather than questioning the validity of Freud's
theory of sexuality, Firestone understood it as a step-by-step, "how-to" account of the creation of two distinct, neurotic, and repressed "sex classes"
that were bound together through the biological imperative to reproduce
the species.

Firestone's account of Freudianism granted it the status of sociological truth. That truth, she qualified, became clear only when studying
Freud through the filter of feminism. "I submit that the only way the
Oedipus Complex can make full sense is in terms of power."[52] Like
Marcuse and Brown, she argued that the incest taboo organized polymorphous sexuality into genital sexuality, and ultimately children into
two opposing sexes and genders. The patriarchal family structure created a sexual desire for the mother in both male and female children, but
only the son would inherit a woman "like his mother" in the future. In
denying women their original sexual object (the mother), the family en-

forced heterosexuality and damaged women's sense of their original and healthy "human" sexuality.

As with Millett, Firestone argued that psychoanalysis articulated the psychic structure internalized by children in western societies. Yet unlike Millett, Firestone used psychoanalysis to show how the family and its repressions produced a historically specific form of sexuality. The nuclear family, and the law of the father that upheld it, separated emotion from sexuality. Children learned that certain forms of intimacy with the mother were inappropriate and called sexual, whereas other intimacies remained acceptable and were labeled emotional. Society thus singled out sexuality as a special experience, a set of tabooed feelings against which a heavy weight of repression was leveled. Thus the distinction between sexuality and emotion that the oedipal situation created became the foundation for both (hetero) sexual identity and sexual repression.[53]

In *The Dialectic of Sex*, Firestone envisioned a society without oppressive heterosexuality as its foundation. To undo patriarchy required the undoing of the nuclear family. To undo the nuclear family required undoing the link between families and reproduction, a link that depended on women. "We have seen how women, biologically distinguished from men, are culturally distinguished from 'human.' Nature produced the fundamental inequality—half the human race must bear and rear the children of all of them—which was later consolidated, institutionalized, in the interests of men." The burden of reproduction "cost women dearly," psychologically, emotionally, and physically. "Continuous childbirth led to constant 'female trouble,' early aging, and death."[54] The solution Firestone offered was radical: free women by freeing them from reproduction. Through artificial reproduction, Firestone proposed, society could breed its own offspring, in public institutions, and thus free individuals from the institution of the family. The feminist revolution must liberate women from "the tyranny of their reproductive biology by every means available, and the diffusion of the childbearing and childrearing role to the society as a whole, men and women."[55]

Firestone thus used psychoanalysis to envision a world where gender no longer set the parameters of sexuality. In Firestone's new society, women would at last become "human" because they would be no longer burdened with reproduction. "In our new society, humanity could finally revert to its natural polymorphous sexuality—all forms of sexuality would be allowed and indulged. The fully sexuate mind, realized in the past in only a few individuals (survivors), would become universal."[56] If the family repressed polymorphous ungendered sexuality, then a feminist revolution must eradicate the family and with it any enforcement of heterosexuality for both men and women. Without biological reproduction and the family, men and women would become free to pick and chose partners and practices based on pleasure alone. Heterosexuality would revert to polymorphous sexuality, "women" to "human," and families to communities.

Firestone used Freudianism as both a historical record of patriarchal heterosexuality in families and a theory that could lead to a genderless world. Firestone added reproduction and sexuality to the analysis first offered by Marcuse and Brown. So doing, she offered a unique vision of a postrepressive society where polymorphous sexuality would shatter the remnants of the two sex classes and the mental straight jacket of masculinity and femininity.

Friedan, Millett, and Firestone each critically engaged with and transformed Freud's work on women. In their unprecedented theories of the origin and perpetuation of women's social, political, and sexual marginalization, these major theoreticians of feminism renegotiated the line demarcating the personal from the political. The triad of ideas forged through feminists' paradoxical engagement with Freudian psychoanalysis—the social construction of femininity, the psychological origins of patriarchy, and the political nature of heterosexuality—lay the theoretical groundwork for a wide range of feminist analyses of sexuality. The foundational concepts promulgated by Friedan, Millett, and Firestone helped to recast the vaginal woman of Freudianism, once held up as the definitive vision of women's mental health and stability, as a fiction at best. At worst, the ideal woman of Freudianism became a sign of the bruising misinformation campaign generated by decades of misogynist practices through which generations of women had suffered.

The critique of Freudianism also enabled feminists to refashion the sexual and reproductive potential of the female body. Feminists declared that women's bodies were no longer for the sole purposes of bearing children and pleasing their male partners' sexual needs. Rather, adjusting the mantle of a new sexual revolution, feminists reclaimed the female body as both the symbolic location of and source for women's true social and political liberation. At the same time, feminists' attention to sexuality and the body as the source of women's oppression and of their liberation also downplayed and, at times, outrightly ignored other sources of women's oppression. The experiences of racism, of poverty, and of homophobic attacks, for example, did not figure as prominently in Friedan, Millett, or Firestone's conceptions of women's oppression as did sexuality. The emphasis on the intersection between sexuality and gender, in itself, racialized this moment of feminism as white; for only white middle-class women had the privilege of focusing on a single axis of identity and oppression.

Rewriting Female Pleasure

Women have . . . been defined sexually in terms of what pleases men; our own biology has not been properly analyzed. Instead, we are fed the myth of the liberated woman and her vaginal orgasm—an orgasm which in fact does not exist.
—Anne Koedt[57]

While Freud's theory is inconsistent with female anatomy, it is excellent evidence in support of the theory that the concept of sexual intercourse is a political construct reified into an institution.
—Ti-Grace Atkinson[58]

As feminists engaged with psychoanalysis, they also adopted and reworked sexology. The radical feminist engagement with sexology proved enormously productive. Foremost, it enabled feminists to claim the clitoris as a uniquely female form of sexuality that had the potential to transcend the narrow and pathologizing classifications of male experts. Specifically, feminists used the sexological remapping of the female body, with its attention to the clitoris, to overturn the Freudian emphasis on the vagina. By focusing on the clitoris, feminists made the first modern case for women's sexual autonomy. The clitoris bequeathed by sexology and reworked by feminists provided a break, at last, out of the legacy of female sexual dependency enshrined for decades by experts. In the hands of feminists, sexological information became a way to reinvent an authentic female sexuality out of which new, more equitable gender roles could be forged.

Radical women who had grown tired of the male-centered culture of the student protest movements and the civil rights movement began meeting together as early as 1967. Some groups of women met as women's caucuses within larger movements, others met independently. Women who began to call themselves radical feminists came together to study, to raise their consciousness about the condition of women's lives, to plot actions, and to generate theory. For example, feminists in Boston's Cell 16 began meeting in 1968 and started generating theory and publishing one of the first feminist underground journals, *No More Fun and Games*.[59] Roxanne Dunbar and Dana Desmore, the group's theoreticians, generated a radical body of writing that set forth some of the movement's emergent agenda. In the first issue of *No More Fun and Games*, Dunbar envisioned groups like Cell 16 as agents in a historic social revolution. "A vanguard of women must operate to show women the possibility of a new society. . . . We shall not fight on the enemy's grounds—on his streets, in his courts, legislatures, 'radical' movements, marriage, media."[60] Similar groups sprang up in cities across the country, including the Feminists, New York Radical Women, Redstockings, Berkeley's Women's Liberation, WITCH, SCUM, Chicago's Women's Liberation, and Women's Majority Union, Seattle.

One Boston-based women's liberation group, The Boston Women's Health Course Collective, began as a small discussion group on women and their bodies at a conference in 1969. In a process that soon characterized the journey of much feminist writing, the project began to educate the members and evolved into a much larger event.

> We had all experienced similar feelings of frustration and anger towards specific doctors and the medical maze in general. . . . We decided on a summer project—to research those topics which we felt were particularly pertinent to learning about our bodies, to discuss in the group what we had learned, then to write papers individually or in small groups of two or three, and finally to present the results in the fall as a course for women on women and their bodies. . . . At the end of the twelve week session we found that many women felt both eager and competent to get together in small groups and share what they had learned with other women. We saw it as a never-ending process always involving more and more women.[61]

The collective first handed out mimeographed copies of the papers to their students. As the demand grew, they turned to the New England Free Press to publish inexpensive copies. The growing number of requests soon swamped the press, and the collective took it to a commercial press in 1971, which made *Our Bodies, Our Selves* into one of the movement's most popular and best-selling books.[62] Many feminists writings took this path from mimeograph copies, to intermediate small-run or underground print runs, to mainstream publishing. This trajectory both testified to and helped produce the wildfire momentum of the women's liberation movement in the late 1960s and early 1970s. It also marked how marginal radical feminists transformed themselves into a new breed of experts whose views on a range of topics, from sexism to orgasm, entered into and changed the mainstream.

Groups like Redstockings, New York Radical Women, Cell 16, and the Boston Women's Health Course Collective based their expertise on the lived experiences of their group members. This process became known as consciousness-raising. Kathie Sarachild of New York Radical Women described how the group coined the phrase *consciousness-raising* and revolutionized what had previously been seen as idle talk.

> I just sat there listening to her describe all the false ways women have to act: playing dumb, always being agreeable, always being nice, not to mention what we had to do to our bodies with the clothes and shoes we wore, the diets we had to go through, going blind not wearing glasses, all because men didn't find our real selves, our human freedom, our basic humanity "attractive." And I realized I still could learn a lot about how to understand and describe the particular oppression of women in ways that could reach other women in the way this had just reached me. The whole group . . . decided on the spot that what we needed . . . was to raise our consciousness some more.[63]

Through methodologies like consciousness-raising, radical feminists politicized the identity category "woman." According to feminists, this category had been socially created by experts like doctors, religious leaders, and teachers and elaborated upon by magazines, movies, and novels. It was also a creation of an individual's home life and the particular views of womanhood enforced by parents and families. And, as radical feminists pointed out in groups across the country, these messages about "womanhood" had been internalized and become intimate components of individual women's sense of self. Thus, according to New York Radical Women, part of women claiming their authority lay in the larger process of, first, overturning male experts and oppressive socialization and, second, speaking their own truth about their experience. Knowledge discovered in this way, and contributed to by all members, would provide the basis for a new feminist theory of women's lives. According to Sarachild, "the decision to emphasize our own feelings and experiences as women and to test all generalizations and reading we did by our own experience was actually the scientific method of research."[64] Consciousness-raising (CR) thus provided a new way to produce expert knowledge.

A key element of how radical feminists marked the category "woman" as political came through their emphasis on sexuality. Feminists thinking about sexuality critically examined the ways in which women learned to act with men, socially and sexually. While they looked at reproductive rights, such as access to birth control and abortion, and racist sterilization practices, they had a tendency to concentrate on sexual practice and the "sexual politics" between women and their partners. Women in the CR groups discovered that many of them faked orgasm or never had had one; many felt their partners' were indifferent to their desires; many felt exploited by the free love spirit of the sexual revolution; and many felt desires for other women that they didn't understand. Radical feminists hoped that by speaking truthfully about their experiences they could both overturn the "universal" oppression of female sexuality and reinvent female sexuality.

However, radical feminists did not uniformly adopt the emphasis on sexual freedom and the counterhegemonic possibilities of a liberated female sexuality. For radical women of color, the emphasis on sexuality was problematic. Sexuality between minority men and women was not seen only as a site of oppression but also as one of strength and empowerment. Francis Beal, in 1969, argued that white women's groups must define overlapping structural forms of racial and sexual oppression, and not conceptualize oppression only as the "vicarious pleasure" men derive from "consuming [women's] bodies for exploitative reasons." Without such an analysis, black feminists "cannot unite with [white women] around common grievances or even discuss these groups in a serious manner because they're completely irrelevant to the black struggle."[65]

Radical black women like Linda La Rue dismissed the revolutionary possibility of white feminism precisely because its reliance on the fiction of the universal woman. In 1971, La Rue wrote that "the American white woman has had a better opportunity to live a free and fulfilling life, both mentally and physically, than any other group in the United States, with the exception of her white husband." She rejected any attempt to discuss the oppression white women might face as having "the validity of comparing the neck of a hanging man with the hands of an amateur mount climber with rope burns."[66] For her, racism defined her gendered identity as powerfully as did sexuality. Without an analysis of the intersections of class and race with sexuality, white feminists' emphasis on sexual pleasure alone could not speak to black women.

Many black women found their revolutionary struggle for liberation to lie with the civil rights and black power movements more than with the women's liberation movement. Facing sexism and homophobia from their male colleagues, on the one hand, and racism from white women, on the other, by the mid-1970s black radical women found themselves in an undeniable paradox where "all the women are white, all the blacks are men, but some of us are brave," as the title of a historic anthology of black feminism later put it.[67] While black feminists claimed sexual pleasure as a right and as important to female empowerment, they did so out of a history of sexual exploitation and violently racist denial of their privacy and bodily integrity. This history shaped black feminism as it emerged in the 1980s.[68]

In the years between 1967 and 1973, radical feminists sought to move beyond the white middle-class women who comprised most of the groups. But they met with limited success. Part of their inability to speak to more racially diverse women lay in the very methodology they utilized to revolutionize women. Basing the new feminist expertise on lived experiences, which tended to be filtered through an emphasis on sexuality, and drawing insights from experiences through discussion and writing was unintentionally exclusionary. Not all women felt comfortable openly discussing sexual topics, nor did all women feel as articulate as the university-trained white women who, for the most part, made up the groups. Differences based on class, race, and sexual orientation divided women within the movement. Thus radical women of all sorts sought out groups of like-minded women who shared similar worldviews and political agendas. This created, from the very beginnings of radical feminism, different groups with different trajectories, each of whom claimed the mantle of feminism.

FRIEDAN, MILLETT, AND FIRESTONE, whose works had become flash points in the media coverage of the "battle of the sexes," set forth the central theoretical foundations for second-wave feminist thought. Their ideas fed from and supplied what was rapidly becoming a specifically radical feminist discourse on women's sexual pleasure. This discourse started at the margins and gradually entered the mainstream. As it did, it propelled some feminists—including Betty Friedan, Kate Millett, Gloria Steinem, and Erica Jong—into notoriety and recast them as new experts on women.

Although radical feminists argued that male experts had never understood women's authentic sexuality, they nevertheless drew on and reworked the tradition of American sexual thought they criticized. Foremost, feminists used Masters and Johnson's new research on the clitoris to overturn oppressive Freudian views of women's sexual dependency. *Human Sexual Response* had depicted female sexuality as super-responsive and not dependent on intercourse with a man. This new view of the clitoris enabled feminists to reclaim the sexual ambiguity first introduced by Freud in the 1920s and later pathologized by Freudians in the thirties and forties. Feminists used the health of the clitoris, established in sexology, to breathe new life into Freud's account of the instability of female heterosexuality. Rather than the problem it had been for Freudians, women's difficult passage into heterosexuality became, for radical feminists, proof of its unnaturalness. According to many radical feminists, it was a strength of women to exist beyond the categories of hetero- and homosexuality imposed by experts. In this way, they positioned "feminism" as a third term between lesbianism and heterosexuality.

Anne Koedt and Ti-Grace Atkinson were among the first feminists to explore the potential of the clitoris to destabilize expert accounts of female heterosexuality.[69] Koedt used the findings of Masters and Johnson to challenge the Freudian ideal of the vaginally orgasmic woman, which she claimed naturalized and depoliticized heterosexuality. Similarly, Atkinson, the former protégé of Betty Friedan, argued that the vaginal orgasm functioned as a form of psychological bondage that perpetuated patriarchal control over women.[70] Both Koedt and Atkinson complained that myths like the vaginal orgasm tangled women in an obsessive concern about their psychological health instead of their political servitude.

In "The Myth of the Vaginal Orgasm," first distributed as a mimeographed essay, then published in an underground journal, finally mass-marketed in the commercial anthology *Radical Feminism*, Koedt wrote that "the worst damage was done to the mental health of women who either suffered silently with self-blame, or flocked to the psychiatrists looking desperately for the hidden and terrible repression that kept them from their vaginal destiny."[71] Koedt rejected psychoanalytic explanations of frigidity that refused to see women's sexual dysfunction as related to the larger societal dysfunction of sexism, homophobia, and enforced heterosexuality. Psychoanalysis, she complained, had pathologized women instead of addressing the problem of male indifference to women's desires. "Rather than tracing female frigidity to the false assumptions about female anatomy," wrote Koedt, "our 'experts' have declared frigidity a psychological problem . . . diagnosed generally as a failure to adjust to their role as women."[72] According to Koedt, women must become full sexual agents, responsible for claiming their own pleasure.

> What we must do is redefine our sexuality. We must discard "normal" concepts of sex and create new guidelines which take into account mutual sexual enjoyment. . . . We must begin to demand that if certain sexual positions now defined as "standard" are not mutually conducive to orgasm, they no longer be defined as standard.[73]

Koedt strategically avoided setting forth new standards for authentic female sexuality. Rather, she embraced sexual self-determination as a feminist value. By refusing to define the bounds of female sexuality, she left radical feminist sex theory productively open-ended, potentially flexible enough to encompass all women and all that they desired.

In "The Institution of Sexual Intercourse," Atkinson also critiqued the psychoanalytic ideal of the vaginal orgasm. She complained that it naturalized the "patriarchal social institutions" of marriage and the family by viewing female sexuality solely as an expression of reproduction.[74] If women did not find heterosexual intercourse pleasurable, she reasoned, it was because, as an institution of patriarchal control, sexual intercourse was not suited to fully stimulate or satisfy women's (clitoral) sexuality. Like Friedan and Millett, Atkinson noted that psychoanalysis believed female sexual "dysfunction" resulted from women's failure to adjust to their social roles. A feminist analysis, she countered, reversed this view and insisted that women's social roles caused women's sexual "dysfunction." By freeing women from oppressive social roles, women would be freed to explore the true nature of their desires, outside of patriarchal phallic intercourse.

Koedt and Atkinson proposed that women throw out male experts' views of women's so-called sexual nature, all accounts of proper sexual techniques, and any assertion about sex not made by a woman herself. For women to be truly liberated, they must choose not to know the boundaries of sexual pleasure in advance. Not knowing, Koedt and Atkinson implied, was an enormous improvement on the years of misinformation that had previously smothered women's authentic sexual expression.

Koedt and Atkinson further extended Millett's concept of sexual politics by analyzing sexual intercourse as a practice that upheld men's social power over women. For them, intercourse stood in for the patriarchal denial of women while the clitoris embodied the implicit promise of women's full sexual autonomy. According to Koedt, male experts denied the centrality of the clitoris to women's sexuality because they felt threatened by the prospect of women as separate desiring subjects.

> It seems clear to me that men in fact fear the clitoris as a threat to their masculinity. . . . The establishment of clitoral orgasm as fact would threaten the heterosexual institution. For it would indicate that sexual pleasure was obtainable from either men or women, thus making heterosexuality not absolute, but an option. It would thus open up the whole question of human sexual relationships beyond the confines of the present male-female role system.[75]

Through her analysis of female orgasm, Koedt articulated the links between patriarchy, male experts, and accounts of normal heterosexuality. She argued that the specter of an independent female sexuality, signified through the clitoris, threatened to alter the meaning of gender itself. If women did not depend on the penis for sexual pleasure, then heterosexuality itself would become a matter of choice and not a natural inevitability. This in turn threw into question the existence of unchanging, dichotomous, and complementary gender identities.

Koedt and Atkinson were not alone in exploring heterosexuality as a political formation. In "The Politics of Orgasm," published in *Sisterhood Is Powerful* (1970), Susan Lyndon of the activist group Berkeley Women's Liberation argued that society found "something indispensable" in the view of women as dependent on men for their sexual fulfillment.[76] Before Masters and Johnson, she wrote, female sexuality had been "objectively defined and described by men," and the "subjective experience of women had had no part in defining their own sexuality." She clearly articulated the links feminists made between the clitoris and women's sexual autonomy.

> If woman's pleasure was obtained through the vagina, then she was totally dependent on the man's erect penis to achieve orgasm; she would receive her satisfaction only as a concomitant of man's seeking his. With the clitoral orgasm, woman's sexual pleasure was independent of the male's, and she could seek her satisfaction as aggressively as the man sought his, a prospect which didn't appeal to too many men. The definition of normal feminine sexuality as vaginal, in other words, was

a part of keeping women down, of making them sexually, as well as economically, socially, and politically subservient.[77]

Feminists like Lyndon and Koedt believed the clitoris was the site of liminality for women, the point at which male experts' categories broke down. Clitoral stimulation resulted in orgasm for women, and this clitoral orgasm, whether stimulated by men or women, became the marker of "the feminist."

To liberate women from the Freudian view that women were naturally maternal rather than sexual, many feminists emphasized women's capacity for orgasm and enjoyment of sex. Psychiatrist Mary Jane Sherfey argued in 1970 that women required "frequent prolonged coitus" to satiate their intense and biological drive for multiple orgasms. Ironically, she proposed that modern civilization was based on the repression of "women's inordinate sexual demands."[78] Liberating women, she and others proposed, depended on liberating female sexuality from the confines of male control. "No doubt the most far-reaching hypothesis extrapolated [from Masters and Johnson] is the existence of the universal and physically normal condition of women's inability ever to reach complete sexual satiation." Theoretically, she explained, "a woman could go on having orgasms indefinitely if physical exhaustion did not intervene."[79]

Feminists who claimed sexual pleasure for feminism insisted that women could transform society by claiming full sexual entitlement and agency. Germaine Greer, in her 1970 best-seller, *The Female Eunuch*, embodied, quite literally, the connections between sex radicalism and radical feminism.[80] An Australian-born sex radical, Greer was committed to both sexual freedom and women's liberation. She had been part of the editorial group that founded *Suck*, a publication dedicated to the belief that sexual relationships should be open and nonpossessive. Founded to counter *Screw*, which she and others saw as denigrating to women, *Suck* set out to liberate pleasure, not to celebrate penises. For example, Greer frequently railed against the missionary position in her editorials, complaining that it gave men all the control and women none of the pleasure. For her, intercourse, done properly, enabled women to claim their full sexual power.

Any woman can be a good fuck lying on her back, but poised over her man . . . she must proceed with sensitivity and control, and with all her strength. . . . She can control the degrees of penetration . . . fluttering and squeezing him with her vaginal muscles which are now free to respond to her desires, instead of being deadened by the impact of the heavy male body. She is at last conscious of female potency, the secret power of her lovely, complex genitals.[81]

The message of *The Female Eunuch* was simple: women must harness the power of sexual pleasure to feminism. "It is dangerous," Greer asserted, "to eschew sex as a revolutionary tactic because it is inauthentic and enslaving in the terms in which it is now possible." Sex provided women with "the principle confrontation in which new values can be worked out."[82] For Greer, heterosexual women's sense of political agency and emotional empowerment rested on their sense of sexual entitlement. And yet, while Greer appreciated the research of Masters and Johnson, she also saw it as limited and limiting. In a 1971 issue of *Suck,* she complained that Masters and Johnson lacked imagination. "To know cunt, it is also necessary to know how it works and what to do. While Masters and Johnson have done much to dispel those absurd presumptions about cunt, they could not be better than their subjects, and there is no reason why we should believe that what American middle-class women taped to electrodes could do, is all that could have been done."[83] Likewise, in *The Female Eunuch*, she wrote against mistaking genital stimulation for true sexuality. Sounding a theme first set out by Marcuse and Brown, Greer envisioned sexual liberation as a return of polymorphous sexuality and a reanimation of the total body.

> Many women who greeted the conclusions of Masters and Johnson with cries of "I told you so!" and "I am normal" will feel that this criticism is a betrayal. They have discovered sexual pleasure after being denied it but the fact that they have only ever experienced gratification from clitoral stimulation is evidence for my case, because it is the index of the desexualization of the whole body, the substitution of genitality for sexuality.[84]

Greer saw the radical potential of liberating the female body from outdated views of women's nature. At the same time, she dismissed the feminist view of the vagina as patriarchal by insisting that the vagina was at the heart of female bodily responsiveness. Rather than an insensitive organ, unresponsive and nonorgasmic, the vagina uniquely allowed women to be "filled up" with sensations and, as such, opened them to a far more powerful and transformative sexuality. Greer wrote that "satisfaction" could not be simply located in a tiny cluster of nerves but rather must be found in "the sexual involvement of the whole person. . . . If we localize female response in the clitoris we impose upon women the same limitations of sex which has stunted the male response." Women's social marginalization, she insisted, resulted from their alienation from the power and pleasure of their bodies. In adopting men as the standard for all "human" existence, feminists ran the risk of making themselves "eunuchs," powerless, stripped of the knowledge from their bodies and their authentic "feminine" nature. For Greer, women's bodily difference was the source of women's power and pleasure and not simply the site of their oppression.

Even within white radical feminism, many women argued that celebrating sexual pleasure as key to women's liberation did not necessarily eradicate the sexism they faced from "liberated," "with-it," men.[85] Dismayed by the hypersexualized woman of the sexual revolution, many radical feminists pointed to what seemed to be an endemic confusion in the 1960s between women's liberation and sexual liberation. They called for liberating women from sexuality. Dana Densmore, a member of Cell 16, explained in 1971 that women were as oppressed by sexual liberation as they were by sexual repression. She wrote that instead of being intimidated by psychiatrists for their lack of vaginal sexuality, women now found themselves oppressed by an "orgasm frenzy."

> Our "right" to enjoy our own bodies has not only been bestowed upon us, it is almost a duty. . . . Everywhere we are sexual objects, and our own enjoyment just enhances our attractiveness. We are wanton. We wear miniskirts and see-through tops. We're sexy. We're free. We run around and hop into bed whenever we please. . . . And people seem to believe that sexual freedom (even when it is only the freedom to actively offer oneself as a willing object) is freedom.[86]

Another feminist explained that in the eyes of their male peers women were "too sick to appreciate the benefits of free love" and needed enlightenment.[87] "Suddenly men became concerned with my hang-ups and insistent that I accept their offers of instant liberation. Sexual exploitation was now disguised as participating in the new society."[88] Roxanne Dunbar, also of Cell 16, complained that sexual liberation had come to mean "the 'freedom' to 'make it' with anyone, anytime."[89] Introducing what would become a crucial theme of seventies feminism, she argued that women's liberation could not simply be equated with sexual freedom since many

women experienced sex not just as an arena of pleasure but as "brutaliza-
tion, rape, submission, [and] someone having power over them." Like
Koedt and Atkinson, Dunbar saw that what experts had defined as "normal" was, in fact, what men found erotic. "Let us openly admit that we
have all been brainwashed so that what is called 'pleasure' is not really, and
is actually often oppressive and humiliating."[90]

Situating radical men in the culture of male dominance, feminists complained that leftist men were guilty of the same exploitative uses of the sexual revolution. Radical men, they argued, criticized monogamy more out
of their desires to be "free" to have sex with whomever they wanted than
out of a desire to bring down the nuclear family. Barbara Leon, a member
of New York's activist group Redstockings, wrote in 1971 that radical men
used the "ideology" of sexual freedom "to exploit women individually."[91]
"Smashing monogamy is nothing new for men. They've been doing it for
centuries. . . . Now," continued Leon,

> our brothers are offering us freedom . . . freedom from love; freedom
> from emotional support; freedom from sharing the material privileges
> they have enjoyed for so long. What these men are essentially demand-
> ing is that women continue to perform all the usual services expected of
> us, but without asking anything in return.[92]

Black feminists also offered scathing critiques of the sexual politics of
black male revolutionaries. Beal complained that radical black men adopted conservative views of gender in their revolutionary rhetoric. Where the
black radical "see[s] the system for what it really is for the most part . . .
when it comes to women, he seems to take his guidelines from the pages
of the *Ladies Home Journal*." She argued that black men's sexism was
"counterrevolutionary."[93] Similarly, Mary Ann Weathers claimed that
"women's liberation is an extremely emotional issue. . . . Black men are still
parroting the master's prattle about male superiority."[94] In 1970, revolutionary men, black and white, maintained deeply gendered ideas about
leadership, woman's proper place, and a dismissive attitude toward the
analysis of women's oppression as women; revolutionary women, black
and white, called them to task for it.

Feminists dubious about the revolutionary potential of sexual pleasure
reintroduced the idea that what women really wanted from sex was not
orgasm but intimacy and love. Drawing on and reworking a tradition of
American sexual thought that emphasized romance over orgasm for wo-

men, as set out by Van Der Velde in the 1920s, elevated and celebrated by Deutsch in the 1940s and tacitly reaffirmed by Kinsey in the 1950s, these feminists theorized psychological intimacy as a unique and unappreciated form of female sexuality. Rejecting traditional concepts of sexual pleasure, these radical feminists sought to open up all feelings and sensations as potentially sexual for women. They suggested the desire for intimacy was authentically female while the desire for something as tangible as orgasm was an oppressive feature of male-dominated society.

Once again, feminists symbolically attributed autonomy to the clitoris and then used it to reinvent sexual freedom for women. For example, Densmore made a case that physical pleasure was not the most important feature of sex for women. Citing Masters and Johnson's finding that with clitoral stimulation a woman could have multiple orgasms, she wrote,

> An orgasm for a woman isn't a release in the same sense that it is for a man, since we are capable of an indefinite number, remaining aroused the whole time, limited only by exhaustion. The release we feel, therefore, is psychological. . . . Without denying that sex can be pleasurable, I suggest that the real thing we seek is closeness, merging, perhaps a kind of oblivion of self.[95]

Atkinson also referred to Masters and Johnson's research on the clitoris when she argued that sex between individuals was not a physical necessity. "If masturbation has such strong arguments in its favor . . . on what grounds is an outside party . . . a positive addition to the experience?"[96] She believed that, once existing heterosexuality had been transformed, the goal of mutual sexual pleasure would no longer be orgasm but a sense of belonging and social bonding. This more authentic desire for psychological intimacy, she asserted, had been falsely sexualized by patriarchal heterosexuality.[97]

In stressing emotional intimacy over sexual pleasure, feminists offered a new way to imagine women's sexual agency and self-determination. They made a case for opening up the definition of "sex" and sexual practice to include a wider range of stimulation, including emotions. Once again, the clitoris helped constitute a third identity between heterosexuality and homosexuality, that of "the feminist" who was sexually autonomous and free from the psychological bonds of male standards. Feminists like Atkinson and Densmore gendered the desire for orgasm as masculine and the desire for intimacy and merging as feminine. Thus, they returned to and radicalized the historic link between emotion and women's orgasm, this time in order to liberate women from expert discourse and male standards. Whereas Van Der Velde counseled his readers that women needed love to reach orgasm and Alex Comfort claimed that love helped women overcome any technical mishaps between a husband and wife, feminists like Atkinson and Densmore argued that orgasm simply was not the point of sex. Intimacy, social bonding, full body sensuality constituted authentic, nonoppressive human sexuality. No longer was a woman who did not reach orgasm frigid; she was existing beyond the terms of male sexual standards.

The feminist analysis of women's sexual independence, developed through their symbolic reworking of the clitoris, also revolutionized the meaning of lesbianism. This new version of lesbianism emerged out of the unmooring of female sexuality from heterosexual phallic sex. Once feminists reintroduced the idea that psychological intimacy was the true origin of female sexual pleasure, the line demarcating heterosexual and lesbian women all but disappeared. If sexual intercourse was an instrument of patriarchal control, and orgasm a male myth, then emotional closeness became the basis for all sexuality. In this light, lesbianism was a form of resistance to male oppression, not an illness one hid shamefully. However, while the view of female sexuality as an expression of emotional and not physical need appealed to many feminists, it was fostered in an atmosphere of hostility to and ambivalence over the issue of lesbianism and its relationship to feminism in both radical and liberal circles.

From its inception, lesbianism had been a difficult and contentious issue within the women's liberation movement. Yet, because of the centrality of sexuality to second-wave feminists, many women in the new movement believed that lesbianism could neither be dismissed as "reactionary" nor marginalized as deviant. As one woman explained, "On a gut level, the women's movement has to be about sexuality. . . . If sexuality is the base, then lesbianism is totally relevant."[98] Salvaging lesbianism from a long history of medical and psychiatric pathologizing, many feminists felt committed to joining lesbianism and feminism.[99]

The Lavender Menace, a group that later became the Radicalesbians, offered one of the most important challenges to the homophobia in the movement in a position paper entitled "The Woman-Identified Woman."[100] This paper theorized lesbianism as an emotional and political choice rather than a (deviant) sexual object choice. It also helped secure the centrality of lesbian feminist theory to seventies feminism. Women-identification or women-loving-women emphasized the centrality of mutuality, equality, and sensuality for women. A woman-identified woman, the paper explained, did not place hetero- or homosexuality at the center of her identity, rather, she put her emotional relationships with other women first.

> Only women can give to each other a new sense of self. That identity we have to develop with reference to ourselves, and not in relation to men. This consciousness is the revolutionary force from which all else will follow, for ours is an organic revolution. For this we must be available and supportive to one another, give our commitment and our love, give the emotional support necessary to sustain this movement.[101]

The "woman-identified woman" built on and elaborated the idea of "the feminist" as occupying a liminal space between sexual categories. Part of how it accomplished this was by emphasizing that emotions were sexual for women. In this set of associations, genitality and orgasm were devalued as "male" and intimacy, sharing, and merging were celebrated as uniquely "female." Political and sexual commitments became one for women-identified-women. For example, Sue Katz argued in "Smash Phallic Imperialism" (1971) that for her lesbianism

> meant an end of sex. . . . Physical contact and feelings have taken a new liberatory form. And we call that sensuality. . . . Physicality is now a creative noninstitutionalized experience. It is touching and rubbing and cuddling and fondness. . . . Its only goal is closeness and pleasure. It does not exist for the Big Orgasm.[102]

Liberated from the tyranny of the "big orgasm," feminists celebrated the blurring of all boundaries; emotional closeness transcended sexual categories like lesbian and heterosexual, minimized interest in orgasm, and eradicated male experts' oppressive definitions of women's mental and sexual health. Intimacy thus became the basis of woman-centered solidarity.

In replacing genital sex with sensuality, feminists like Katz found a way to unify their political commitment to women with their sexuality. By insisting on the emotional and political viability of lesbian relationships, lesbian feminists invited their straight sisters to identify with other women and to value the support and empathy women felt for each other. Lesbianism, they insisted, must not be seen as merely a sexual alternative to heterosexuality but as an emotional way of life and a form of resistance to patriarchy. Katz articulated a central premise of lesbian feminism when she wrote that "the sensuality I feel has transformed my politics, has solved the contradiction between my mind and my body because the energies for our feminist revolution are the same as the energies of our love for women."[103] In this conception, lesbianism was very much a part of the feminist project of empowering women to be full sexual and social agents.

Feminists who claimed intimacy and not orgasm as the centerpiece of female sexuality again reworked sex expert discourse. They radicalized what on the surface seemed like the return of the asexual Victorian woman. Yet, unlike sex experts, feminists explained that emotional closeness was sexuality for women, or as much a part of sexuality as the orgasm. The feminist analysis of psychological intimacy as sexual, then, was a gesture toward liberating women from the confines of an expert discourse that many women-identified feminists believed had deliberately misunderstood female sexuality for most of the century. Those intent on elevating emotional closeness as an expression of women's deepest desire saw themselves as opening up the range of women's sexual self-determination.

The discussion within feminism over the significance of the female orgasm created a radical body of writing that both acted as an intervention in American understandings of sexuality and generated new accounts of the female body. The productivity of this extended moment in early feminism, between 1967 and 1973, rested on feminists' willingness to embrace the liminal space between lesbianism and heterosexuality as the space of women's sexual and social empowerment. By claiming sexual self-definition as a goal, second-wave feminists chose to move beyond experts' accounts of the pathology of lesbianism and the neurotic hysteria of female heterosexuality. They opted instead to use ambiguity to unsettle the link between gender and sexuality, focusing on the links between healthy/liberated heterosexual femininity and vaginal/multiple orgasms found in expert and alternative discourses.

Radical feminist sexual theory both drew on and opposed earlier discourses in which female sexuality had been cast as a defining metaphor that justified women's social subordination. Freudians in the interwar years distilled into their theories of sexuality a view of women as fundamentally dependent on men, emotionally passive and naive, and essentially maternal. Armed with the postwar sex studies of Kinsey and Masters and Johnson, feminists set out to unravel the symbolic ties between women's social and sexual subordination. Drawing as well on countercultural critiques of Freudianism and new symbolic investments in the idea of sexual liberation, feminists offered a counterhegemonic model of female sexuality by infusing it with the new values of self-determination, autonomy, and equality.

While feminists drew from psychoanalytic and countercultural models of sexuality, they were also limited by the very terms of these discourses. The psychoanalytic distinctions between orgasm and emotion, sexual objects and sexual identities, and the clitoris and the vagina as indicative of homo- and heterosexual tendencies set the terms from which feminists began the process of rewriting female sexuality. Likewise, the counterculture's murkiness on women being "like" or "unlike" men and its difficulty in integrating sexual freedom with an appreciation of women's historically different experiences of sexuality set much of the feminist agenda for a generation. Further, the assumptions of psychoanalysis and sexology were also the assumptions of whiteness. White radical feminists did not acknowledge the privileges implicit in seeing sexuality as the primary source of identity. They simply absorbed the category of sexuality, a category forged by experts, in the early years of the century, who themselves did not attend to its racial specificity.

At the same time radical feminists set out to build the political category woman, they minimized the intersection of sexuality with other axes of identity, namely, race and class. The implied woman of radical feminism remained white and middle-class. Without more knowledge of and commitment to the diverse experiences of women, radical feminism's historic project of politicizing pleasure as the basis for feminism also nurtured what would in the 1980s become divisive and painful fissures between feminists.

For a few years, feminists rallied around the value of female sexual autonomy as a way to transcend the lines between straight and lesbian women, between pleasure and danger, liberation and exploitation, in the name of expanding women's self-determination. They also succeeded in infusing female sexuality with the symbolism of women's full social, political and sexual equality unbounded by either difference from or similarity to men. For these women, then, the third term between heterosexuality and homosexuality was feminism.

The radicalism of feminist sex thought during this period of ferment and impending fragmentation emerged, to no small degree, out of the state of not knowing the boundaries of female sexual pleasure. After dismantling what they viewed as the reigning oppressive constructs about female sexuality, feminists in the late 1960s took the radical position of questioning everything, trusting women's desires wherever they might lead, and sabotaging any theory that proposed to secure, at last, the true nature of female sexual pleasure.

Four
DESIRES AND THEIR DISCONTENTS

Feminist Fiction of the 1970s

y the early 1970s, it was virtually impossible to miss that sex had finally arrived, belatedly perhaps, as the last great guest of the sixties revolutions. Whether Americans encountered the imagery of sexual freedom in mainstream erotic magazines like the pornography of *Playboy* or *Hustler*, engaged in new sexual styles in singles clubs and discos, or read, in the quiet of their homes, the media coverage on the "outbreak" of sexual expressiveness loosely labeled the sexual revolution, it was clear that sexual liberation had come to occupy a privileged place in the national consciousness.[1]

Feminists were regular participants in the national conversation about the significance of sexuality to liberation, to health and happiness, and to modern selfhood. Betty Friedan, Kate Millett, and Shulamith Firestone had, in some cases reluctantly, become spokeswomen of a new movement committed to women's sexual self-determination. Robin Morgan's 1970 blockbuster anthology of feminist writings, *Sisterhood Is Powerful*, and the arrival in 1972 of *Ms.* magazine, headed up by the glamorous Gloria Steineim, marked the further reach of feminism into the mainstream.[2]

The early 1970s also marked the arrival of soon-to-be-classic novels about female sexual liberation. In 1972 Alix Kates Shulman published *Memoirs of an Ex-Prom Queen*, and Margaret Atwood, *Surfacing*. In 1973, Erica Jong published *Fear of Flying*, Rita Mae Brown, *Rubyfruit Jungle*, and Barbara Raskin *Loose Ends*. In just a few years, a veritable treasure trove of popular novels appeared, all of which had a tentative and often uneasy connection to feminism. These included Lisa Alther's *Kinflicks*, Sara Davidson's *Loose Change*, Marilyn French's *The Woman's Room*, Shulman's *Burning Questions,* and Marge Piercy's *Vida*, to name only a few.[3] These novels, which almost universally took sexuality as both their main focus and the central event of the heroine's development, also participated in the extension of white middle-class feminist views of sexuality into the mainstream.[4] Written against what many felt to be the paradox of female sexual freedom in a sexist society, these fictional accounts of women's sexual development introduced many nonactivist women to an emergent perspective loosely labeled "feminist" by publishers and reviewers alike.[5] As *Newsweek* explained, it was difficult to miss that women's liberation had become a literary genre of its own. "Anyone who reads contemporary fiction is by now familiar with the heroine who in the course of the novel graduates from the role of victim to that of guerrilla warrior."[6]

While literary scholars debate whether or not novels like Jong's *Fear of Flying* or French's *The Woman's Room* can legitimately be called "feminist" or not, the appearance of these novels in the 1970s must be accounted for historically.[7] Most histories of the second wave of feminism do not focus on these novels at all or, at best, make a passing reference to them. Some literary scholars have argued that these novels compromised feminist ideals because of their reliance on conventional narrative strategies like the picaresque or the romance. Others have pointed out that the unquestioning heterosexual standpoint of many of the novels ultimately made their messages conservative. Despite such criticisms, these novels remain crucial to our histories of the second wave precisely for the ways they provide, despite their flaws, a window onto how feminism and sexuality became bound together, at times problematically, in the 1970s.[8] For their unwillingness to cede heterosexuality to patriarchy, for their detailing of the psychic burden of feminine socialization, and, finally, for their ambiguous conclusions about the nature of liberation, these novels deserve a place in our histories of the second wave.

Much of the fascination these novels held for readers was the ways in which they made the need for feminism "come to life" for heroines. How women came to see the need for feminism was a related yet somewhat different story from the production of feminist theory. This history can be found in a variety of places including memoirs, oral histories, accounts of consciousness-raising groups, and in popular feminist fiction of the seventies. Feminist theories that explored the problems of sexual repression, on the one hand, and sexual liberation, on the other, often missed representing the rich texture of lived contradictions that brought many nonactivist women into feminist consciousness.

At the same time, popular feminist fiction did not perform the work that feminists who wrote about fiction did. For example, in *Sexual Politics*, Kate Millett devoted the final section of her analysis to reading what she deemed classic examples of male literary chauvinism, which included D. H. Lawrence, Henry Miller, Norman Mailer, and Jean Genet. In her hands, literature by men about women provided the basis for her theory of patriarchy and a blueprint of the psychology of male domination. Erica Jong's heroine Isadora Wing also learned about women through the writings of men. "I learned about women from men," Isadora explained. "I learned what an orgasm was from D. H. Lawrence, disguised as Lady Chatterley. . . . I learned from Shaw that women never can be artists; I learned from Dostoyevsky that they have no religious feeling. . . . But what did all this have to do with me?"[9] The question Jong poses was precisely the point Millett made. Yet, unlike *Sexual Politics*, feminist fiction like *Fear of Flying* did not propose a theory about the origin of women's oppression or of the production of gendered identities that figured so centrally into feminist theoretical writings. Instead, novels that took up some relationship to feminism described and elaborated upon the experiences of their female heroines with an eye toward what in their social environments enabled them to flourish and what restricted them to a narrow round of domestic activities.

While the connection between theories of feminism and novels classified as "feminist" cannot accurately be charted in any simple cause-effect way, the fiction and the movement of feminism were nevertheless bound together through popularization. The contradictions associated with women's sexual freedom in the seventies became increasingly visible as feminism took up more space in the public world of news magazines, motion pictures, blockbuster publishing events, and literary circles.[10] The visibility of women's now-very-named problem, and of feminism itself, established an association between feminist theory and so-called feminist fiction, if not by the authors explicitly, then by readers and reviewers.

Feminist sex novels of the seventies shared a number of features. Most centrally, they told the story of white middle-class educated women and their journeys into feminism. They did so by moving the heroine through two related developmental narratives. The first was a personalized history of women from the upset of the World War II homefront, through the mushrooming of white suburbs in the 1950s, and to social revolutions of the 1960s. This structure offered a way for the heroine, and, implicitly, readers, to think about the historic events surrounding their own lives. This historic sweep also offered an avenue for the heroines to examine the continuities and discontinuities between generational experiences of sex and marriage.

The second developmental narrative these novels utilized was the evolution of an individual woman's self-awareness. Such a structure offered a way for readers to come into consciousness about themselves as women by "displaying," or producing, a set of experiences deemed "growing up female in the U.S." Thus these novels propelled their plots forward by detailing the classic arch of feminine development: growing breasts, first menstruation, first crush, first kiss, first intercourse, first marriage, and often, first divorce. The novels conflated the heroines' awareness of themselves as women and their oppression as women since, in these novels, growing up female and becoming a feminist followed the same trajectory. Together, the overlapping stories of an individual coping with life cycle upheavals and a nation coming to grips with social and political crises converged in feminist fiction to produce stories of Everywoman as a historical agent caught up in revolutionary forces of repression and liberation.

For the majority of popular feminist novels, the white middle-class woman they universalized became another site for the production of white women as "all women" and the implied subject of feminism. Once again, sexuality provided white feminists with the sense of shared oppression and commonalty that proved necessary to the movement in the seventies. This everywoman of feminist fiction was both a problematic example of universalism and an attempt to show readers that gender mattered. Feminist sex fiction, then, cannot be read as indicative of all women and their relationship to heterosexuality or feminism. Done in an unreflexive spirit of sisterhood before that word and its contradictions imploded, feminist novels, explicitly or not, offered readers lessons in how to see the world and their lives in primarily gendered terms.[11]

Feminist sex novels of the 1970s became popular at the same time the women's liberation movement began to actively engage with the meaning of lesbianism and racism; these debates would intensify as the decade wore on.[12] Audre Lorde's *Zami: A New Spelling of My Name* (1982) and Alice Walker's *Meridian* (1976) and *The Color Purple* (1982) gained wide readership against the backdrop of a fast-growing multicultural, multiracial cultural feminism.[13] Such novels utilized multiple identifications, not only gender, in their heroines' searches for selfhood. The feminist work they performed in the late seventies and early eighties took place in a distinctively different moment than that of the white feminist sex novels of the early seventies. Sexuality for white feminists was the ground on which the movement sought to define womanhood. Novels like Jong's *Fear of Flying* and Brown's *Rubyfruit Jungle* participated, in various degrees, in the radical feminist effort to make sexuality meaningful as a point of solidarity between feminists. This premise itself was dismantled by the eighties, in part through the work of novelists of color like Lorde and Walker.

The popular feminist novels of the early seventies, as novels, operated in several contexts simultaneously. These novels were in dialogue with early radical feminist sex theory and the liberation rhetoric of the counterculture. But, at the same time, they were also in a conversation with the male literary heritage of sex and sexuality in which women were almost never the subject. While Jong and French wove critical literary histories of the representation of women into their novels, most popular feminist novels did not. But they did self-consciously operate in a world male writers had made. Authors of feminist fiction also operated in a gendered literary marketplace. Pulp and popular novels written by women portrayed women and their desires through romance. Heroines searched for love, sexual union, and emotional nurturing. Critics and readers did not classify women's popular novels as "literature," in part because of their literary style, in part because of their content, and in part because "lady writers" wrote them, as Norman Mailer quipped in 1971. Authors of feminist fiction, then, negotiated both literary worlds in an attempt to rewrite women's desires.

Motifs of Liberation

How much longer do I go on conducting these experiments with women? How much longer do I go on sticking this thing into the holes that come available to it—first this hole, then when I

tire of this hole, that hole over there . . . and so on. When will it
end? Only why should it end! To please a father and mother?
To conform to the norm? Why on earth should I be so defensive
about being what was honorably called some years ago, a bachelor? So what's the crime? Sexual freedom? In this day and age?
—Philip Roth, *Portnoy's Complaint* (1967)[14]

There is no such thing as love, the way you talk about it. You'll
only find that kind of love in cheap movies and novels.
—Jacqueline Susann, *Valley of the Dolls* (1966)[15]

With the flagship of high literature leading the way, sex in novels became graphic and fashionable in the 1960s. The literary sexual revolution
started when D. H. Lawrence's *Lady Chatterley's Lover*, Henry Miller's
Tropic of Cancer, and Allen Ginsberg's *Howl* became widely available at
bookstores across the country.[16] Like feminists who engaged with and
transformed expert knowledge about female sexuality, authors of feminist
fiction in the 1970s similarly absorbed and reworked the available and, at
times, competing narratives of sexual liberation.

The literary context of the 1970s with which white feminist novelists
like Jong, Brown, and Shulman engaged was one that celebrated what one
literary scholar called the "newly enshrined masculinist metafiction" of the
late sixties and the seventies.[17] Celebrated popular American writers included such notables as John Updike, John Cheever, William Styron, Norman Mailer, Saul Bellow, Philip Roth, Joseph Heller, and Thomas Pyn-
chon. According to an observer in 1968, modern American writers like
these adopted comedy and parody as their tools and "social alienation and
absurdity as their twin themes." They assumed that "society is at best
malevolent and stupid, at worst wholly lunatic. The gods are dead and
their graves untended, morality is a matter of picking one's way between
competing absurdities." Part of this worldview involved stripping sex of
"its pretensions to holiness, love, mystery and galactic consequences."[18]

The popular literary imagination of sexual freedom, to which feminists
offered an alternative, took men as the conscious and unconscious subject.
Male protagonists in the novels sought out women with whom not only to
have sex but through whom they could find meaning and greater self-
knowledge. At the same time, male novelists portrayed women as embodying the shadowy threat of stifling repetition, deadening obligation,
and sexually repressive marriage. For example, in an essay published in

1963, John Updike explained his view of what women symbolized for men: "A woman, loved, momentarily eases the pain of time by localizing nostalgia: the vague and irrecoverable objects of nostalgic longing are assimilated, under the pressure of libidinous desire, into the details of her person."[19] Norman Mailer, in a 1962 interview, also characterized sex with women as a self-communion, if perhaps in more egalitarian terms:

> All I know is that when one makes love, one changes a woman slightly, and a woman changes you slightly. . . . One has had an experience which is nourishing. Nourishing because one's able to feel one's way into more difficult or more precious insights as a result of it. One's able to live a tougher, more heroic life if one can digest and absorb the experience.[20]

For Mailer and Updike, women and their sexuality offered men an existential shelter that they desperately needed. Such conceptions left little room for women possessing an active, subjective desire.

Male modernist fiction broke barriers about sexual explicitness, particularly in its discussion of masturbation, oral sex, adultery, and swinging. For example, Philip Roth's 1969 *Portnoy's Complaint* helped to create new space for sex in the public sphere. Roth's hugely popular novel chronicled Alex Portnoy's effort to have as much sex as he could without succumbing to that dreadful state of matrimony. Alex's story, told as a transcript of a psychoanalysis, was organized both around his efforts to elude the controlling influence of his Jewish mother and to appease the endless desires of his insatiable penis. The novel gave Roth ample room to detail an animating fantasy of women in the age of sexual freedom. For example, when riding in a bus going through a tunnel, Alex couldn't ignore his little commander who was brought to life by a sleeping woman sitting next to him.

> "Jerk me off," I am told by the silky monster. Here? Now? "Of course here and now when would you expect an opportunity like this to present itself a second time. Maybe she's just faking being asleep. Faking it but saying under her breath, 'Come on Big Boy, do all the different dirty things to me you ever wanted to do.'"[21]

He imagined that the woman who appeared to be sleeping was in fact daydreaming about Alex in the very same way he was dreaming of her. This fantasy view of women as sexually available regularly appeared in the popular imagination of sexual freedom. However, it was crucial for Alex to view women as ready and willing sexual partners since, for him, sexual freedom was about having as much sex as he could have. He reveled in his role of bachelor and was in no hurry to get married or raise a family. He needed women who would agree to have sex, lots of sex, without the promise of marriage.

Frank discussions of sex became a mark of being modern. However engaging in frank sex talk did not mean the same thing to every author. Norman Mailer rejected the view of masturbation as benign sexual self-expression. Alluding to the Vietnam War, Mailer explained that "masturbation is bombing. It's bombing oneself." It was "a miserable activity," a waste, a crippling activity. "If one has, for example, the image of a beautiful sexy babe in masturbation, one still doesn't know whether one can make love to her in the flesh. All you know is that you can violate her in your brain. . . . But if one has fought the good fight or the evil fight and ended with the beautiful sexy dame, then . . . one has something to build on. The ultimate direction of masturbation always has to be insanity."[22] Masturbation was insanity because it left the man with "nothing to build on" whereas sex with real women left him empowered.

In the novels of Roth, Mailer, Updike, and others, women literally and symbolically carried the double freight of sexual ecstasy and the burdens of marriage. Roth vividly captured the ambivalence that was "woman" for sexual liberationists. On the one hand, Alex's psychoanalytic discourse rendered every woman a glorious receptacle. "Still can't get over the fantastic idea that when you are looking at a girl, you are looking at somebody who is guaranteed to have on her—a cunt! They all have cunts! Right under their dresses! Cunts—for fucking!"[23] On the other hand, girlfriends, no matter how glorious, never stayed girlfriends for long. They all eventually tried to get married. Pleading his case to his (male) analyst, Alex accidentally stumbled upon the double bind sexual liberation offered women:

> In the end, I just cannot take that step into marriage. But why should I? Why? Is there a law saying Alex Portnoy has to be somebody's husband and father? Doctor, they can stand on the window ledge and threaten to splatter themselves on the pavement below, they can pile the Seconal to the ceiling—I may have to live for weeks and weeks on end in terror of these marriage-bent girls throwing themselves beneath the subway train, but I simply cannot, I simply will not, enter into a contract to sleep with just one woman for the rest of my days. . . . How can I give up what I have never even had,

for a girl, who delicious and provocative as once she may have been, will inevitably grow as familiar to me as a loaf of bread? For love? What love?[24]

Updike's 1968 best-selling novel *Couples* also explored the connections between self, sex, and freedom. However, he explored it not through the single life of a bachelor but through a tightly connected social circle nestled in suburbia. Updike's suburban couples try to infuse their marriages with the utopian possibilities of sexual liberation, but by the novel's end discover such liberation an illusion at best. Updike portrayed his couples as part of the sixties generation who did not march in Selma or protest the Vietnam War. "They belonged to that segment of their generation of the upper middle class which mildly rebelled against the confinement and discipline whereby wealth maintained its manners during the upheavals of depression and world war."[25] In contrast to their parents, these couples turned away from upper crust formality and set up a closed social circle in which each member could express him or herself more fully. For Updike's couples, self-actualization was the point of tension.

Updike's vision of suburbia cast it as a space not constituted solely by domestic obligations. Rather, the home became a location for sexual experimentation. The tight group of friends, who shared homes, drinks, dinner, and shuttling their children about, soon slipped into sharing their spouses. Updike portrayed couple swapping as a small yet significant step from adultery. Here, couples managed the threat of the other woman or other man by incorporating them into a decisively modern and flexible family/home. Such an arrangement appeared to solve the problem of reconciling pleasure and responsibility. Sexual experimentation was suddenly harmonized with the potentially deadening experience of marriage when two couples, for all intents and purposes, became one. Updike's portrait of adultery, rendered in the extreme by couple swapping, cast it as a search for meaning in a world where older codes of behavior and significance have gone flat. After all, God "packed up," according to another husband of the circle, Freddy Thorne, and sex was all that was left of morality. Updike interrogated sex as the last meaningful resource available in the godless age of consensus politics.

Oral sex carried an assortment of literary meanings in the late 1960s. Alex Portnoy detailed his fantasies of women performing fellatio as the height of narcissistic liberation. For him, women's mouths became the ultimate replacement for the masturbating hand. For Updike, oral sex sat at the juncture of changing sexual mores. It was a practice that carried with it a hint of the repressed, defined as both deviant and pleasurable. The acceptability of oral sex, or its shifting status as part of an acceptable repertoire of heterosexual practice, functioned in Updike's novel as a sign the times were changing. As one husband tells another,

> I like it to be long, to take forever, have a little wine, have some more wine, fool around, try it on backwards, you know, let it be a human thing. She comes too quick. She comes so she can get on with the housework. I gave her the *Kama Sutra* for Christmas and she wouldn't even look at the pictures. The bitch won't blow unless she's really looped. What did the Bard say? To fuck is human; to be blown, divine.[26]

Updike's attention to sexuality won him some dismissive and gendered criticism. One reviewer complained that Updike's novel was an upper-middle class *Peyton Place,* filled with sexual scenes "remarkably explicit even for this new age of total freedom of expression" and a cast of characters one needed a chart to keep track of. The *Nation* called it a miniature domestic drama characteristic not of modern American literature but of "a kind of literature of the fifties that no one wants to defend any more," vacant of the "experimental prose" and "Large Statements in fiction."[27]

While *Peyton Place* author Grace Metalious and Jane Austin had little in common beyond their gender, Mailer's dismissive comment about "lady writers" yoked them together. His comment also spoke volumes about how women's writing existed in a world apart from "literature."[28] Such dismissal of women's writing was not new to the sixties.[29] Despite the marginalizing of women's writing, women writers wrote about sex throughout the 1950s and 1960s. Feminist fiction writers of the 1970s engaged with this tradition as well. Lesbian pulp fiction writers wrote about female desire in mass-marketed novels that readers could pick up at corner bookstores and newsstands.[30] Metalious's *Peyton Place,* published in 1956, was a best-seller known for its steamy account of women's passions.[31] Yet it was business-savvy Jacqueline Susann, with her 1966 *Valley of the Dolls,* who fully capitalized on this genre of women's writing. According to *Life,* "More than 8,500 Americans each week are paying $5.95 each to buy *Valley of the Dolls* and with each purchase Miss Susann is enriched by $1.35."[32] Susann and her business partner-husband Irving Mansfield helped revolutionize publishing by cranking the publicity machinery to record-high levels. According to Mansfield, "If you want a book to be a bestseller you can't just reach the book-buying people, you have to get to those who never bought a book before in their lives. You advertise on the entertainment pages, not just the book pages."[33]

Yet Mansfield's innovative techniques for promoting *Valley of the Dolls* did not alone account for its popularity. The novel explored in great detail the personal desires and aspirations of three women in the fifties and six-ties on their own in New York City. The heroine, Anne Welles, finds New York exhilarating and full of possibilities that are simply unimaginable in her small hometown. Yet new opportunities for work and for dating as many men as she wants clash with her deeply felt desire to find love and be loved. The three women's efforts to navigate sexual freedom with their desire for romantic love, family, and emotional intimacy made up the fab-ric of the novel. The Harlequin romance style of the sex scenes, in which emotion and sensation were conflated and mystified, also situated Susann's novel in the growing pulp (heterosexual) romance fiction tradition.[34] Sex was supposed to lead to commitment, in this genre, even if many plot twists and turns were to be expected. At the same time Susann utilized the soap opera format of romance fiction, her novel was different in its por-trayal of the women's dashed dreams, the men they had sex with not liv-ing up to their hopes for romance, and the self-destructive behaviors such disappointments caused. Romance, while held up as the plot line of a woman's life, was also cast, by Susann, as a form of addiction, not unlike the "dolls" the threesome swallowed to cope with their lives.

Feminist fiction writers, then, found themselves negotiating two fields of literary production. One, the male "literary" world peopled with au-thors like Mailer, Roth, and Updike, problematically infused sexuality with masculine self-development and a quest for meaning. The other, the female "popular" romance world peopled by writers like Metalious and Susann, problematically represented women's sexual desire as identical to romance. Writers of feminist fiction borrowed from each literary world motifs of liberation and satisfaction, of sex and romance, of subjectivity and selfhood. To that combination, they added a new element: feminism.

Growing Up Female, Growing Up Feminist

Motifs of liberation that circulated and gained readership in the six-ties and seventies shared little in common beyond an agreement that sexu-ality had become both primary architect of and location for modern self-hood. White feminist fiction writers deliberately set out to claim sexuality for a new sort of female selfhood—this one independent of romance and of abstracting, objectifying imagery.

The blurring of gender consciousness and selfhood in novels about young women was the primary way they "taught" readers how to see the world "like a feminist."[35] These novels were structured by a woman's emergent sense of self/feminism as she faced the fraught waters of growing up female in America. Sasha, the heroine of Alex Kates Shulman's first novel, *Memoirs of an Ex-Prom Queen* (1969), narrated her life as first a girl and, by the novel's end, a woman hungry for feminism. Her story began by describing a slow and steady restriction of her mobility and her activities as she entered the rough and tumble world of elementary school. Girls like Sasha learned at a tender age lesson feminists of the 1970s took for granted: boys hate girls. Such girlhood realizations functioned like a protofeminist flash of insight, planting seeds that over the course of the novel Shulman and the reader harvested as the foundation for their politics. Describing the boys who attack any girl who crosses into their territory, Sasha accounted for the hostility she faced. "They did it for fun. They did it to prove themselves. They did it because they hated us. . . . There was only one thing to do: stay in the shadow. Prudently I gave up football, trees, and walking to school unaccompanied for acceptable 'girl's things,' until, before I was ten, like everyone else I unquestioningly accepted the boy's hatred of us as 'normal.' "[36]

Ginny, the heroine of Lisa Alther's novel *Kinflicks* (1975), also came to see that being a girl meant giving up a whole range of activities. Like Sasha, Ginny faced a crucial moment when she learned that being a girl harnessed her to all things domestic. Wanting nothing but to be a defensive left tackle for the Oakland Raiders, the thirteen-year-old Ginny articulated the "bitter lesson" feminists already knew: "Women led their lives through men. . . . I must have suspected what was cooking, deep in the test kitchen of my unconscious, because my football playing had the desperation of the doomed to it. My tackles were performed with the fervor of a soldier making love on the eve of a lost battle."[37]

The never ending quest to fit in became the only available outlet for girls like Ginny and Sasha. For Ginny, fitting in involved giving up her dreams of playing football. For Sasha, fitting in was symbolized by beauty, which functioned in Shulman's novel as the symbol for the entire arsenal of feminine training and personal affect. The feminine beauty culture acted like a wedge between girls, displacing the feminist dream of women's "natural" allegiance to each other. Girls replaced innate sisterhood with a socialized competition for suitors' attentions. For example, in a sorority meeting at her high school, fourteen-year-old Sasha was schooled in the laws governing female friendship. She experienced a form of consciousness-raising about femininity that was not only detached from feminism but was its shadow opposite, as the Alpha Phi Beta sorority met to censure one of its members. "As the last few sisters spoke, we shifted on our pastel skirts and plucked at our sweaters, combing our hair and checking our bras again, till finally, circle completed, we were back to the President." The mean-spirited and power hungry president turned to Sasha and reminded her that beauty was not a license for autonomy but came with duties. "You think that just because you're beautiful you can do anything you please and get away with it. But you can't! Someday it'll all catch up with you and then you'll pay! You'll pay for everything!"[38]

Shulman evoked a distopian CR group where allegiance to the laws of femininity, not sisterhood, became the measure against which all members were judged. The scene implanted in both Sasha and the reader a memory of feminine friendship soured by the pressures to compete for men. This negative encounter group begged for new content, a fresh angle through which the bonds of women could be transformed into nurturing connections that sustained women, not tore them down. Ironically, Sasha's response to her "sister's" attack measured the extent of her "feminine illness." Rather than feeling rebuked and censored, Sasha found longed for reassurance that she was, in fact, "beautiful." Such reassurances empowered her to feel superior to her sisters and to pick from the many suitors waiting to get near her. Beauty cut both ways for Sasha in that it at once held her to a terrible insecurity about herself over whether or not she was worthy and inspired her to feel good by invoking the same insecurity in other women.

Like Shulman's novel, Jong's 1973 *Fear of Flying* also explored the ways girls learned to replace larger life goals with the empty pursuit of beauty. Isadora recalled her own growing up as being intimately bound up with advertisements that conflated beauty with love and narcissism with fulfillment.

What litanies the advertisers of the good life chanted at you! what curious catechisms! "Be kind to your behind." "Blush like you mean it." "Love your hair." "Want a better body? We'll rearrange the one you've got." "That shine on your face should come from him, not from your skin . . . " What all the ads and all the whoreoscopes seemed to imply was that if only you were narcissistic enough, if only you took proper care of your smells, your hair, your boobs, your eyelashes, your armpits, your crotch, your stars, your scars, and your choice of scotch in bars— you would meet a beautiful, powerful, potent, and rich man who would satisfy every longing, fill every hole.[39]

For Jong and for Shulman, part of seeing like a feminist involved prob-lematizing the message of the beauty culture ("Be kind to your behind") and analyzing the effects of beauty (separating women through competi-tion). Readers who traveled through the heroines' budding feminism saw elements of female socialization made unfamiliar and strange rather than glossed over as normal and unremarkable.

Examining the feminine role and feminine beauty standards became central elements in white novelists' investigations of heterosexuality for women. The promise of love, fulfillment, and a place in the social order that came with marriage motivated the heroines to learn the painful les-sons of growing up female. Yet while the erotic promise of love constitut-ed the main events of girls' interpolations into the narratives of heterosex-uality, erotic disappointments became the pathway out to feminism. As the heroines discovered, the pleasures of sex with young men were paradoxi-cal. Pleasure was both elusive and wonderful, came too easily and yet was costly. As with white radical feminists, these novelists mobilized a belief that sexuality was the common experience that could bring a variety of women together. Heterosexual pleasure, in both arenas of feminism, pulled women into embracing an array of confining gender roles (in the hope of being found attractive) and ironically, simultaneously, fueled their desire for feminism.

Feminist novels explored how women came to know their heterosexu-al desires in an erotic environment organized primarily around men. In this environment, the vagina and men's access to it defined the parameters of "sex," but the clitoris defined the boundaries, secretly at times, of pleas-ure. The novels utilized the classic scenario of sexual brinkmanship, cast-ing women as the preservers of their virginity, which, as a precious asset, they must protect against both their own and their partner's desires. Along the way, the authors questioned the very organization of "sex" by con-trasting the heroines' very different responses to foreplay and to inter-course. For many heroines, heavy petting, where boys and girls "replaced" intercourse with touching each other's bodies, was often more erotically engaging than intercourse. However, the heroines soon learned that these pleasures were not truly "sex." In this definition of what counted for "real sex," clitoral sexuality was cordoned off as mere foreplay to the main event. As Sasha recounts, "Gone were those long, voluptuous hours of kissing on my living-room sofa or in the car at Shaker Lakes when I could abandon myself to Joey's sweet mouth. . . . The kissing and French kissing and petting I had so enjoyed had been reduced to a five-minute warm-up before the struggle, and I had been forced to trade abandon for vigilance."[40] Sasha's anxiety over protecting her reputation made any encounter with her desire frightening. "Passionate as I was, I looked for excuses to go straight home from a date."[41] Under pressure to "give into" Joey and her own desire for Joey's "voluptuous" kissing, Sasha finally agrees to throw caution to the wind and have intercourse with Joey. Again, in a classic moment of feminist sex fiction, Shulman described the non-event of first penetration.

> I didn't get to remove my underpants, so eager was Joey to cross my threshold. He stretched the elastic of one leg and slipped his organ in; then with a little moan of joy he began humping me the same as always. . . . This is it! I said to myself. This is love! Enjoy it! . . . I tried to enjoy it, as least to attend to this celebrated moment in the most touted of acts. . . . It wasn't unpleasant with Joey inside me, but it wasn't particularly pleasant either. It didn't even hurt. . . . Watching him move up and down on me in the darkness, I wondered: is this all there is to it? I had loved Joey to the melting point, but now I resented him. I received each thrust of his body like a doubt. Really all? When it was over a few moments later and Joey came groaning into his handkerchief as always, it struck me as hardly different from our usual sex. The only thing to recommend it was that it was ultimate. But, really, kissing felt much nicer.[42]

Sasha discovered that her main sexual problem was that the teenage boys with whom she had sex didn't know how to have sex with women. They treated sex with women like an extension of their solitary masturbation. Unfortunately, the heroines' solitary masturbation, which educated them to the techniques that gave them pleasure, were not speakable, at least not until the heroines could see like a feminist. The teenage Sasha and her literary sisters were shocked to learn that intercourse in the back of a car stood in for "sex," with all its promises of feminine self-fulfillment. Sex with boys, it appeared, was a bust.

Alther's novel questioned in a much more profound way the categorization between real and inauthentic sex than did Shulman's. In fact, Ginny's clitoris, who touched it and why, constituted the thread of feminist/lesbian continuity across the novel. Ginny's first experience of intercourse with Clem bore little resemblance to the months of pleasurable foreplay with former boyfriend Joe Bob that had preceded it. Intercourse, billed as the culmination of desire, was reduced to the mere mechanics of penetration.

> I found it hard to believe that this was what Joe Bob and I had spent almost two years building up to. "You meant that's it?" I asked with dismay. It hadn't been unpleasant, except for the first pain, but I couldn't exactly view it as the culmination of my womanhood. Frankly, the rupturing of my maidenhead had been just about as meaningful as the breaking of a paper Saniband on a motel toilet.[43]

Eventually Ginny gave up heterosexual sex as being a waste of time and energy. "Honestly. I'm through with men. They're just one disappointment after another. . . . Believe me, I just want to be left alone with my vibrator."[44]

Women's struggle to reconcile their desire for sexual pleasure with the narrow range of activities labeled "sex" constituted a central problem explored by the soon-to-be feminist heroines. Unlike Shulman or Jong, Alther presented lesbianism as an alternative to frustrating sex with men and implicitly argued that any woman could make the same choice. Ginny's new friend Eddie literally rubbed new life into her in the women's shower in their college dormitory. In a passage surprising for its narrative restraint, Alther spelled out the solution to Ginny's problematic desires. "We spent that night in Eddie's narrow lumpy institutional bed, sleeping in each other's arms until after lunch. I woke up delighted finally to know who put what where in physical love between women."[45] For Ginny, the authenticity of her (clitoral) sexuality led her away from men and intercourse to women and lesbian feminism.

The clitoris hovered in the feminist sex novels as a site of authentic sexuality that many women lost track of as they pursued men and intercourse. For some heroines, like Isadora, the clitoris and its pleasures became explicitly linked to autonomy. Sexual desire for men confused Isadora since, according to everything she had learned, it led inevitably to domestic entanglements for women. The lesson learned in high school was clear. Good girls waited to have sex or were gossiped out of school. In contrast, bad girls didn't wait and got pregnant. Isadora hoped celibacy/masturbation would ensure her safe passage to autonomy, but, she discovered, it did only at a price.

I wouldn't have known how to say it then, but Steve's finger in my cunt felt good. At the same time, I knew that soft, mushy feeling to be the enemy. If I yielded to that feeling, it would be good-bye to all the other things I wanted. "You have to choose," I told myself sternly at fourteen. Get thee to a nunnery. So, like all good nuns, I masturbated. "I am keeping myself free of the power of men," I thought, sticking two fingers deep inside each night.[46]

Other heroines, like Sasha, viewed masturbation as a dirty secret, a sign of her ill health. She felt like she was the only one who knew of the pleasures the private "button" could give. "Between my legs I had found an invisible button of flesh, sweet and nameless, which I knew how to caress to a nameless joy. I was pretty sure no one else had one, for there was no joy button in the hygiene book and there was not even a dirty name for it."[47] The lack of a "dirty name" for the clitoris reinforced an implicit message of Shulman's novel. The clitoris was truly a terrain untainted by fumbling teenagers or inept men, a new land on which to build a new woman.

The clitoris for many feminist heroines represented the only genuine form of sexuality they experienced. And yet, like the feminist sexual theory set forth by Millett, Koedt, and Atkinson, the authors of feminist novels similarly charted the ways that girls and women learned to see the clitoris and its pleasures as immature and deviant. Isadora explained how she learned that clitoral sex was inauthentic. Citing her analysis with a veritable horde of psychiatrists, Isadora learned first that "there is no such thing as rape. Nobody can rape a woman unless she consents at the last minute." The second, that there are two kinds of orgasm: vaginal and clitoral. "One is 'mature' (i.e. good). The other is 'immature' (i.e. evil). This pseudo hip, pseudopsychological moral code was more Calvinistic than Calvinism."[48] While the heroines did not give up clitoral stimulation, they learned that they should not talk about what they liked and that liking what they liked set them apart from "normal" women. Paralleling the sense of disjuncture that came from seeing like a feminist, the heroines of these novels experienced the secret of their clitoris as yet another disjuncture. Feminism, then, for these heroines, manifested itself as the capacity to see and to want something that lay outside the bounds of normal heterosexuality, as it was constituted and transmitted in the late fiftiess and the sixties. It was also at moments like these, where the novels reach for universal experiences that all women share, that they inadvertently produced racially and class-specific accounts of womanhood. Womanhood for heroines like Sasha, Ginny, and Isadora was defined primarily through gendered, not racial, lessons about sex and sexual desire.

The heroines' difficulties in defining their sexual desires and in shaping heterosexual practice were the major events on their journey into feminist consciousness. Many heroines attempted to shed the frustrations they encountered as sexual beings by turning to the mind. On the one hand, intellectual pursuits offered the heroines both relief from the burden of living in a female body and access to a privileged realm of ideas where the body theoretically did not matter. Heroines embraced and later discarded intellectualism as a haven when they come to see the promise of equality through merit and hard work to be a sham. For Alther and Shulman, intellectualism meant philosophy; for Jong, it meant existentialism and psychoanalysis. The novelists further marked their heroines' marginality and thus their nascent feminism by their intelligence. Heroines desired mastery over bodies of knowledge—secretly, at times. Intelligence, clitoral pleasures, and desiring what lay outside the bounds of normal femininity became a cluster of related characteristics that lay the groundwork for the heroines' capacity to see like a feminist.

For example, Shulman's novel explicitly eroticized the promise of ideas for Sasha and other protofeminists. In college, Sasha fell into philosophy and the history of ideas like a love-struck girl. "Somewhere during my sophomore year . . . I fell hopelessly in love with philosophy."[49] Sasha's romance with philosophy, like Ginny's and Isadora's, gave her a feeling of order and control over not only her body and its disorders but of the universe.

> I plunged in, pursuing the ideas deep into ancient texts, losing myself among subtle distinctions. Nothing else mattered. I analyzed with Aristotle and flunked my French midterm. I synthesized with Augustine and stopped eating everything but Cheezits and black coffee. Discovering with Spinoza the connectedness of things, exploring with Kant the mind that thinks so, I stopped going to chapel or gym and eventually stopped sleeping at night. My brain was in a constant state of intoxication. . . . The more I studied, the less sure I was of anything.[50]

Feminist heroines reveled in ideas and mistakenly hoped that intelligence would transcend their limited, sexualized female body. Isadora, Ginny, and Sasha each stop eating at some point in college, literally giving over their bodies to their minds. Ginny detailed her regime of study, which had become tangled up with her desires to please a female professor, nicknamed "the Head." "I devoted myself with ardor to my studies. My typical day began at seven. . . . I had classes all morning. . . . I studied all afternoon at the library. . . . After supper I went to my room and studied until midnight. . . . I was like a nun. This was my novitiate."[51] The Head promoted such devotion, challenging Ginny to give up empty sexual pursuits for a life of the mind. " 'You see,' Miss Head explained, 'the human organism has only so much energy at its disposal. . . . If you squander your vital energies on your emotional life, as you have been doing, plan to be physically and mentally bankrupt, as it were.' "[52] Miss Head epitomized first-wave feminists, women who devoted their lives to the mind at the cost of their bodies. Eventually, Ginny, like other second-wave feminists, came to see that sexual desire needed a place to exist, and it was not the "enemy of the mind" that Miss Head saw it to be.[53]

For Isadora, the struggle became how to reconcile intelligence with lust. This became tangled up with her feminism as well. "When I was sixteen . . . I used to dream of a perfect man whose mind and body were equally fuckable. He had a face like Paul Newman and a voice like Dylan Thomas. He had a body like Michelangelo's David. He had a mind like George Bernard Shaw. . . . I never met him. At sixteen, my not meeting him seemed unbearable."[54] Isadora attributed her feminist "radicalization" to a teenage date in 1955 who asked her if she planned to be a secretary. Isadora, who had much grander plans for herself, found the problem to be "how to make your feminism jibe with your unappeasable hunger for male bodies. It wasn't easy."[55]

Similarly, Sasha's quest to become an intellectual led her not to transcending her body but, rather, into an affair with her philosophy professor, Donald Alport. Sasha believed Alport's sharp intelligence would see through her body to her true essence.

> He was so far above the petty concerns that corrupted every shallow young man I knew that I didn't care if he was forty or one hundred and forty. I loved him for his mind that knew everything—a provocative mind whose experienced eye could penetrate through layers of mask, clothes, skin, muscle, and bone, straight to the center of me where my untutored mind, now a quivering mass of jelly, lay waiting to be given form and life.[56]

For Sasha, the desire to transcend the limits of her femininity slipped into the desire to be seen, and her hopes to be an intellectual into being a partner to this new—better—man.

With Alport, Sasha experienced intercourse that did not take place in a car and that gave her her first orgasm from oral sex. Here at last was a man with whom Sasha could integrate her ambitions to be a philosopher with her bodily desires for sex. Symbolically, Sasha's orgasm promised a relationship in which she could cease hiding, stop her obsession with beauty as her life goal, where at last she could be a full subject. But the affair and its promise of integration ended when Sasha realizes she isn't the first or the last "little friend" in the professor's life. The novel can't imagine a place for Sasha to exist, fully integrated and empowered, mind and body, selfhood and sexuality intact. Instead, it replicated a gendered dynamic of sexual dependency with Sasha's mind, like her body, reduced to a "quivering mass of jelly" waiting to be shaped by a man.

Feminist fiction writers, like those feminists who wrote sex theory, turned to and dismissed psychoanalysis as an answer to the problem of female desire. The account offered by so-called experts neither took women's desires seriously nor supported them in their quest to be independent and equal subjects. Eliding class and racial specificity in the name of sisterly oppression at the hands of bad experts, Shulman has Sasha face down a psychiatrist. When Sasha, now married, tells the psychiatrist she fears she is frigid, she is told, like Isadora, that she herself is the problem. As Sasha saw it, sex remained divided into foreplay and intercourse, girl time and boy time, clitoris and vagina. "It was as it had always been. If I wanted to kiss and snuggle and embrace, I had to be prepared to screw. One thing had to lead to another, whether there was only a little time or a lot. Touching and holding, for which I yearned, were only prelude for men."[57] The doctor declared that Sasha suffered from penis envy. He offered her a classic Freudian interpretation of what Sasha suspected is a much deeper problem in the nature of women's sexual desire in a sexist society.

> Didn't everything, he asked, reduce for me to queen versus king? My belligerence, my seductions, my willfulness? Did they not all point to a profound conflict within my nature? Was I now always attempting to conquer where I should yield? take where I should give? Did I not identify with my father instead of my mother? Were not my very ambitions (to be a lawyer! a philosopher!), my rejection of maternity, my fantastic need to excel, my unwillingness to achieve orgasm—were they not all denials of my own deepest, instinctive self—my feminine self?[58]

Like Sasha, Isadora came to see that the psychoanalytic account of women as reactionary, as part of what Friedan called an "orchestrated" cultural message that bound women to men's view of ideal femininity. Isadora concluded that

> analysts were such unquestioning acceptors of the social order. Their mildly leftist political views . . . were just camouflage. When it came to the crucial issues: the family, the position of women, the flow of cash from patient to doctor, they were reactionaries. As rigidly self-serving as the Social Darwinists of the Victorian Era.[59]

The message, one echoed across feminist theory and fiction of the 1970s, was that men—experts and husbands—didn't understand what women wanted from sex. Again, the clitoris, with its links to authenticity and autonomy, came to stand in for and, in crucial moments, to produce feminist consciousness.

Novels such as those by Shulman, Alther, and Jong explored the double vision on which feminism in the early seventies rested. Problematic for their attention only to gender and sexuality, the novels made white women's experiences paradigmatic for all womanhood. Learning to know oneself as a woman was, in these novels and in radical feminism, nearly identical to learning to know oneself as a feminist. This conception of womanhood and, by extension, feminism as emerging out of white middle-class experience would prove divisive later in the decade.[60] But, in 1973, the convergence between coming-of-age stories and stories of budding feminist consciousness taught readers to interpret the once unremarkable story of female development as the very stuff of revolution.

Sexual Freedom: Visions of Liberation

Feminist sex novels detailed the problem of female desire in a heterosexual world. Young male lovers were ignorant, husbands indifferent, the heroines themselves unsure what they wanted from sex and romance, much less from men and marriage. Yet these novels did not only describe the limits placed on women's self-development. In the manner of feminist theorists who wondered what sexual freedom for women would look like, feminist novelists also imaginatively engaged with the question of sexual liberation for women.

The heroines in the two most famous novels of the period, Rita Mae Brown's *Rubyfruit Jungle* and Erica Jong's *Fear of Flying*, offered their readers visions of what female sexual fulfillment and freedom would look like. The differences in their visions, in many ways, paralleled those found in feminist sexual theory. Brown's novel made women's sexual freedom inseparable from dismantling obligatory, homophobic, and patriarchal heterosexuality. For Jong, women's sexual freedom depended on women's capacity to move out of the romance narrative that conflated sexual pleasure, selfhood, and marriage. Whereas Brown critiqued compulsory heterosexuality, Jong critiqued heterosexual women's sexual and psychological dependency on men. Importantly, both Jong and Brown offered their readers visions of the interconnections between sexual freedom and women's liberation.

In *Rubyfruit Jungle* (1973) Rita Mae Brown's chronicled her heroine Molly Bolt's journey into lesbian feminist liberation. Molly, however, had no need to come into feminist consciousness, for she somehow possessed it instinctively. In this way, Molly perfectly embodied the conflation between "the lesbian" and "the feminist" endemic to seventies feminism. Brown, according to one literary scholar, deliberately alternated between two representational strategies in her portrayal of Molly. On the one hand, she crafted Molly to show heterosexuals the problems, conscious and unconscious, of homophobia; on the other hand, she offered a supremely self-confident Molly, whose native intelligence and spunk made any prejudice against her seem outrageously ignorant, as an affirmation for her lesbian readers. The feminist work the novel performed, then, came from precisely the way in which it had "designs on both lesbian and heterosexual readers' consciousnesses."[61]

Molly's self-respect, wildly out of step with those around her, enables her to dismiss the range of obligations associated with womanhood. Molly and her stepmother, Carrie, fight over Molly's outright refusal to master the arts of women's domestic work. Carrie aggressively polices the young Molly in part out of her anxiety about Molly's "mixed blood." Brown deliberately left the race of Molly's biological mother ambiguous, a move that strategically allows Brown to emphasize Molly's broad allegiances with marginalized people of all sorts. Within the novel, Molly's ambiguous racial heritage ultimately becomes a place of her self-empowerment even as it creates obstacles for her to overcome, one being the stress it introduces into her relationship with her stepmother. For example, after giving Molly a beating, Carrie complains to her husband that Molly "don't act natural." Brown made the concept of "natural" into something quite paradoxical. Being assertive and independent was what came "naturally" to Molly. For Carrie and the others Molly faced, this was precisely the problem with Molly.

> I don't give a goddamn how brainy she is, she don't act natural. It ain't right for a girl to be running all around with the boys at all hours. She climbs trees, takes cars apart, and worse, she tells them what to do and they listen to her. She don't want to learn none of the things she had to know to get a husband. Smart as she is, a woman can't get on in this world without a husband.[62]

Carrie can't decide which was Molly's worst crime—that she assumes the privileges of men ("runs around with boys at all hours") or that she disrupts men's rightful authority ("she tells them what to do and they listen to her").

Brown's novel proposed that true sexual freedom rested on all people—men and women—opening their minds to what made them feel the most pleasure. As Molly explained to her cousin Leroy as they were about to embark on their first experience of heterosexual intercourse, getting "screwed on rules other people make" was a waste of time. "I can do whatever I want. I feel like playing with you and I'm gonna do it. Why don't you lie down and shut up?"[63] Molly's sexual philosophy is "just do what you damn well please."[64] In this way, Brown offered a vision of sexual freedom as living beyond the scripted sexual choices that came with "compulsory heterosexuality."[65]

> Yeah, maybe I'm queer. But why would people get so upset about something that feels so good? Me being a queer can't hurt anyone, why should it be such a terrible thing. Makes no sense. But I'm not gonna base my judgment on one little fuck with ole Leroy. We got to do it a lot more and maybe I'll do around twenty or thirty men and twenty or thirty women and then I'll decide. I wonder if I could get twenty people to go to bed with me.[66]

Molly is a regular advocate of women's rights to desire whomever they want. She also has an early and uncanny capacity to separate sexual desire from gender roles. As a girl in elementary school, Molly mused on her schoolmate Leota. "I began to wonder if girls could marry girls, because I was sure I wanted to marry Leota and look in her green eyes forever. But I would only marry her if I didn't have to do the housework."[67] Molly's early sexual experimentation with Leota left her feeling full of strangely satisfying sensations. "We threw our arms around each other and kissed. My stomach felt funny. . . . We kissed again and my stomach felt worse." When her cousin Leroy demanded to be let into the kissing club taking place in the woods after school, Molly decided to test her belief in sexual democracy by letting him join. "How does your stomach feel?" the girls ask him after he kisses Molly. "Hungry," he replies. "Maybe it's different for boys," the girls concluded in another emblematic moment of the slippages between self-consciousness and feminist consciousness produced in many feminist sex novels.[68]

Brown's novel was one of the first to evaluate the social, psychological, and sexual nature of obligatory heterosexuality. Through a range of secondary characters like Leroy and Leota, Brown mapped out her view of sexuality as a straightforward desire for pleasure that did not "naturally" adhere to the social classifications of heterosexuality. While Molly was surprisingly comfortable living inside sexual contradictions, others were less so. As a teenager, cousin Leroy wondered how he could reconcile his feelings about certain male friends with his adamant desire to be simply heterosexual. He found sex with women to be confusing and wondered about alternatives. Similarly, Molly's sixth grade lover Leota wrestled for a brief time with her "instinct" or desire to touch and kiss other girls. However, neither Leroy nor Leota could withstand the social pressure pushing them into "normality." Both turned away from whatever "polymorphous" feelings they had as children to fit into the adult patterns of "mature"(stifling) heterosexuality.

Brown's conception of authentic "polymorphous sexuality" marked out a crucial space of sexual freedom. In her novel, polymorphous sexuality stood in for the capacity to find anyone erotically charged, any body satisfying, any personality attractive. The term also marked Brown as coming out of the counterculture and its celebration of nongenital, pre-/postgenital sexuality.[69] For counterculture rebels, including some feminists like Shulamith Firestone and Germaine Greer, polymorphous sexuality resexualized the entire body, not merely the genitals.[70] For Brown and other lesbian feminists, polymorphous was a way to authenticate all sensations and practices as "real" sex and not just intercourse with a penis.

At the same time, Brown's choice to use polymorphous sexuality as an ideal instead of bisexuality was shaped as much by the battles raging among lesbian feminists in the 1970s as by the ideals of the counterculture. Many lesbian feminists dismissed bisexuality as a deeply compromised identity and argued that bisexuals were confused women who drew precious energy away from the beloved community. Bisexuals destabilized a line that lesbian feminists proudly reasserted and policed in the early seventies: lesbians were no longer the pathological minority but constituted the vanguard of a revolutionary feminist movement.[71]

Brown's novel also explored how homophobia seeped into otherwise progressive individuals. Molly understands, without consciously learning it, that sexuality provided the illusory though sacred bedrock of an individual's gender identity. By extension, she understands the origin of homophobia, or why people felt threatened by gays and lesbians. When her best friend Connie learns that Molly is a lesbian, despite having a boyfriend, she is surprised by her own horrified reaction. "All this time I thought I was this progressive thinker . . . now I find out I'm as shot through with prejudice as the next asshole." Connie voiced the age-old anxiety nonheterosexuals provoked in heterosexuals: "I don't know if I can be your friend anymore. I'll think about it everytime I see you. I'll be nervous and wonder if you're going to rape me or something." When Molly tells her she is simply wrong, Connie's stunning response highlights Brown's view of homophobia as a painful social disease that separats otherwise reasonable people: "I know that, but it's in my head. It's me, not you. I'm sorry. I really am sorry."[72] As Connie walks away, the sisterhood of three is shattered much like the reaction of heterosexual women to lesbianism within feminist organizations destroyed illusory forms of "sisterhood" in the early years of the women's liberation movement. At the end of the novel, Molly reluctantly embraces her solitude and marginality, and decides to wait until the times caught up to her. "My bitterness was reflected in the news, full of stories about people my own age raging down the streets in protest. But somehow I knew my rage wasn't their rage and they'd have run me out of their movement for being a lesbian anyway. . . . Damn, I wished the world would let me be myself."[73] For Molly, neither her poverty nor her biracial heritage shaped her sense of self to the degree that her desire and homophobia did.

Brown's novel tiptoed through the battlefield of competing interpretations of what women's sexual freedom would look like. Committed to ending both homophobia and sexism, she tried hard to join sexual liberation and women's liberation through Molly's (theoretical) acceptance of sexual pleasure as an inalienable right. Molly's message that women should be free to pick whomever they wanted to have sex with could only have reached the popularity it did among lesbian feminists in the 1970s if Molly herself preferred to sleep with women. Brown's message of polymorphous sexuality required the messenger to be the alpha lesbian feminist Molly proved to be.

Jong, in *Fear of Flying*, also problematized heterosexuality for women. She, however, concentrated not on destabilizing the line between lesbian and straight women in the name of sexual freedom but on the destabilizing effects unruly desires had on the search for security. Jong's heroine operated well inside the heterosexual imperative, without seriously contemplating lesbianism or bisexuality as real alternatives. Yet Isadora's unquestioning heterosexuality did not limit the effectiveness of Jong's critique of femininity and the dilemmas it posed for women. For Isadora, security means a husband (Bennett), children, and plans that mapped out a secure, if dull, future. Her sudden desire for Adrian Goodlove at a psychoanalytic conference in Vienna catapults her into a frenzy of lusty attraction that threatens not only her marriage to Bennett but also her belief in security itself. Her desires for Adrian became tangled up with her desires for liberation from domestic obligations and feminine constraints.

Jong's most famous contribution to American sexual thought was Isadora's fantasy of the "zipless fuck." This fantasy was about two strangers who had incredibly good sex on a train as it traveled through a tunnel. "The zipless fuck was more than a fuck. It was a platonic ideal. Zipless because when you came together zippers fell away like rose petals, underwear blew off in one breath like dandelion fluff. Tongues intertwined and turned liquid. Your whole soul flowed out through your tongue and into the mouth of your lover." For her, the tunnel and the anonymity of the encounter added up to sexual self-discovery, a sensuous freedom from self-consciousness and inhibition that only a stranger (ideally) could give. "For the true, ultimate zipless A-1 fuck, it was necessary that you never get to know the man very well. I had noticed, for example, how all my infatuations dissolved as soon as I really became friends with a man. . . . I might enjoy his company . . . but he no longer had the power to make me wake up trembling in the middle of the night."[74]

Anonymity for Isadora meant a lack of entanglement in someone else's problems and imperfections that might tarnish the contact between (equally) lusting bodies. In her fantasy, sex "is free of ulterior motives. There is no power game. The man is not 'taking' and the woman is not 'giving.' . . . No one is trying to prove anything or get anything out of anyone. The zipless fuck is the purest thing there is."[75] Jong's effort to clear a nondomestic space free of care-taking obligations for Isadora to experience her desire was very much a part of the feminist work the novel performed.

Yet at the same time, Jong's novel complicated any simple separation between sexual pleasure and relationships. Throughout the novel, Isadora muses on the problem of reconciling her "cunt" with her "head," pleasure with marriage, romance with freedom:

> I was not against marriage. I believed in it in fact. . . . But what about all those other longings which after a while marriage did nothing much to appease? The restlessness, the hunger, the thump in the gut, the thump in the cunt, the longing to be filled up, to be fucked through every hole, the yearning for dry champagne and wet kisses, for the smell of peonies in a penthouse on a June night, for the light at the end of the pier in *Gatsby*.[76]

Isadora fetishizes and critiques romance. She is captured by it and at the same time sees it as a trap. Thanks to years of psychoanalysis (with sexist analysts) and to the endless parade of disappointing men, Isadora wrestles with the chimera that is romantic love. After many lovers and two failed marriages, Isadora realizes that marriage does little to tame the sexual longing or the existential fulfillment women need.

> And what about those other longings which marriage stifled? Those longings to hit the open road from time to time, to discover whether you could still live alone inside your own head, to discover whether you could manage to survive in a cabin in the woods without going mad; to discover, in short, whether you were still whole after so many years of being half of something.[77]

Isadora's metadiscourse on the contradictions of femininity positioned sexual freedom in opposition to security. Herein lay Isadora's capacity to "see like a feminist." But seeing the inequities of being a woman and actually transcending them were quite different enterprises, as Isadora soon discovers.

> At times I was defiant and thought I had every right to snatch whatever pleasure was offered to me for the duration of my short time on earth. Why shouldn't I be happy and hedonistic? What was wrong

with it? . . . But no sooner had my defiant mood passed than I would be seized with desolation and despair. . . . I wanted to run to Bennett and plead forgiveness, throw myself at his feet, offer to bear him twelve children immediately, promise to serve him like a good slave in exchange for any bargain as long as it included security. I would become servile, cloying, saccharinely sweet: the whole package of lies that passes in the world as femininity.[78]

Isadora's trouble is that she cannot reconcile a tangle of binaries produced by the contrary experiences of being a woman. She cannot find a way to make peace between her desire to write and her desire for children, her longing for excitement and her need for security. Isadora sees that these oppositions are deeply and problematically gendered. While setting out the problem Isadora faces in gendered terms, Jong did not offer simple formulas or obvious solutions. Unlike Molly Bolt, whose lesbian feminism guides her through her life troubles, Isadora muddles about in the messy overlay of her search for love, sexual fulfillment, and individuality. Like other heterosexual feminists, most notably Germaine Greer, Jong's narrative of self-development/feminist development is productively complicated by her passion for men. In some moments, Isadora's love of men, of sex, of security become obstacles on her journey toward becoming a writer. At other times, her longing to write and to be free of emotional entanglements block her efforts to find happiness, with either Bennett or Adrian.

Through most of the novel, Isadora is motivated by her desire for sex, an act that represents to her the most gratifying way of reconciling her writing and her need for a man. Isadora, like Jong, writes erotic poems about women's desire that earn her prizes and notoriety. Isadora experiences sex as the point of intersection between her competing quests for self and for pleasure and cannot stop herself from following her unruly desire for Adrian. Jong cleverly complicated what could be a relatively straightforward equation between Bennett as the symbol of security and Adrian as the symbol of unregulated pleasure. Ironically, Isadora has wonderful intercourse with Bennett and almost none with Adrian. "Adrian was only at half-mast and he thrashed around wildly inside me hoping I wouldn't notice. I wound up with a tiny ripple of an orgasm and a very sore cunt. But somehow I was pleased. I'll be able to get free of him now, I thought; he isn't a good lay. I'll be able to forget him."[79] Yet the opposite happens. Isadora's lust transforms into something else, a different sort of intimacy that is bound up with his philosophy of self-reliance and self-centeredness.

On these terms, new to Isadora, Adrian offers a zipless fuck of the mind. "His limp prick had penetrated where a stiff one would never have reached."[80] Despite not having satisfying intercourse, Isadora is hooked on the heady mix of Adrian's "existentialist" approach to a life without plans, maps, or safety nets as well as on his "dizzying wet kisses."

The novel's structure replicats the division between pleasure and autonomy with which Isadora herself wrestles. It does so through Adrian's impotency and his critique of romance, both of which undercut Isadora's attempt to make him into her ideal man. At every turn in their journey to nowhere, Adrian eludes Isadora's efforts to make him into a romantic hero who would rescue her. In a dialogue they replay in their numerous campsites and cafés, Isadora and Adrian debate romantic love, which comes to stand in for the larger gendered struggle between relationships and autonomy. Isadora tries to explain why she feels she needs love. "It's just that I want to really feel close to someone, united with someone, whole for once. I want to really love someone." Adrian refuses her entire narrative that finding the right man, a man who would reconcile her competing desires for romance and for freedom, would solve her problems. "Look—why don't you just stop looking for love and try to live your own life?" Isadora cannot help but be trapped by her ambivalence. "Because what sort of life do I have if I don't have love?" she asks in response. "You have your work, your writing, your teaching, your friends . . . " "Drab, drab, drab, I thought."[81]

Adrian's rejection of the role of romantic hero, his rejection of sex as an answer, and ultimately his rejection of Isadora leave her, at last, at the center of her own life. Alone in a dirty, run-down French hotel room, Isadora confronts herself and the terror of being alone. She gives herself a talking to, trying to work her way out of her "fear of flying," of being by herself, self-reliant, and satisfied, even if she cannot find the man of her dreams or, by this point in the novel, of her illusions. Rather than have Isadora burst free of the binaries that structure the narrative and metadiscourse of Jong's feminism, Jong shows Isadora tolerating contradiction.

> Me: And you know that men and women can never wholly possess each other.
> Me: I know.
> Me: And you know that you'd hate to have a man who possessed you totally and used up your breathing space . . .
> Me: I know—but I yearn for it desperately.
> Me: But if you had it you'd feel trapped.

Me. I know.

Me: You want contradictory things.

Me: I know.

Me: You want freedom and you also want closeness.

Me: I know.[82]

The novel's metadiscourse, which centers on moments like these in which Isadora's need for sex, autonomy, and selfhood clash, constituts the point at which the novel performs its most feminist work. Isadora, like Molly, can see like a feminist. In this case, Isadora ses that her desire to be loved is a symptom of her femininity and the cultural messages that replace women's larger life goals with the quest for romantic love. Yet, unlike Molly, for Isadora the problem with seeing like a feminist is that it offers no simple solutions or pathways out of the complicated ambivalence of a woman's life. Seeing like a feminist does not, in and of itself, present a map for Isadora to follow. Thus Adrian and his critique of plans, order, and security function as much as a critique of gender as does Isadora's search for sexual pleasure. Adrian's ironic contribution to the feminist work of *Fear of Flying* lies in his refusal to be a solution for Isadora, either by being a romantic hero (and giving her a home and children in which to lose/find herself) or by giving her satisfying sex that ultimately obscures her deeper search for selfhood. The novel, by its ambivalent weave of existentialism and feminism, ultimately and paradoxically dismisses sexual pleasure as the vehicle of a woman's liberation.

The novel ends with Isadora floating in a warm bathtub in Bennett's London hotel room. She determines to neither beg him to take her back nor to fantasize about Adrian or any other idealized and ultimately nonexistent man who would alleviate her from the burden of her own existence. At last Jong delivers to her readers the only solution the novel's critique of sex and romance could offer. "I thought of my crazy notions that Adrian was my mental double and how wrong it had turned out to be. That was what I had originally wanted. A man to complete me. . . . But perhaps that was the most delusional of all my delusions. People don't complete us. We complete ourselves."[83]

Feminist novels of the 1970s explored in rich detail the problems of heterosexuality for white middle-class women. In these accounts, like those found in feminist theory of the late 1960s and early 1970s, the authors viewed heterosexuality not simply as a sexual object choice. Rather, they understood it as a social system that trained girls in the art of femininity—

the replacement of larger goals with narrow narcissistic concerns like the shape of their bodies, the makeup on their faces, and the proper way to behave with boyfriends. The life lessons the heroines absorbed taught them that being the right sort of girl would lead them to being the right sort of woman. The right sort of woman ideally would find sexual and personal fulfillment in marrying and having children.

However, as the novels suggested, girls' social training schooled them equally well in self-denial. On the way to becoming proper women, the heroines found themselves mastering the problematic art of dissembling, of not articulating who they felt themselves to be and not specifying the kinds of sexual behaviors and practices that they found most erotic. The heroines of feminist sex novels learned to hide the pleasure they took from masturbation, from petting, and, eventually, from foreplay. They tried hard to find the groping intercourse with teenage boys and, later, husbands to be the pinnacle of fulfillment they had been promised it was by experts, parents, and peers alike. The novels explored in bittersweet detail the meaning of a female heterosexual identity organized primarily around men and their desires. For these heroines, feminine gender identity shaped in quite tangible ways sexual desire and its expressions.

The painful comings of age/coming into feminism stories the novels explored, however, were not only about men's sexual misunderstanding of women. Often, the problems the heroines faced were themselves generated by the heroine's own acceptance of the terms not only of the sex they had with men but of the personalities they assumed. The heroines, in short, misunderstood themselves. They had replaced their own desires with a set of messages that identified what they should want. The novels, then, were propelled by the heroines' various quests to unlearn the terms of femininity they had unwittingly taken in too well and discover their own "unique" path to fulfillment and selfhood. For many heroines, most notably Isadora Wing, that meant remaking heterosexuality to better fit their emergent selves. It also meant remaking the boundaries of normal femininity, and thus of gender itself.

The feminist project of remaking heterosexuality to better accommodate women and their desires was not identical for women discovering their sexual passion for and political commitment to women. According to both feminist theorists and novelists, remaking heterosexuality was about making room for the clitoris in heterosexual practice, renegotiating the line between foreplay and intercourse, and redefining what constituted "real sex." Most important, remaking heterosexuality involved women imagining what sexual freedom could be. As the feminist sex novels of the 1970s so vividly document, feminism became identified as the space of women's self-definition.

Feminist sex novels also helped to produce the subject of feminism as white. In their attention to the intersections of gender with sexuality, the novels elided other categories of identity that also powerfully shaped desire. While Brown productively cast Molly as possibly "colored," gender and sexual difference overshadowed racial difference throughout the novel. Molly, raised as white, feels the root of her oppression to lie in ideas about normal womanhood, not in the experiences of living in a racist society. As with early radical feminist theory, sexual oppression occupied a privileged site for the production of feminist consciousness.

While the white heroines in seventies feminist novels did not always find what they were looking for, the process of looking for what they wanted, of identifying what gave them pleasure, enacted what became known popularly as "feminism." The discontentment the novels explored—the multiple obstacles women encountered on their way to becoming themselves, the misguided advice offered by teachers, parents, and boyfriends, the sheer amount of bad sex they experienced—added up to a mainstream critique of heterosexuality. This critique of heterosexuality shared much with feminist sex writing of the late sixties and early seventies. Such seeding between novels and theory, between activists and readers, helped to create a discourse about sexuality and about (white) feminism that profoundly joined one to the other.

CULTURAL FEMINISM

Reimagining Sexual Freedom, 1975–1982

In October 1974, one year after the publication of Erica Jong's *Fear of Flying* and Rita Mae Brown's *Rubyfruit Jungle*, the New York City branch of the liberal National Organization for Women (NOW) sponsored a conference on sexuality. In many regards, the conference literally embodied the popular association, made by novelists, blockbuster anthologies, and a new breed of feminist experts, that feminism itself was the space of women's sexual self-definition. The conference planners self-consciously attempted to speak to *all* women—gay and straight—about sexual practice and sexual pleasure. The event began with a "speak out" about sex. Participants could then choose to attend workshops on various sexual practices, orientations, and identifications. A film series ran throughout the day, showing films that included graphic accounts of heterosexual technique, group, gay, and lesbian sex. While New York NOW was among the most radical of all the NOW branches, the frank sex talk the conference facilitated spoke volumes about the acceptability of the once radical, now commonplace view that women lusted for plea-sure as much as men.

However, not all feminists embraced the event or the spirit of sexual egalitarianism it promoted. A number of lesbian feminists denounced the conference as too heterosexual, too reformist, too soft on pornography, and too focused on orgasm. Critics of the conference, writing in the feminist journal *Off Our Backs* (*OOB*), complained that the conference simply paid too much attention to pleasure. In doing so, *OOB* critics complained, par-ticipant depoliticized sexuality. "It's frightening," wrote three feminists, "that such a large proportion of the supposedly non-sexist 'liberated' men and women of NOW accepted wholeheartedly the 'everyone's got their own thing isn't it wonderful (and anti-political)' liberal sexual propaganda served up by the organizers." According to these authors, sexual pleasure looked suspiciously like opium for the masses, a distraction to keep wo-men's attention off the pervasive problem of male domination. "At the 'Speak Out,' " these critics complained, "we were treated to the various joys of group marriages; open marriages, group masturbation; bisexuality; bestiality; sado-masochism; pissing in someone's mouth; celibacy; again and again the vibrator, which was presented as the messiah—everywo-man's dream come true (only $19.95)."[1]

The coverage by *Off Our Backs* of the NOW conference marked the be-ginning of a new moment in the evolution of second-wave feminism. It signaled a consolidation of a new vanguard—the lesbian feminist. Taking their lead not from Anne Koedt or Kate Millett, the new vanguard em-braced Andrea Dworkin and Adrienne Rich. According to *OOB*, only les-bians dealt with the political nature of sexuality. Claiming the mantle of radical feminism as theirs, they viewed lesbian separatism as the only log-ical outcome of radical feminism.

> As Andrea Dworkin pointed out, it is important to go beyond the sexu-al as purely personal (it only happens to me) and take the next step to re-alizing the commonality with other women of our sexual problems and joys as a direct product of the male patriarchal culture. The NOW con-ference, however, has not yet heard of Kate Millett, much less being able to hear Andrea Dworkin—it's much to busy lying on its back.[2]

As the responses to the NOW conference indicated, sexual pleasure, un-defined and self-determined, was fast evaporating as a point of common-ality between feminists. Radical feminism, refracted through lesbian separatism, rendered the goal of sexual self-determination for all women misguided. Ironically, *OOB* contributors rejected the conference's focus on women finding pleasures in a variety of ways with a variety of partners as apolitical. One author dismissed as "overworked" the ideas of "enjoying masturbation, being sex positive and having sex with other women while being straight."[3]

Such criticisms, centered in lesbian feminism and the burgeoning antipornography movement, began the decade-long project of sketching out lines of disagreement between feminists over the meanings of sexual desire and sexual practice. Contributors to *OOB* forecasted the terms of what would, eight years later, become a full-blown "sex war" between feminists at the Scholar and the Feminist Ninth Conference, "Towards a Politics of Sexuality," held on April 24, 1982, at Barnard College in New York City. At the Barnard conference, feminists did what in the heyday of radical feminism would have seemed unthinkable: they picketed and protested other feminists over their competing definitions of sexual freedom. How and why had sexuality, which once provided radical feminism with a utopian vision of women's liberation, become so contentious and divisive?

The 1974 sexuality conference vividly captured the transition underway within feminism over the meaning of sexual freedom and sexual liberation for women. This transition, which ushered in a new moment of feminist activism and theory, had complicated roots that lay within feminism itself and within broader changes in the social and political climate of the seventies. By 1974, the country had begun to feel the full assault of a popular backlash against feminism. Four years after establishing women's constitutional right to abortion, the U.S. Supreme Court ruled that women could not use Medicaid funds for abortions, once again making abortion a privilege of those who could afford it.[4] At the same time, passage of the Equal Rights Amendment, which had appeared to be all but secured, met serious and mounting opposition from conservative groups.[5] Spurred onto activism by feminist victories, the New Right mushroomed and organized both locally and nationally around defense of the family, marriage, and the sanctity of motherhood.

As many Americans rejected what they viewed as the excesses of the sexual revolution, feminists started to interrogate the very terms of feminism, its political goals and its theoretical understandings of womanhood, sexuality, and equality. Long-standing conflicts and disagreements between feminists intensified as many in the movement turned away from the elusive ideal of equality and toward exploring women's unique experiences and knowledge. More and more, feminists began to emphasize the failures of sexual liberalism and the dangers women faced from unrestrained male sexuality. Cultural feminism, lesbian separatism, and the antipornography movement converged by the late seventies to produce accounts of female sexuality as decidedly unlike male sexuality: instead of pleasure, women pursued connection; instead of orgasm, women focused on intimacy; sex became touching, looking, and kissing. A new sexual prescription emerged. Truly feminist sex was antiphallic, antirole-playing, and fundamentally egalitarian.

While cultural feminism was on the rise, it had no better success in uniting feminists than had its predecessor, radical feminism. The mainstreaming of key elements of radical feminism, such as the definition of feminism as the space of women's sexual self-determination, the popular acknowledgment of male chauvinism and sexism, and the political significance of everyday life, contributed to the usefulness, and thus the multiplicity and fracturing, of the movement. Core values forged in 1969 had, by 1976, been edited, expanded, and transformed as feminism itself became useful to more and more women. Values like sexual self-determination, which provided a unifying vision to early radical feminism, increasingly came to mean different things to different feminists. What did sexual freedom mean to battered women? To poor women? To prostitutes? To minority women? To middle-class married women? To black lesbians? Fissures multiplied at a breathtaking rate.

The legacy of radical feminism—that the category of "woman" was itself political and based on the patriarchal uses and misuses of female sexuality—had bequeathed not only historic accounts of women's oppression but deep divisions within the movement. In 1974, feminists of color began their historic critique of feminism as white, as middle class, and as implicated in the colonialist and imperialist project of the U.S. in relation to the third world. The lesbian separatist movement grew in the mid-1970s and positioned itself as a feminist vanguard. Together, racial and sexual diversity challenged previously useful radical feminist theories of women's liberation. The utopianism of radical feminism in 1969 and 1970 held sexual freedom to be a universal goal, universally applicable to all women, no matter their social location. Yet as lesbian feminists and minority feminists argued, sexuality was too much implicated in women's historically different social experiences to be simply or naively promoted as the basis of women's liberation. As women of color clamored for a profound restructuring of the very terms of feminism, lesbian feminists, black and white, hoped that a woman-centered multicultural feminism would provide a new basis for an authentic sisterhood among women.

The 1974 NOW conference, with its emphasis on pleasure and plural-ism, as well as the angry responses it triggered in many lesbian feminists, marked the beginning of yet another chapter in the evolving meaning of sexuality to second-wave feminism. Bookended on one side by the NOW conference and on the other by the more infamous 1982 Feminist and the Scholar conference at Barnard, these years marked a fundamental re-working of radical feminism and its legacies. Different groups claimed different parts of radical feminism as their own. Antipornography femi-nists took up the critique of patriarchy as a form of psychological and sex-ual domination of women and applied it to pornography; lesbian feminists took up the critique of the orgasm as a male fantasy and advocated that women needed love and intimacy from their sexual partners, not merely orgasms; psychologically minded feminists returned to psychoanalysis to reimagine the mother-child bond as a model for women's empowerment; women of color pushed feminist radicalism to include race and class in the structuring of women's sexual identities; straight and gay, minority and white sex radicals took up the revolutionary potential of women's sexual pleasure and advocated for even greater acknowledgment of women's unique sexual desires within feminism.

All these impulses had existed in and animated radical feminism. They coexisted, uneasily at times, but resulted in a productive moment of activism, theory making, and mainstreaming where feminists re-claimed sexual pleasure, broadly defined, as every woman's right. But by 1982, competing groups of feminists, each with their own definitions of sexual freedom, authenticity, and even of feminism, claimed the legacy of radical feminism.

Radical Feminism as Cultural Feminism: Defining Women's Difference

Lesbian feminists played a decisive role in the development of cul-tural feminism and its view of female sexuality. Whereas generations of psychologists, doctors, and other experts had produced accounts of les-bianism as a form of sexual and gender deviancy, a new generation of les-bian feminists recast it as an emotional and political alternative to hetero-sexuality. These so-called political lesbians did not always prioritize sexual desire for women as the primary motivation for lesbianism.[6] Lesbian-feminists found each other through political groups and at meetings, both of which became the center of their community life, rather than at the bars.[7] They rejected butch/femme relationships as an anathema to feminism. Many embraced Jill Johnston's dream of a "lesbian nation" where women would create a safe and empowering space for each other apart from men and their institutions.[8] For women emerging from destroyed marriages, failed relationships, and heady doses of consciousness-raising, the all-woman environment of lesbian feminist groups seemed to hold out the promise of a refuge where they could find intimacy and equality. For others, lesbian feminism enabled a better integration of lifestyle and politics.

Lesbian separatism, which began in 1971, offered an important critique of heterosexuality as an expression of internalized male domination.[9] One group in particular, the Furies, in Washington, D.C., introduced and defined the term *heterosexism* as a form of domination based on the assumption that heterosexuality was the only "normal" form of sexuality. They advocated that women should sever ties with men and reject the privileges heterosexuality brought them. Charlotte Bunch, one of the group's leaders, argued that lesbianism was more than a sexual preference; it was a revolutionary act. "It is a political choice . . . because relationships between men and women are essentially political . . . [and] involve power and dominance. Since the Lesbian actively rejects that relationship and chooses women, she defies the established political system."[10] As a normative identity, Bunch went on, heterosexuality offered straight women the privileges of economic and emotional security, which "give heterosexual women a personal and political stake in maintaining the status quo."[11] Lesbianism, she continued, "is key to liberation and only women who cut their ties to male privilege can be trusted to remain serious in the struggle against male dominance. Those who remain tied to men, individually or in political theory, cannot always put women first."[12] According to the Furies, "any woman relating to a man cannot be a feminist. Women who give love and energy to men rather than women obviously think men are better than women."[13]

The Furies envisioned lesbian separatism joining women of all races and classes. They critiqued reform-minded straight feminism for using "sisters of color" to win advances for middle-class white women. For example, in "Taking the Bullshit by the Horns," written in 1972, Furies member Barbara Solomon identified straight white women as the common enemy of minority and lesbian feminists.

Straight women tried to rally us all together under the "Sisterhood is groovy" banner to win abortions. Straight privileged women said that sex, class or race issues would be divisive and would keep us from winning. Then they proceeded to use us to win abortions that are totally irrelevant to Lesbians, can be used as genocide against Third World women, and are too expensive for poor women to afford. Oh, sisterhood is so groovy.[14]

The Furies' combination of separatism and antiracism did not necessarily perform the unifying work that they hoped it would. Separatism from men was a racially divisive issue between lesbian feminists. For many minority women, it implicitly rested on white privilege in that it narrowly defined women's emotional and material resources as coming only out of their relationships with other women. For many minority women, white women had mistreated them as much as men had.

Black women had long felt suspicious about the women's liberation movement. In 1970 black feminists Francis Beal, Mary Ann Weathers, and Linda La Rue forged a distinct black feminist standpoint premised on the belief that all women had autonomous selves that were distinct from the social roles of wife, mother, and girlfriend. For example, La Rue complained that the rhetoric of black liberation problematically embraced a conservative gender politic. "Upon the rebirth of the liberation struggle in the sixties, a whole genre of 'women's place' advocates immediately relegated black women to home and babies which is almost as ugly an expression of black Anglo-Saxonism as is Nixon's concept of 'black capitalism.'"[15] Weathers, too, argued that women must see themselves as more than "someone's personal sex objects, maids, baby sitters, domestics, and the like in exchange for a man's attentions." While race and class separated women, Weathers went on, women nonetheless had "female's oppression in common."[16]

Such points of commonality, however, did not result in the grounds for a simple alliance between black and white women. By the late 1970s, women of color saw less and less binding them with white women who were apt to profess their antiracism but had difficulty seeing the ways in which racial privilege shaped their feminism.[17] The Combahee River Collective's 1977 "A Black Feminist Statement" advocated that minority women organize around their own experience of simultaneous and overlapping systems of racial, gender, and sexual oppressions.[18] By the 1980s feminists like Audre Lorde, Barbara Smith, and bell hooks had produced a significant body of theory that challenged the assumptions of class and race in feminist conceptions of gender oppression.[19]

The Furies' decision to express their feminism by separating from men and any woman who did not share their vision was simply unworkable for many minority feminists. Whereas Soloman wrote that "I am just stating that I personally am going to keep my distance from men and straight women," the Combahee River Collective rejected separatism as a strategy. "As we have already stated, we reject the stance of lesbian separatism because it is not a viable political analysis or strategy for us. It leaves out far too much and far too many people, particularly Black men, women and children." According to this group, black women found allies with black men in their battle against racism. They questioned "whether lesbian separatism is an adequate and progressive political analysis and strategy, even for those who practice it, since it so completely denies any but the sexual sources of women's oppression."[20] The dream of establishing a form of multicultural sisterhood based on a rejection of men and patriarchy proved unworkable even in the heyday of the lesbian nation.

Lesbian separatist theory emerged out of the feminist counterculture which mushroomed in select cities throughout the 1970s.[21] Lesbian and straight feminists viewed the building of an alternative woman's culture as an extension, not a retreat from, of their political vision. For many, establishing feminist institutions was about lending scarce resources to more women as well as offering women images of themselves that were positive and untainted by patriarchy. According to one woman who participated in the counterculture of the seventies, "We believed that we were creating a whole new world, a world that lived by different values. We didn't buy into the capitalist ideology. We treated each other the way we wanted others to treat us. It was incredibly heady, empowering."[22]

Drawing on the radical feminist battle cry "The personal is political," lesbian feminists viewed cultural institutions and women-centered products like music, books, and art as political interventions. According to one group of prominent cultural feminists, the growth of alternative feminist institutions proved the righteousness of the feminist vision.

> While the male politics of the sixties grow less relevant in the rhetoric to people's lives, women move on. This is a period of rapid expansion and outreach for the Women's Movement as Feminism finds form in new health centers, community women's centers, women's studies programs, rape crisis lines and similar projects.[23]

Likewise, *The New Woman's Survival Source Book* (1975) claimed that "what we call 'women's culture' . . . is perhaps the most profound and ultimately far reaching expression of our politics—the incredibly difficult and moving discovery of a woman's world view that will inform the conception and reality of women's power to change their lives and their culture."[24] Within the feminist counterculture, specifically lesbian institutions developed, including, journals, small presses, bookstores, women's music festivals, and record companies.[25]

Women's music delimited both the positive and the negative elements of the lesbian counterculture. On the one hand, women's music was one of the most popular elements of the women's counterculture of the 1970s. Made predominantly by lesbians like Holly Near and Chris Williamson, feminist musicians politicized both what one could sing about and the process of musical production. According to Near, "Women's music was not just music being done by women. It was music that was challenging the whole system. . . . It was like taking a whole new look at systems and societies and letting a music rise out of those systems."[26] Done in opposition to the "cock rock" of disco and male bands like the Rolling Stones, women's music promoted a belief in universal sisterhood based on women's identification with each other. Women's music festivals around the country became mini lesbian nations for a weekend as women gathered to hear music written and performed by women. These festivals also became hot spots for coming out, for breaking up, and for engaging in sex with multiple partners.

At the same time women's music provided an important rallying point for lesbian feminists, many felt excluded by the sense of sisterhood women's music produced. By the late 1970s, feminists of color complained that women's music had become, for all intents and purposes, European women's music. Albums and tours by black artists on women's music labels like Olivia did not attract the necessary money and audiences, confirming for many minority women their sense of being marginalized by white feminists.[27] Still others felt confined by the enforcement of taste and preferences implied as part of the lesbian community. According to one participant, "The lesbian community to me is all those women who go to Holly Near concerts, and I just don't identify with that at all. I like rock and roll. . . . I find women's music boring."[28] While women's institutions like music festivals and recording companies helped to create the sense of a women's community, they also produced boundaries that excluded and marginalized women.

The convergence of lesbian separatism and the women's counterculture helped reshape radical feminism into cultural feminism. A key arena that both reflected and produced this transformation was theory making, elevating yet again another set of feminists into experts. Adrienne Rich and Audre Lorde set out the major themes of cultural feminist theory. They, along with theologian Mary Daly and activist Jane Alpert, promoted a new vision of women's bodies as the source of female power.[29] Rich, with her account of mothering, and Lorde, with her account of the power of the erotic, successfully developed a portrait of the female body whose sexuality was no longer bound by genitals, that found liberation in the mystical powers of reproduction, and whose lived experience of racial and sexual oppression had crystallized into a woman-centered knowledge.

The cultural feminist project of revaluing women's difference from men involved two at times competing impulses, both of which had roots in radical feminism. One impulse was to celebrate lesbianism as a pure and authentic connection between women that was essentially counterhegemonic and thus revolutionary. The second impulse was to celebrate women's bodies as unique and their sexuality as independent of "male models" of genital sex. In radical feminism, nongenital, nonorgasmic forms of sexual connection existed side by side with a call for clitoral orgasm, multiple orgasms, and better sexual technique from partners. By the mid 1970s, under the influence of an ascendant lesbian feminism and a growing antipornography movement made up of gay and straight women, sexual pluralism no longer seemed like a workable goal for feminism.

In her acclaimed 1976 *Of Woman Born*, Adrienne Rich used the fiery political rhetoric of early second-wave feminists to argue that control over reproduction was the primary motivation of patriarchy.[30] Sounding like Shulamith Firestone, Rich proposed that society controlled women by controlling their bodies, specifically their reproductive capacities and the material organization of bearing and raising children.[31] But, unlike Firestone, Rich did not call for women to end their role in reproducing the species. Rather, she exhorted women to reclaim from patriarchy the power "inherent" in their biology. "I have come to believe," she wrote, "that female biology—the diffuse, intense sensuality radiating out from the clitoris, breasts, uterus, vagina; the lunar cycles of menstruation; the gestation and fruition of life which can take place in a woman's body—has far more radical implications than we have yet come to appreciate."[32] Rich elevated women's capacity to bear children both as the source of women's power and men's desire to control them. "Patriarchy's control over women through heterosexuality and motherhood," she wrote, provided "the sexual under-structure of social and political forms."[33] Rich endowed the female body with the power to transform society because of its capacity to reproduce. The capacity to reproduce life, dismissed as oppressive by Firestone in 1970, became for Rich, by 1976, the source of women's empowerment.

The stable categories of men, women, and patriarchy in Rich's work lent force to her analysis of the gendered workings of power. Part of its force also came from her use of two opposing constructions of women. She at once claimed women as all-powerful, life-giving mothers and as scorned, victimized, and powerless. Rich used both constructions brilliantly. On the one hand, Rich claimed women's biology provided them with the power of nurturing life, of thinking beyond dualisms, of managing power over a weaker person with grace and compassion. Her reclaiming of motherhood as a source of power affirmed many women's experiences and harnessed constructions of femininity as nurturing to her feminist vision. On the other hand, Rich equally drew on the power of the victim's position. As victims of patriarchal logic that viewed them as inferior, Rich asserted that women had no responsibility for the cruel workings of society. She explained that "women's primary experience of power till now has been triply negative: we have experienced men's power as oppression; we have experienced our own vitality and independence as somehow threatening to men; and, even when behaving with 'feminine' passivity, we have been made aware of masculine fantasies of our potential destructiveness."[34]

Rich boldly asserted that women had no meaningful relationships to social (male) power and suggested that feminism must generate an entirely new understanding of power based on women's knowledge and bodies. She proposed a new definition of power based on matriarchy. "There is a new concern for the possibilities inherent in beneficent female power, as a mode which is absent from the society at large, and which, even in the private sphere, women have to exercise under terrible constraints." This alternative power originated from the simple fact that "we all carry in our earliest imprints the memory of, or the longing for, an individual past relationship to a female body, larger and stronger than our own, and to female warmth, nurture, and tenderness."[35] In Rich's feminism, the "beneficent" mother would replace the patriarchal father as the basis for social relations.

Rich's vision of the powerful mother, who ruled society in the same way as a mother nurtured her children, politicized the female body toward the goal of liberating women. Yet this vision left little place for sexuality as defined through pleasure. Eliding female sexuality was productive for Rich. Sexuality had the potential to link men and women together in pleasure that disrupted the primary dyad of her analysis, the mother and child. By viewing women's bodies solely in relationship to actual or potential reproduction and children rather than sexual pleasure, Rich made a decisive break from radical feminism.

In revaluing what patriarchy devalued, Rich tightly associated women with a set of traits earlier feminists like Betty Friedan and Kate Millett strenuously denied had any essential relationship to women.[36] Rich argued that "masculine intellectual systems" lacked the "wholeness that female consciousness, excluded from contributing to them, could provide. . . . Truly to liberate women, then, means to change thinking itself: to reintegrate what has been named the unconscious, the subjective, the emotional with the structural, the rational, the intellectual . . . and finally to annihilate those dichotomies."[37] In contrast to radical feminists like Anne Koedt, Rich did not claim that the binaries were false or that society generated misinformation about women.[38] Rather, she argued that the fundamental structures of society and knowledge excluded feminine thinking and women's values.

Rich's analysis essentialized psychological traits like emotion, nondualistic thinking, subjectivity, and irrationality as unique to all women and helped produce a universal, ahistorical, and fundamentally maternal woman as the subject of feminism. In the last page of her book, Rich linked her view of women's unique natures to the project of social change.

> The repossession by women of our bodies will bring far more essential change to human society than the seizing of the means of production by workers. The female body has been both territory and machine, virgin wilderness to be exploited and assembly-line turning out life. We need to imagine a world in which every woman is the presiding genius of her own body. In such a world women will truly create new life, bringing forth not only children but the visions and the thinking necessary to sustain, console, and alter human existence—a new relationship to the universe.[39]

Rich's vision of women's bodies as the site of authenticity and power was one that many cultural feminists shared, including poet Audre Lorde. Lorde's 1978 essay "Uses of the Erotic" shared Rich's sense of the female body as a resource for feminism.[40] Like Rich, Lorde's understanding of sexuality was one that reclaimed the entire body as a source of postgenital sexual pleasure. In "Uses of the Erotic," Lorde proposed a return to seeing sexuality as a life force. The erotic stood in opposition to the merely sexual or pornographic.

In a complicated rewriting of Freud's concept of the libido, Lorde viewed eroticism as a feminine life force that women could claim for themselves. This authentic life force had the potential to reanimate all aspects of life, from writing poetry to political activism. As did Freud and radical feminists before her, Lorde understood the erotic as providing the central component of a woman's identity. Despite its centrality, or because of its centrality, the female erotic life energy was something men had "misnamed" and taken away from women. This made the female erotic essentially counterhegemonic, a force whose power lay in its outsider status. "The erotic has often been misnamed by men and used against women. It has been made into the confused, the trivial, the psychotic, the plasticized sensation. For this reason we have often turned away from the exploration and consideration of the erotic as a source of power and information."[41] Lorde wrote that the erotic was "a resource within each of us that lies in a deeply female and spiritual place, firmly rooted in the power of our unexpressed or unrecognized feeling." At the same time, men denigrated the erotic as feminine. "On the one hand the superficially erotic has been encouraged as a sign of female inferiority—on the other hand women have been made to suffer and to feel both contemptible and suspect by virtue of its existence."[42]

Lorde's conception of the erotic combined radical feminism and cultural feminism in new ways. Lorde emphasized sexuality as both pleasurable and a bonding experience between women. "When I speak of the erotic, then, I speak of it as an assertion of the life force of women; that creative energy empowered, the knowledge and use of which we are now reclaiming in our language, our history, our dancing, our loving, our work, our lives."[43] In her "biomythography," *Zami: A New Spelling of My Name* (1982), Lorde narrated her life of loving other women and their bodies as a political journey into multicultural, woman-centered feminism.[44] For example, in a passage where the narrator made love with Afrelete, her first lover, for whom Africa figured as a source of empowerment, Lorde presented sexual pleasure as a form of personal empowerment. "Our bodies met again, each surface touched with each other's flame, from the tips of our curled toes to our tongues, and locked into our own wild rhythms, we rode each other across the thundering space, dripped like light from the peak of each other's tongue."[45] For Lorde, sexual pleasure helped bring women together to create a space outside of patriarchal oppression.

Lorde shared with other cultural feminists the gendering of violence and bodily alienation as male and the erotic life force as female. As important, Lorde racialized the binaries and situated pornography as a product of white manhood. In "The Power of the Erotic," she wrote that

> the need for sharing deep feeling is a human need. But within the Euro-pean-American tradition, this need is satisfied by certain proscribed erotic comings together, and these occasions are almost always characterized by a simultaneous looking away, a pretense of calling them something else, whether a religion, a fit, mob violence, or even playing doctor. This misnaming of the need and the deed gives rise to that distortion which results in pornography and obscenity—the abuse of feeling.[46]

Lorde saw women's sexuality as essentially feminine in nature, oppositional to the powers of oppression and capable of uniting women. At the same time, she saw the erotic existing in a world marred by racism. Thus, her project of instilling the female body with a mythical and ancient power attempted to overturn centuries of racist conceptions of the black female body. According to Lorde, the black female body was no longer a resource to be claimed by racist white men or disempowered black men. Rather, it was a force for black female empowerment. "For not only do we touch our most profoundly creative source [through the erotic] but we do that which is female and self-affirming in the face of a racist, patriarchal and anti-erotic society."[47]

Lorde's lesbian feminism, which celebrated women's bodies and embraced women's difference, offered a vision upon which feminism could strengthen connections between women. Yet, her vision of lesbian feminism could not fully transcend the real differences that existed between women. For example, in her 1979 "An Open Letter to Mary Daly," Lorde boldly broke out of the cultural feminist sisterhood she had helped to construct. Focusing on Daly's recently published *Gyn/Ecology*, Lorde complained that Daly's vision of women's inherent power drew only on European images and mythologies. In doing so, Lorde wrote, Daly had "dismissed my heritage and the heritage of all other non-european [*sic*] women, and denied the real connections that exist between us."[48] Lorde pointed out that Daly used the works of black women only when speaking of genital mutilation. Such racism severed what Lorde saw as the real connections between women—the "female strength and power that nurtures each of our visions"—which also had roots in Africa and other non-Western countries. Forcefully, Lorde exposed the rifts that plagued lesbian feminism.

> Have you read my work, and the work of other black women for what it could give you? Or did you hunt through only to find words that would legitimize your chapter on African genital mutilation in the eyes of other black women? If so, then why not use our words to legalize or illustrate the other places where we connect in our being and becoming? If, on the other hand, it was not black women you were attempting to reach, in what way did our words illustrate your point for white women?[49]

Lorde concluded her letter by carefully weaving her way through the racism she sought to expose while holding on to a unifying vision that could empower all women regardless of race. For Lorde, the dilemma of commonalty and difference could only be resolved through acknowledging both.[50] Lorde concluded her letter by reminding Daly and other white cultural feminists that while "the oppression of women knows no ethnic nor racial boundaries . . . that does not mean it is identical within those boundaries. Nor do the reservoirs of our ancient power know these boundaries either. To deal with one without even alluding to the other is to distort our commonalty as well as our differences."[51]

Cultural feminist theory drew on the lesbian feminism of Rich and Lorde to affirm a view of women as essentially different from men. At the same time, as a discourse, cultural feminism remained focused on the differences between men and women more than on the differences between women. In their search for a positive view of woman-as-difference, white cultural feminists continued to marginalize the powerful analysis made by feminists like Lorde, the Combahee River Collective, Barbara Smith, and others about the racism that continued to plague feminism. As cultural feminist Alice Walker complained in "One Child of One's Own," even Judy Chicago's artistic celebration of women's vaginas, "The Dinner Party" (1975) could only image vaginas as white. Walker recounted her dismay at discovering that the Sojourner Truth plate was the "only one in the collection that shows—instead of a vagina—a face. In fact, three faces." "It occurred to me," wrote Walker, "that perhaps white women feminists, no less than white women generally, cannot imagine Black women have vaginas. . . . Sojourner Truth certainly had a vagina, as note her lament about her children, born of her body, but sold into slavery."[52] Walker, like Lorde and Rich, celebrated women's bodies as powerful and transcendent. Yet she too decried the tendency in feminism to render the sexuality of minority women only in terms of victimization and not as the resource reserved for white women's bodies. "Note [Truth's] comment that when she cried out with a mother's grief, none but Jesus heard her. Surely a vagina has to be acknowledged when one reads these words. (A vagina the color of raspberries and blackberries.)"[53]

Cultural feminist theory, starting with Jane Alport's "Mother Right" in 1973, building with Rich in 1976 and Lorde in 1978, shifted the focus of feminist theory off what many viewed as a problematic emphasis on sexual liberation.[54] As more and more cultural feminists rejected the idea that exploring women's sexual desires could lead to women's empowerment, the movement looked for and found in abstracted notions of motherhood a potential rallying point for all feminists.[55] The cultural feminist emphasis on maternalism, rather than sexuality, had the potential to bring lesbian and heterosexual feminists as well as black and white feminists together.[56] Since the days of the black power movement of the late 1960s, African American feminists had seen in the role of the mother women's enduring commitment to survival and love in the face of intense racism. Particularly in the wake of Daniel Patrick Moynihan's 1965 report on the black family, African American traditions of motherhood, extended families, and care taking of children had been discursively placed at the center of the black feminist project.[57] Cultural feminists, then, hoped both to heal the wounds between competing groups of feminists as well as to transform the experience of mothering into the foundation for a new feminism. The difference that mattered, the difference all women shared, gay and straight, black and white, was the potential to mother. Cultural feminism's shift to motherhood, then, sought to energize a flagging sisterhood and to generate a positive account of women's difference from men.

The cultural feminist affirmation of women's difference and the replacement of the sexual body with the mother's body took place not only in lesbian feminism. Feminist-inspired psychologists, sociologists, and educators in the seventies generated a new paradigm of women's difference that drew on and extended cultural feminism. Psychological explorations of women's difference, produced by psychologists Dorothy Dinnerstein and Jean Baker Miller, sociologist Nancy Chodorow, and educator Carol Gilligan, had by the mid-1980s became the dominant form of both scholarly and popular feminism.

New psychological theories of women's difference synthesized trends in feminism with those in the social sciences. Feminist psychologists explored the power of the mother through the prism of the preoedipal child. Feminist interest in the preoedipal mother developed out of changes in the discipline that had led practitioners to explore the early years of life, the years before Freud's oedipal drama culminated. Following the rise of ego psychology in the 1940s, American psychologists had begun to embrace a wider array of psychological theories, loosely categorized as "contemporary psychoanalysis," that helped to decenter Freudian authority. Further, the influence of the women's liberation movement had begun to be felt in the discipline as more practitioners conceded the problematic legacy of misogyny in Freudian theories.[58] In this post-Freudian moment, psychologists retooled Freud's drive theory from sex and aggression to what they viewed as an essential drive toward attachment and objects, or people in the infant's world. These changes culminated in what one historian called "an entirely new narrative of psychological development . . . that spotlighted the first three years of life."[59] This new narrative of development was deeply relational and no longer sought to examine the role sexuality played in identity but to explore the origin of sexual difference itself.

Like Rich and Lorde, psychiatrist Jean Baker Miller took women's social marginalization as a powerful source of knowledge that gave women a unique vantage point and a distinctive set of values. In *Towards a New Psychology of Women*, published in 1976, Miller described the process by which power and social domination of men over women created gender roles and identity traits. She explained that dominant groups enjoyed the privilege of defining the traits of the subordinates. "Once a group is defined as inferior, the superiors tend to label it as defective or substandard in various ways." Dominants also defined specific roles for subordinate groups. "Out of the total range of human possibilities, the activities most highly valued in any particular culture will tend to be enclosed within the domain of the dominant group; less valued functions are relegated to the subordinates." Powerful groups defined what constituted "reality," meaningful activity, important personality traits, and set out systems of knowledge that justified their worldview.[60]

Within this framework of inequality, Miller theorized that many of the traits typically understood as essential attributes of women were, in fact, a result of their social marginalization. "It follows that subordinates are described in terms of, and encouraged to develop, personal psychological characteristics that are pleasing to the dominant group. These characteristics form a certain familiar cluster: submissiveness, passivity, docility, dependency, lack of initiative, inability to act, to decide, to think and the like. . . . If subordinates adopt these characteristics they are considered well-adjusted."[61] Social inequality between men and women produced in women highly sensitive awareness of men and of their social position as a survival mechanism. Thus subordinates, wrote Miller, "become highly attuned to the dominants. . . . Here, I think, is where the long story of 'feminine intuition' and 'feminine wiles' begins."[62]

Miller's call for a "new" psychology of women involved two related yet potentially contradictory analyses that provided cultural feminism with a key aspect of its political vision. First, Miller argued that the division of the world into dominants and subordinates, in this case men and women, weakened society and men. Gender weakened society by the fact that only one group's values shaped its goals, its priorities, and its philosophies. Specifically, Western society valued competition, autonomy, rationality, and power. Miller argued that the division of the world into dominants and subordinates weakened men because society encouraged men to reject any traits associated with the subordinates, or with women. Such traits included emotionality, intimacy, attunement, mutual dependency, and an emphasis on relationships. This left men incomplete, out of balance, and ultimately unable to integrate major aspects of the "human experience." The psychological divisions of traits between the sexes made equality a profoundly disturbing notion for men because it would require men to absorb a set of feelings they had been psychically organized against.[63] Thus, men manage their vulnerability and weaknesses through managing women who symbolized and embodied such traits.

The second, and more pressing goal of Miller's analysis was to offer a new reading of the values associated with women. Specifically, Miller read the attributes of vulnerability, weakness, helplessness, emotions, cooperation, and creativity as strengths and not signs of psychological inferiority and ill-health despite the fact they were developed as a response to women's social subordination. She argued that women's capacity to tolerate feelings of weakness and vulnerability—experiences both men and women had—made them more in touch with reality than men. "By being in this closer connection with this central human condition, by having to defend less and deny less, women are in a position to understand weakness more readily and to work productively with it."[64]

Like Rich, Miller's analysis drew on, and struggled to reconcile, two conceptions of women. Explicitly, Miller argued that society denigrated women's strengths by calling them weaknesses. At the same time, she also argued that traits associated with women were effects of their social marginalization and defined any division between subordinates and dominants as unhealthy. However, her vision of a more equitable society implicitly depended on her assumption that women's fundamental psychological difference from men would persist even when women were no longer classified as subordinate. In a more equal society, Miller reasoned, women would feel good about being different from men. But women would continue to carry a specific set of values and traits, traits that would spring from women's unique psychology and not the experience of social marginalization. Miller's social constructionist analysis of power, then, rested on a form of psychological essentialism. Women's view of the world, simply, would remain unique and different even after social equality had been achieved.

With this, Miller set out an important theme of cultural feminism, that equality between the sexes did not mean that women would model themselves on men or simply adopt the attributes of masculinity. Rather, sexual equality meant that women's unique values and knowledge would be acknowledged and incorporated into the mainstream of society, in institutions, in psychology, and in the domestic sphere. Her view of feminism, then, was not to dismantle the markers of sexual difference but to celebrate them as a unique and significant contributions to human civilization.

The theme of difference in cultural feminism was paradoxical. Many conceived of women's difference as both a sign of society's sexism and masculinism and as the source of female empowerment. Cultural feminists utilized both conceptions of womanhood, despite the contradictions they introduced into their feminism. Such ambiguity proved to be productive for cultural feminism in that it allowed those who believed in women's difference as empowering and those who saw difference as a product of sexism to unify under one banner.

Along with Rich and Miller, psychologist Dorothy Dinnerstein also theorized the paradox of women's difference and partook of a psychologically based form of essentialism. In *The Mermaid and the Minotaur: Sexual Arrangements and Human Malaise* (1976), Dinnerstein examined the origins and implications of gender identities in societies where women mothered and raised young children and, like Rich, emphasized the heritage of desire, rage, and ambivalence between the vulnerable human infant and its caretaker, specifically the mother.[65] Together, Dinnerstein's and Rich's competing views of the preoedipal mother explored the power and the danger of the mother-infant bond for feminism.

Dinnerstein wrote that the dependency of all humans on female mothers produced in both sexes a deep ambivalence about women and femininity. In the transition from infancy to childhood and adulthood, men and women lost bodily and emotional unity with the attuned and responsive ("good") preoedipal mother. The loss of such bodily and psychic intimacy left children with an unconscious desire for the pleasures they once enjoyed. This tale of human misery was one that Freud first articulated, Herbert Marcuse and Norman Brown explored in the 1950s, and Millett, Firestone, and Koedt radicalized as a way out of patriarchal (genitally organized) heterosexuality. Dinnerstein's contribution to this tale was her exploration of the fact that the body to which all infants attached, and to which all humans desired ultimately to return, was female. Unlike Atkinson and Koedt and other early second-wave feminists for whom the clitoris symbolized female emancipation and liberation and for whom the sexual body was the feminist body, Dinnerstein, like Rich, envisioned the female body as primary the mother's body.

Drawing on Melanie Klein and Donald Winnicott, Dinnerstein explained that the current organization of motherhood allowed children to avoid working through the anxieties associated with being small, weak, and powerless.[66] Dinnerstein argued that children carried into adulthood infantile ambivalence about the mother's power both to engulf and gratify the vulnerable and powerless child. Desiring freedom from the mother, yet afraid of their own existential autonomy, children raised by women turned away from the all too-powerful and frightening mother of their infancy. Crucially, children turned to the father (and eventually society) for protection and security since men had no associations with infant care and as a result did not evoke the primitive fantasies of infancy. Unlike earlier radical feminists, Dinnerstein argued that both men and women feared the mother and willingly fled to patriarchy as a way to gain protection from the father. As long as women mothered, concluded Dinnerstein, "woman will inevitably be pressed into the dual role of indispensable quasi-human supporter and deadly quasi-human enemy of the self."[67]

Dinnerstein's analysis of the frightening, encompassing preoedipal mother was a far cry from Rich's account of the mother as a resource for feminism. For Dinnerstein, women's psychic freedom required that they break their identification with the mother's body. Unlike Rich, Dinnerstein viewed women not only as the powerful preoedipal mother but as having been the vulnerable infant. Dinnerstein also continued a radical feminist interest in women's sexual self-determination in her attempt to free women to be fuller sexual agents by enabling them to engage in non-romantic sexual relations if they so choose. Breaking out of the burden of romance, of the need for "magical fusion," would render heterosexual sex more authentic for no longer being a passageway back to preoedipal bliss at the breast. Dinnerstein's work thus marked both a continuity with radical feminism when she envisioned women in relationships with men as well as with children and a break from radical feminism in her emphasis on reproduction as providing the foundation for gender roles.

The significance feminists placed on the preoedipal mother had complicated roots. On the one hand, second-wave feminists, like other countercultural revolutionaries, utilized psychoanalytic theory to imagine a polymorphous body freed from the psychological constraints of gender and genitality. A trajectory in American sexual thought contained within the preoedipal infant authenticity and the source of liberation, both sexually and psychologically. For Marcuse, Brown, Firestone, and Greer, liberation lay in reclaiming an intimate connection with the polymorphous body of the preoedipal infant. Some early radical feminists had imagined sexual liberation as a return to a sexuality that was not organized around genitals but instead around merger, psychological attunment, and intimacy. Others had imagined sexual liberation as a return to bisexuality, or a sexuality that transcended the classification of sex experts.

Cultural feminists' attention to the preoedipal mother continued within this psychoanalytic trajectory of American sexual thought. Cultural feminists also believed that the early bond between mother and infant lay the foundation for gender and sexual identity. However, Rich and Dinnerstein diverged from earlier sexual revolutionaries in that they returned to the preoedipal moment to explore fear and loathing of "woman" and the ambivalence attached to the mother's body. They emphasized how and why men hated women and how patriarchy took root in the alternating feelings of love and hate infants experienced at the mother's breast.

Feminist interpretations of the preoedipal mother culminated in the work of Nancy Chodorow.[68] In *The Reproduction of Mothering* (1978), Chodorow proposed that gender differences were created and re-created in the early mother-infant bond. Mothers encouraged their boys to be independent, to identify with their fathers, and, toward those ends, helped them distinguish themselves as different from them. Sons raised by women, Chodorow wrote, learned to define themselves as "that which is not female—not mother." As a result of mothering by women, negation underwrote masculine gender identity. She theorized that such instability became the psychological source of men's sexism and their "psychological in-vestment in [maintaining] difference."[69] Chodorow explained that women raised by women faced an entirely different set of negotiations with the preoedipal mother. Women tended to confuse themselves with their daughters. They encouraged their daughters to identify with them while not promoting the same degree of separation-individuation as they did in their sons. Thus the mother-raised daughter did not base her identity on negation of the mother, or the feminine, but rather on similarity and con-tinuity with the mother. Women's personalities, as a result, tended to be more oriented to emotions, personal relationships, and intimacy. These skills, Chodorow argued, made women better equipped to parent. As with Dinnerstein, Chodorow believed that if men became more involved with parenting children of both sexes could experience merging with the same-sexed parent and the opposite-sexed parents. The relationality undergird-ing Chodorow's theory of gender echoed trends not only in American psy-chology but within feminism itself. Intimacy and relationships, hallmarks of women's difference, no longer appeared to be the signs of female inferi-ority but of women's strength.

A relatively underexplored aspect of *Reproduction of Mothering*, howev-er, was the conclusion Chodorow reached about the nature of heterosexu-ality for women, a feature of her analysis that pulled it more in line with Rich and other lesbian feminists writing in the 1970s. In her final chapter, Chodorow explained that women's heterosexual orientation was never simply toward men but always formed "in dialogue" with both oedipal (fa-ther) and preoedipal (mother) issues. Here again, Chodorow's attention to mothering cast heterosexuality as a search not for sexual pleasure but for the lost mother.

> Women's heterosexuality is triangular and requires a third person—a child—for its structural and emotional completion. For men, by con-trast, the heterosexual relationship alone recreates the early bond to their mother; a child interrupts it. Men, moreover, do not define them-selves in relationship and have come to suppress relational capacities and repress relational needs. This prepares them to participate in the affect-denying world of alienated work, but not to fulfill women's needs for in-timacy and primary relationships.[70]

Chodorow argued that heterosexuality for women left them emotional-ly unsatisfied. To attain the emotional and psychological intimacy they craved, women must have children with whom they can be affectively connected. Sexuality, subsumed within mothering, could only haunt her account of women's emotional dissatisfaction. Updating Freud's concept of penis envy by filtering it through cultural feminism, Chodorow asserted that women's triangular psychic structure meant that sexual pleasure could not "fill" women. Only children could do that. Like Dinnerstein, Chodorow's analysis of heterosexuality as problematic for women did not lead her to advocate lesbianism or to emphasize women's need to recreate in the present the love and intimacy of the past connection with the mother. But it did securely position her in a longer history of feminist critiques of heterosexuality.

Chodorow's emphasis on the two-parent nuclear family for her theory of gender also situated her in a longer tradition of psychological experts that reproduced racial ideologies. Chodorow's model for the family was not universally applicable to all children or parents, many of whom lived in differently configured homes. Without marking the "family" she created as middle-class and white, Chodorow produced a theory of gender that neglected all but sexual identifications. This elision of race was not unique to Chodorow but characterized much of the cultural feminist theory that became widely popular in the 1980s.

Mothering-by-women theories accounted for gender domination in the institutions of motherhood and the personalities nurtured within it. This focus enabled feminists to call for men to take up more of the psychological work of parenting. Their account differed from that of radical feminists, whose calls for men to share in the work of parenting came out of their analysis of the gendered nature of work. At the same time, mothering-by-women also enabled feminists to value the psychological traits and values culled in mothering, as seen in Rich and Chodorow, who both believed that men could be more like women. In that belief, they articulated the paradoxical meaning of difference that became the hallmark of cultural feminism. Difference was both valuable and problematic—the source of women's empowerment and of their oppression. Cultural feminists productively used the murky status of difference to justify transforming men and society to better fit women. Transforming women who had been stunted by society was no longer the guiding vision of feminism. Rather, reclaiming women's "unique values" from social marginalization was.

The psychology of women's difference did important work for legitimizing and popularizing cultural feminism. By the early 1980s, cultural feminists had become the new experts on women, broadly influencing the study of women in the humanities and social sciences. One of the best known and best-selling authors of cultural feminism was Carol Gilligan, whose research into the applicability of developmental and moral theory for women first appeared in scholarly journals in 1979 and culminated in *In a Different Voice* in 1982. *In a Different Voice* became one of the most widely read texts of cultural feminism. In it, Gilligan combined Rich, Miller, and Chodorow to argue that women's history of difference gave them a distinct moral code.[71] Also echoing themes of lesbian feminism, Gilligan asserted that women's moral code centered around care of others, mutuality, and preserving relationships.[72] Cross-over feminists like Gilligan, who found their audience inside and outside the university, thus interpreted difference as a source of women's empowerment, even as their descriptions of women ran the risk of affirming the same set of differences that had historically restricted women to the private sphere. They also reaffirmed, once again, that whiteness as a racial identity was marked in and through silences.

The psychological essentialism found in the work of white feminists in the late 1970s shared a common set of values that they claimed came from women's unique experiences. The portrait that emerged from the texts of Dinnerstein, Chodorow, Miller, and Gilligan was that of a person the dominant values could not fully represent, whose experience of sexism led her to value relationships over separation, mothering over work, love over sex, mutuality over individuation. While feminists affirmed traditional gender associations between women and children, nurturing, and care of others, their analysis also posed the radical possibility of rethinking values associated with masculinity and public success.

However, while theories of women's difference put pressure on the meaning of masculinity, they tended to simply affirm femininity. As such, they did not call for women to change their "different voice" but rather called for an end to the exclusion of that voice from the concert hall, university, and podium. Theories of women's difference thus defined female empowerment as social affirmation of the values, traits, and relationship styles women had cultivated from their experience of social and political marginalization. Such a vision also defined "male values" as the source of women's oppression.

The cultural feminist emphasis on gender and the power of difference elided the earlier radical feminist concern with sexuality and what, in the mid-1980s, would become the basis for a minority feminist movement, race. White cultural feminists who used gender universalism as the glue for their political vision both abandoned sexuality as a resource for feminism and discarded race as a meaningful difference between women. Cultural feminist theory of women's difference thus focused on the gender traits and knowledge they believed women as a group shared, at the cost of not seeing how other differences mattered.

The psychological essentialism outlined in theories of women's difference and their subordination of sexuality to gender proved enormously useful to the other major branch of cultural feminism, the antipornography movement. For these feminists, theories that reaffirmed women's desire for intimacy, mutuality, and care bolstered their critique of pornography and rape as key elements of an oppressive form of heterosexuality. Antipornography feminists utilized the same set of traits outlined in theories of women's difference toward specifically political ends.

Convergences: Lesbian Feminism, Cultural Feminism, and the Antipornography Movement

At the same time that theories of women's difference gained explanatory value within the disciplines of psychology, sociology, and education, the antipornography movement also came into its own. In the years between 1975 and 1980, feminists turned their attention to sexual violence: rape, the seeming acceptability of sexual assault within marriage and the family, the economic power of pornography, and the near legal sanctioning of violence against women. Feminists active in the antipornography movement used theories of women's difference to outline a distinct view of female sexuality.

The growing antipornography movement incorporated the psychosexual analysis of patriarchy and sexism laid down by Friedan, Millett, and Firestone into new political goals. These goals involved turning to state legislators to protect women from the dangers of living in a male-dominated society.[73] Legal scholar Catherine MacKinnon and activist Andrea Dworkin combined the liberal emphasis of NOW, with its attention to legal and civil rights, with the radical feminist critique of everyday life and sexuality in their approach to the issues of pornography, rape, sexual harassment, and battering.

The new feminist concern with the sexual danger posed by men created a powerful surge of activism. In 1976, the same year Rich and Dinnerstein published their analyses, Women Against Violence Against Women (WAVAW) formed in Los Angles and defaced a Rolling Stones billboard that showed a woman stating, "I'm black and blue from the Rolling Stones and I Love it." Later that year, a conference on violence against women in San Francisco spawned Women Against Violence in Pornography and the Media (WAVPM).[74] These new feminist organizations singled out pornography as a major site in the perpetuation and naturalization of male violence against women. Antipornography feminists argued that male sexual violence constituted a form of political terrorism over women that had the tacit support of male-dominated society. They saw pornography as particularly dangerous because most people understood it as a nonpolitical form of entertainment that had little effect on men's relationships to women. Feminists held the opposite to be true. They argued that pornography encouraged men to mistreat women and served as an implicit threat to keep all women submissive to men and male sexual desires.

However, the legacy of American racism made the politics of the antipornography movement troublesome for feminism. As cultural feminists launched a critique of rape, harrassment, and pornography, black feminists pointed out that rape was a crime that carried not only gendered meanings but layers of racial meaning as well. They refused to separate the history of racist attacks against black men, propped up by false accusions of rape, and the long record of sexual assaults against black women that went unacknowledged. The politics of rape, then, once again played out the problem of difference for cultural feminism.

Susan Brownmiller's *Against Our Will: Men, Women, and Rape* (1975) marked an important theoretical moment in which radical feminist critiques of patriarchy set the terms for a new, highly politicized analysis of sexual violence that came to characterize cultural feminism in the late 1970s and 1980s. Brownmiller, herself an active member in New York Radical Feminists and the 1971 speak out against rape, wrote a tome that was saturated with the founding principles of second-wave feminism: men learn to dominate women through a loosely orchestrated cultural system that indoctrinated them to accept their own superiority and women's inferiority. Such a system taught them to be physical, to dominate, to be aggressive, to disdain vulnerability, and to take what they wanted, whereas the same system taught women to be submissive and passive.

Most centrally, Brownmiller's radical feminism manifested in the connections she made between sex, power, and gender. Like other second-wave feminists, Brownmiller viewed patriarchy as an ahistoric social organization that, at its core, remained unchanged throughout time. As did Friedan, Millet, Firestone, Koedt, and Atkinson, Brownmiller linked so-called sex crimes like rape to the social, economic, and political power of men as a social class.[75] She dismantled the public/private distinction by analyzing what she saw as the sexual coercion of dating and marriage on a continuum with stranger and gang rape. Brownmiller reiterated throughout her analysis that men enacted their domination of women through sex. Rape, then, was not merely an aberrant crime of the sick or violent but an aspect of sexual politics between men and women, be they related by blood, marriage, physical attraction, or abstractly in the social relations between the sexes.

Brownmiller's history of rape marked one important cusp between radical and cultural feminism. Her book, as noted, fit easily into the genre of writing that characterized early foundational texts of the second wave—in its length, its scope, its polemical style, and its sheer ambition. Yet Brownmiller's critique of sexual violence was unlike radical feminist sexual theories in that it did not concern itself with enhancing women's sexual self-determination. Instead, Brownmiller's and other cultural feminist critiques of sexual violence relied on a view of all women as potentially passive victims and of all men as potential aggressors.[76] "Rape," wrote Brownmiller, "is nothing more or less than a conscious process of intimidation by which all men keep all women in a state of fear."[77] The burgeoning feminist politics of rape, in which Brownmiller's book participated and that it came to symbolize, required very specific portraits of men and women's essential natures for its political analysis of sexuality. Whereas the implied subject of radical feminist texts had been an autonomous, sexually confident woman, the woman produced in the cultural feminist analysis of sexual violence was conscious of her victimization under patriarchy, enraged at the flood of sexual imagery that degraded her, and deeply ambivalent about heterosexual desire.

While early radical feminists ad launched scathing critiques of heterosexuality, many refused to cast it off as unworkable and universally bad for women. Rather, feminists like Millett, Koedt, and Greer argued that heterosexuality—as an institution and as a set of sexual practices—must be changed to make it more hospitable to women's sexual pleasure and burgeoning sense of sexual entitlement.[78] Antipornography feminists, in contrast, tended to conflate social power (or, in the case of women, social subordination), heterosexuality, and the unconscious in a way that paralleled theories of women's difference. The antipornography movement interpreted heterosexual intercourse as an expression of men's power over women and the penis as a weapon in the larger effort to keep women submissive to men and male power. These associations joined men's drive for sexuality with their drive for power and control over women. Such an analysis also constructed femininity as an identity created only in relationship to male power and the implicit threat of violence rather than as an identity with resources of its own to mobilize. Antipornography feminists, like feminist psychologists, elided the historic and social differences between whites and minorities, and, in doing so, racialized their theories as white.

Brownmiller's detailed history of rape linked it to the origins of patriarchal civilization. As with many second-wave feminists, Brownmiller argued that the possession and exchange of females by males helped to establish civilization. She added a new feature to this narrative: that men used sexual intercourse specifically to claim ownership over individual females. Without such ownership, women faced "an open season of rape" from other men. Thus, according to Brownmiller, the roots of patriarchal civilization lay buried in the long heritage of males raping females and females' avoidance of sexual terror by exchanging their virginity for protection from individual men.

Brownmiller attempted to show that the experience of rape was a universal one, that women of all races and in all periods of history regularly faced sexual assault from men. She thus situated rape as an enduring feature of patriarchy: she saw it in the interactions between Native Americans and whites, in American slavery between slaves and their owners, between civilians and soldiers in wars from the revolution to Vietnam, and in institutions of the state such as prisons and jails. While Brownmiller argued that these rapes resonated with the overlapping goals of nationalism and masculinity, where men claimed their rights to the property (in this case, women) of another man through rape, she problematically ignored how race figured into the history she constructed. The sisterhood Brownmiller hoped to forge depended on all women identifying soley "as women," and not as members of communities that struggled to survive in a racist society.

Angela Davis argued in her 1981 essay "Rape, Racism and the Myth of the Black Rapist" that white feminists like Brownmiller mobilized racist accounts of the black rapist to support their falsely universal claims about women and rape. As an example of the ways in which Brownmiller's pioneering scholarship utilized racist imagry, Davis noted Brownmiller's analysis of the teenage Emmett Till, who Brownmiller characterized as a near rapist. "While Brownmiller depores the sadistic punishment inflicted on Emmett Till, the Black youth emerges, nonetheless, as a guilty sexist—

almost as guilty as his white racist murderers. After all, she argues, both Till and his murderers were exclusively concerned about their rights of possession over women."[79] Brownmiller's view of Till as predator dangerously if unconsciously replicated the racist jury who acquitted his white murderers. Davis asserted that black women, who were "conspicuously absent from the ranks of the contemporary antirape movement," rejected any such activism that was not actively antiracist as well. Without an analysis of how rape charges were used by whites to frame black men, black women would remain outside the antirape movement. "The struggle against racism must be an ongoing theme of the anti-rape movement, which must not only defend women of color but the many victims of the racist manipulation of the rape charge as well."[80]

Brownmiller's analysis of pornography and rape as expressions of men's hatred of women, along with the work of Susan Griffin, found echoes across the antipornography movement.[81] Particularly resonant was the work of Andrea Dworkin, who became one of the movement's most vocal and important leaders. In 1978, three years after Brownmiller published *Against Our Will*, Dworkin gave a speech at the "Feminist Perspectives on Pornography" conference in San Francisco that marked an intensification of the analysis that men's hatred of women drove them to make, consume, and protect pornography.[82] Dworkin also set forth a view of men that came to characterize much of the antipornography movement in the years between 1975 and 1980.

> We think that we have grasped [men's] hatred [for women] once and for all, seen it in its spectacular cruelty, learned its every secret, got used to it or risen above it or organized against it so as to be protected from its worse excesses. We think we know all there is to know about what men do to women . . . when something happens that simply drives us mad, out of our minds, so that we are again imprisoned like caged animals in the numbing reality of male control, male revenge against no one knows what, male hatred of our very being.[83]

Dworkin's dramatic prose was intended to inspire the large number of women gathered at the conference who afterward left to "take back the night" from San Francisco's pornographers and pimps.

Like Brownmiller, Dworkin viewed the state as a masculine domain where women had no voice and no advocate. She saw it as populated by men who hated women and who used state power to protect their right to dominate women. Two *New York Times* editorials cited her 1978 speech as evidence of feminists "overwrought" and "strident" politics.[84] Dworkin responded with an essay in 1979 titled, "For Men, Freedom of Speech; for Women, Silence Please." Here she explained that both law and pornography, as arenas of male social control over women, "express male contempt for women. . . . Both express enduring male social and sexual values; each attempts to fix male behavior so that the supremacy of the male over the female will be maintained."[85] Rape laws did not function to protect women, she asserted, but rather to uphold a view of women as property by punishing "some men for using women who belong to some other men."[86]

Dworkin, like Brownmiller and Griffin, relied on the conflation of social power, sexuality, and the unconscious for her analysis of men. For her, as well as for others in the antipornography movement, no difference existed between violent pornography and unchecked, or "natural," male sexuality. "The most terrible thing about pornography is that it tells male truths," she wrote. "The most important thing about pornography is that the values in it are the common values of men."[87] With all distinctions between men erased, Dworkin claimed that the sole lesson women learned from pornography was that "erotic pleasure for men is derived from and predicated on the savage destruction of women." For antipornography feminists, pornography served both as a visual record of men's deepest fantasies and as a sacred text of the ancient bonds of patriarchal civilization. "Pornography functions to perpetuate male supremacy and crimes of violence against women because it conditions, trains, educates, and inspires men to despise women, to use women, to hurt women."[88]

During these years, Dworkin joined forces with feminist lawyer Catherine MacKinnon to claim some of the state's power for women. Together, they crafted city ordinances outlawing pornography as a violation of women's civil rights.[89] Their reasoning repeatedly circled back to the educational role pornography played in perpetuating male violence: "Pornography exists," Dworkin wrote, "because men despise women, and men despise women in part because pornography exists."[90] The link between pornography and rape, premised on feminist interpretations of pornographic imagery as identical to men's sexual desires, set the terms for many cultural feminists' wholesale rejection of First Amendment protection for pornography.

Brownmiller soon became a vocal supporter of antipornography measures. Writing after her participation in a 1978 panel on pornography and the First Amendment, Brownmiller's "Let's Put Pornography Back in the

Closet," appeared in *Newsweek* and brought even greater attention to feminists' rejection of pornography.[91] In it, Brownmiller explained that the feminist objection to pornography "is based on our belief that pornography represents hatred of women. . . . We are unalterably opposed to the presentation of the female body being stripped, bound, raped, tortured, mutilated and murdered in the name of commercial entertainment and free speech."[92] Such images, which Brownmiller pointed out as standard pornographic fare, "have nothing to do with the hallowed right of political dissent. They have everything to do with the creation of a cultural climate in which a rapist feels he is merely giving into a normal urge and a woman is encouraged to believe that sexual masochism is healthy, liberated fun."[93] Drawing on earlier feminist critiques of the sexual revolution, Brownmiller added a different emphasis: the sexual climate in which women found themselves was saturated with hostile and violent messages that oppressed women.

In this framework, many cultural feminists encoded female heterosexuality as an identity a woman could never freely choose and, if embraced, potentially resonated with her internalized self-hatred.[94] By rendering pornography the authentic sexual unconsciousness of men, antipornography feminists defined female sexuality as its mirror opposite. Cultural feminists implicitly drew on a view of female sexuality that prioritized intimacy over orgasm, sensuality over genitality, psychological bonding over sexual coupling, egalitarianism and mutuality over power and domination. The heritage of radical feminists' rejection of sexuality as a male construct, as with Atkinson and Densmore, found political currency in this new moment of cultural feminist activism.

One of the clearest articulations of how ideas about female sexuality underwrote the antipornography movement came from Adrienne Rich, whose 1980 "Compulsory Heterosexuality and Lesbian Existence" reread theories of women's difference in light of her involvement with the antipornography movement.[95] In this essay, Rich wove together the dominant elements of cultural feminism: lesbian separatism, theories of women's psychological difference, and the antipornography movement. Rich's piece expressed just how tightly woven were the strands of cultural feminism. Her organizing rubric lay in what she called "compulsory heterosexuality." Writing in the feminist journal *Signs* four years after the publication of *Of Woman Born*, Rich offered a stark portrait of sexual difference between men and women. A view of female sexuality as relational, nurturing, sensual, and not genitally oriented and of male sexuality as an aggressive biological drive that relentlessly sought release underwrote her analysis.

Rich's account of heterosexuality drew from and reworked feminists' psychological analyses of gender. While complaining that many psychologists ignored the presence of lesbians, Rich nevertheless shared their view that women valued intimacy, prioritized relationships, offered necessary emotional support, and did not require power over others as their basis for action in the world. From Dinnerstein and Chodorow, Rich took the object relations analysis of women's primary connection to the mother as an enduring feature of their psychological makeup. These contributed to Rich's formulation that women shared a rich and unique bond with each other.

Yet, drawing from her involvement with the antipornography movement, Rich argued that mothering-by-women theories separated analyses of social power from gender arrangements and in so doing depoliticized what she saw as the underpinnings of male power over women. Rich asserted that neither Dinnerstein nor Chodorow adequately accounted for the role of coercion, fear, and sense of powerlessness that she and others in the antipornography movement claimed drove most women to endure heterosexuality as an enforced identity. Rich took the cultural feminist critique of men to the next logical step when she forcefully pointed out that such theories unconsciously assumed heterosexuality as essential to women. "If women are the earliest sources of emotional caring and physical nurture for both female and male children . . . why in fact [would] women . . . ever redirect that search" away from women, she asked. They did so, Rich proposed, not because they were biologically driven to be heterosexual but because they were taught to be. Rich asked why, if heterosexuality was biological and inevitable, "such violent strictures [found in male dominated societies] should be found necessary to enforce women's total emotional, erotic loyalty and subservience to men."[96]

Rich's analysis of pornography wove together her view of patriarchy and compulsory heterosexuality as forms of sexual and psychic domination of women. She detailed pornography to play an important role in creating the awareness of male privilege and power in both men and women. Confusing sexuality and violence, Rich argued that pornography "does not simply create a climate in which sex and violence are interchangeable; it widens the range of behavior considered acceptable from men in heterosexual intercourse—behavior which strips women of their autonomy, dignity, and sexual potential, including the potential of loving and being loved by women in mutuality and integrity."[97]

Rich's critique of heterosexuality, informed both by theories of women's difference and the antipornography movement, led her to return to the radical feminist impulse to reimagine sexual categorization for women. Working from object relations theory as found in Chodorow as well as the concept of women identification from lesbian separatism, Rich argued that all women existed on a lesbian continuum, whether or not they identified themselves as lesbian or consciously desired another woman. By emphasizing relationships between women and by minimizing sexual object choice, she, like others before her, challenged the line demarcating heterosexuality and homosexuality, yet, unlike radical feminists such as Koedt and Millet, Rich located relationships of sisterhood, friendship, and sexuality in the primary, mother-based bond between women. This primary bond between women instilled the potential for lesbianism in all women, not an open-ended transcendent sexuality that had, in 1970, inspired radical feminists.

In one of the most explicit cultural feminist descriptions of authentic female sexuality, Rich returned to a view of a powerful, transcendent female body capable of unifying love and pleasure. Echoing Lorde, Rich described female sexuality as "that which is unconfined to any single part of the body or solely to the body itself, as an energy not only diffuse but . . . omnipresent in the sharing of joy, whether physical, emotional, psychic and in the sharing of work."[98] Women's "anti-phallic sexuality," she wrote, had historically and in the present been a form of resistance against sexual oppression and "a form of subversion of male power."[99] Like radical feminists who questioned male standards of sex, Rich minimized the orgasm, emphasized emotional and psychological intimacy, and conceived of female sexuality as unrestricted to any narrow understanding of sexual identity.

As did many second-wave feminists, Rich proposed female sexuality had the power to unify women across history and sexual orientation. Rich did not organize her view of female sexuality around the clitoris or around sexual self-definition. At the same time, the female body, in fact, rarely figured into Rich's understanding of sexuality or desire. Instead, Rich essentialized lesbianism, or women's bonds to each other, as the "true" or "original" desire that patriarchy and compulsory heterosexuality had obscured or pathologized. Her vision of a liberated woman as "lesbian" also powerfully elided heterosexuality as a viable feminist sexual choice. By erasing freely chosen heterosexuality, Rich's vision implicitly limited the transcendent potential of female sexuality to one true feminist choice: nonviolent, nonhierarchical, relational sex with women.

Rich's view of women as requiring love, intimacy, and mutuality and of men as requiring power over women, a power that they institutionalized through rape, pornography, and compulsory heterosexuality, brought cultural feminist theories of women's values fully in line with the antipornography movement. Together cultural feminist theory and the antipornograhy movement left the competing worldviews of black and white women unexplored. The universal category of "woman" in cultural feminism thus relied upon psychologically essentialist readings of gender that attempted to elide racial differences. A growing minority feminist movement offered important challenges to the gender universalism of cultural feminism by calling for white feminists to be antisexist and antiracist simultaneously. Doing so would push feminists to see women's identities as developing across a number of experiences beside sexual oppression. Such a strategy gained momentum in the 1980s.

CONCLUSION

Negotiating Legacies in the Feminist Sex Wars, 1982

*I*n 1982, two years after Adrienne Rich introduced the idea of a "lesbian continuum" and the same year Carol Gilligan published *In a Different Voice*, feminists gathered at Barnard College for a conference entitled "Towards a Politics of Sexuality." The conference planners intended it as a forum in which feminists could return to what many viewed as the movement's roots: an analysis of sexuality that saw pleasure as a resource for female empowerment. A differently politicized group of feminists began protesting both the methods and the message of the antipornography movement. In 1979 and 1980, Ellen Willis and Deirdre English published anti-antipornography pieces in the *Village Voice* and *Mother Jones*, respectively. Sex radicals and lesbian S/M groups also criticized cultural feminism. They rejected the view of female sexuality underwriting both the antipornography movement and cultural feminism. Samois, a San Francisco collective of sex radicals, published fictional accounts and writings about lesbian S/M in *What Color Is Your Handkerchief* (1979) and *Coming* *to Power* (1981); both caused heated debate in lesbian communities when many women's bookstores refused to carry them.[1]

The 1982 Barnard conference dramatically captured the historic changes that had taken place in feminism since the early days of the movement. Anne Koedt, Kate Millett, and Germaine Greer had argued in 1970 that sexual pleasure mattered to women's sense of empowerment. They did so by emphasizing the political importance of women's sexual self-determination. Sexual freedom and women's liberation were inseparable values. By the late 1970s, cultural feminist theory, lesbian feminism, and the antipornography movement converged to define women's sexual freedom as the freedom from violent male sexuality. Male sexual standards, most graphically expressed in pornography, they argued, poisoned women's subjective experience of sexuality. Feminist liberation involved cleansing the residue of patriarchal sexuality from women's psychology, from their fantasies and desires, and significantly, from their sexual practices.

By the time the Barnard conference took place in 1982, the trajectory from radical to cultural feminism and from sexual liberation to sexual safety was itself under fire. That is, the conference planners, foremost among them Carole Vance, and participants, including Cherríe Moraga, Joan Nestle, and Gayle Rubin, deliberately sought to disrupt the evolution of radical feminist sexual theory into cultural feminist antipornography rhetoric. They intended to return the centrality of sexual pleasure to feminism and to feminist theory. "The intent of the conference planners," Vance described, "was not to weaken the critique of [sexual] danger. Rather, we wished to expand the analysis of pleasure."[2] Vance and others argued that while the feminist analysis of sexual danger constituted an important critique of male power and patriarchy, it could not stand in for feminist sexual theory. It was too oriented to both male sexuality and to seeing women solely as its victims. Returning to a theme of early radical feminism, Vance proposed that sexuality mattered to women's sense of empowerment. "It is not enough to move women away from danger and oppression; it is necessary to move toward something: toward pleasure, agency, and self-definition. Feminism must increase women's pleasure and joy, not just decrease our misery."[3]

Equally historic, the Barnard conference marked the effectiveness of minority feminists' challenge to the universalism that had long plagued the second wave. Unlike early radical feminists whose radicalism came from asserting "woman" as a legitimate and political identity in a moment when the political subject was unmarked by gender, the Barnard conference participants had been through a difficult and painful critique of racism and classism within feminism. They embodied the accomplishment of minority feminists who had marked the unspecified and universal "woman" as white and middle class. Class and race self-consciously marked Barnard participants, and, rather than eliding those differences, they embraced and elaborated them. Further, they asserted that those differences, forged in race and class specificity, were erotic. That is, differences in social location shaped the fantasies and desires of women, and these differences in erotic subjectivities strengthened women's sense of self-empowerment and, ultimately, feminism.

As the papers and workshops of the Barnard conference demonstrated, the feminist commitment to women's sexual self-determination was an ongoing project of expansion, debate, and revision. Feminism in the 1982 was not the same as feminism in 1975 or 1969. Yet, throughout, feminism remained intertwined with the idea of sexual liberation. Through all these periods of second-wave feminism, the commitment to women's sexual freedom propelled feminist theory and activism. Early radical feminism of 1969 took as its backdrop the sexism of the sexual revolution and the student protest movements. Cultural feminism and the antipornography movement in the 1970s resented the increased profits and presence of pornography. The Barnard conference took place against the backdrop of the New Right's assault on sexual minorities, abortion rights, feminism, and any threats against the nuclear family. The debate within feminism and among differently located feminists likewise propelled the evolution of feminist sexual theory. Debates between radical feminists like Kate Millett and Germaine Greer, between cultural feminists like Mary Daly and Audre Lorde, and now between antipornography feminists like Andrea Dworkin and sex radicals such as Gayle Rubin spoke to the enduring part conflict played in the making of feminist theory.

The Barnard Conference: Restoring Sexual Pleasure as Feminist

Cultural feminist theories of women's enduring difference from men, their innate capacity for nurturing, relationships and nongenital sexuality informed new standards of feminist sexual behavior. Within feminist circles, and particularly in lesbian feminist circles, discussions of sexual behavior became explicit, with some behaviors deemed feminist and others "male-identified," patriarchal, and misogynist. Such definitions established a tight weave between psychological essentialism, the antipornography movement, and ideas about proper feminist sexual practice. Construing sex as something men imposed on women, antipornography feminists tended to view sexual desire as alien to women and to conflate heterosexual sex and rape.[4] Such associations between sexuality and misogyny discredited a number of sexual activities, foremost vaginal penetration of any kind. Both lesbian and straight cultural feminists considered any role-playing, in dress or in sex, suspect. Makeup, high heels, dresses, stockings, along with ties, suspenders, and leather boots were seen as "rip-offs" of heterosexuality and rejected for their so-called tacit support of patriarchal power relationships. In terms of behavior, they explained that any use of power during sex was male-identified and thus a form of patriarchal oppression. Such activities, they insisted, stood in direct conflict with the feminist model of sexual egalitarianism.

Cultural feminists, including lesbian separatists, lesbian feminists, and antipornography feminists, believed that sex should be consistent with feminist ethics. Those active in the antipornography movement acknowledged that images of domination, control, and violence had become part of everyone's psychological makeup and so shaped both men and women's sexual fantasies and desires. Yet, they believed that feminists should permit themselves only those sexual fantasies that did not objectify or degrade other women. All fantasies and desires must be scrutinized for misogyny, the self-hatred women learned to turn on themselves and other women in a woman-hating society.[5] For sex to be consistent with feminism, it had to reflect women's values by prioritizing intimacy, nongenital touching, and emotional nurturing. For many feminists, freeing women from genital sexuality was liberation; it offered a wider variety of sexual practices to women. As one feminist articulated it in 1975, "If we are to learn our own sexual natures we have to get rid of the male-model of penetration and orgasm as the culmination of love-making. . . . Holding hands is lovemaking. Touching lips is lovemaking. Rubbing breasts is lovemaking. Locking souls with women by looking deep in their eyes is love-making."[6]

Even the relatively conservative NOW joined in the cultural feminist valuing of some sex as more feminist than others. The 1980 NOW resolution both reaffirmed the liberal feminist support of lesbian rights and, not unexpectedly, condemned pornography, public sex, and sadomasochism. The resolution, which was an important and long coming advance from its earlier homophobic position, stated that "marginal" sexual practices like S/M "have mistakenly been correlated with Lesbian/Gay rights by some gay organizations."[7] NOW defined such issues as exploitation and violence and condemned them on the grounds that they violated feminist principles.[8]

A group of straight and lesbian feminists, calling themselves sex radicals, rejected the new feminist code of sexual behavior. They argued that women would never be truly free until they could be empowered to explore their own sexuality in whatever way they wished. Even before the conference in 1981, Gayle Rubin argued, "By conflating lesbianism (as sexual experience) with feminism (a political philosophy), the ability to justify lesbianism on grounds other than feminism dropped out of the discourse."[9] Rubin argued that sexual desire for other women produced lesbianism, not emotional identification or the psychological need for intimacy. Sex radicals promoted the use of lesbian pornography, sex toys like dildos, S/M costumes, and erotica. Others reclaimed butch/femme roles as a uniquely lesbian form of sexual identity that had little to do with male-dominated heterosexuality. Feminist sex radicals made S/M pornography, published sex manuals, set up businesses that featured a range of sex toys, dildos, and leather outfits. Others promoted more casual sex between lesbians and a handful opened lesbian strip bars in San Francisco.[10]

In response to what they considered the antisex censorship of cultural feminism, lesbian sex radicals publicly debated the meaning of sexual freedom in feminism.[11] They criticized cultural feminists for reenforcing Victorian ideas about female innocence and male sexual aggression, ideals feminists had battled against for decades. These feminists actively reclaimed sexual freedom as instrumental to women's empowerment and thus to feminism. Sex radicals explained that in rigidly defining what constituted feminist sexual behavior cultural feminists had begun to police other women's sexuality. That, they claimed, was much worse for feminism than role-playing.

Given the growing rancor between feminists over the volatile issue of sexuality, the Barnard conference committee's choice of focus, "Towards a Politics of Sexuality," seemed timely and important. Yet, at its inception, the conference faced significant hostility. Almost immediately, the planning committee found itself under assault from antipornography groups who were excluded. In the week leading up to the meeting, members of antipornography groups made telephone calls to New York–area feminists and to Barnard College denouncing the conference organizers for inviting only proponents of "antifeminist" sexuality to participate.[12] Conference organizers justified their decision by explaining that cultural feminists had already dominated much of the debate over sexuality in feminism. Particularly in the wake of NOW's 1980 resolution, they hoped the conference could offer a diversity of views about female sexuality. As the conference's concept paper explained, recent attacks on feminism and sexual freedom by conservatives demanded that feminists not "abandon our radical insights into sexual theory and practice" but rather "deepen and expand them, so that more women are encouraged to identify and act in their sexual self interest."[13]

The conference soon appeared to be a battleground between antipornography feminists, who relied solely on an analysis of sexual danger and sex radicals, and anticensorship feminists, who sought to liberate sexuality or free women to be full self-defining, sexual agents. On April 24, the day of the conference, a line of antipornography feminists formed outside Barnard, from such groups as Women Against Pornography, Women Against Violence Against Women, and New York Radical Feminists. Protesters donned T-shirts with "For a Feminist Sexuality" on front and "Against S/M" on back and passed out leaflets complaining of their exclusion from the conference. Signed by the "Coalition of Women for a Feminist Sexuality and Against Sadomasochism," the leaflet accused conference organizers of inviting speakers who supported "patriarchal" sexuality such as sadomasochism and pedophilia.

> Represented at the conference are organizations that support and produce pornography, that promote sex roles and sadomasochism. . . . Excluded . . . are feminists who have developed the feminist analysis of sexual violence, who have organized a mass movement against pornography . . . who believe that sadomasochism is reactionary, patriarchal sexuality and who have worked to end the sexual abuse of children.[14]

The coalition criticized the conference organizers for "throw[ing] their support to the very sexual institutions and values that oppress all women."[15] The leaflet singled out individuals for specific criticism such as Gayle Rubin for her support of S/M and groups such as No More Nice Girls, which the coalition accused of supporting pornography and child abuse.[16] Before every session, the coalition passed out critical leaflets. Comprised of sessions on sexual practice, S/M, butch/femme roles, pornography, children's sexuality, and sexual therapies, the conference and its protesters generated much press attention.[17] By the end of the conference, when the Lesbian Sex Mafia held a "Speakout on Politically Incorrect

Sex," no one could deny that the conference marked a major breakdown of feminist unity.[18]

With such animosity surrounding the conference, those who actually attended and participated witnessed a new blend of feminist sexual radicalism that explored the overlap of different identifications negotiated by women. Foremost, participants exposed and theorized differences between women rather than suppressing them in an effort to name patriarchal power and ensure female solidarity. Dreams of female solidarity, they argued, produced silences between feminists that undermined coalitions that could exist between differently situated women. Strategically adopting the rhetoric of safety and empowerment used by the antipornography movement, feminist sex radicals transformed the notion of silence to critique what they saw as a restrictively narrow feminism.

Hortense Spillers explored the discursive silences African American women negotiated both within feminism and in American sexual thought more broadly. In "Interstices: A Small Drama of Words," she argued that "black women are the beached whales of the sexual universe, unvoiced, misseen, not doing, awaiting their verb. Their sexual experiences are depicted, but not often by them."[19] This silence was forged primarily through a pervasive racism that rendered black women's sexuality literally unspeakable. She proposed that the silence around black female sexuality came from the symbolic freight black women carried. Within American racial logic, Spillers argued, African American women constituted "the principle point of passage" between the human and the nonhuman world, culture and debased nature. "Her issue became the focus of a cunning difference—visually, psychologically, ontologically—as the route by which the dominant male decided the distinction between humanity and 'other.' . . . In other words, the black person mirrored for the society around her and him what a human being was not."[20]

According to Spillers, feminism shared with dominant white culture the silencing of African American women. She wrote, "Black American women in the public/critical discourse of feminist thought have no acknowledged sexuality because they enter the historical stage from quite another angle of entrance from that of Anglo-American women."[21] Reviewing the trajectory of feminist sexual theory from Shulamith Firestone and Kate Millett to Susan Brownmiller, Dorothy Dinnerstein, Nancy Chodorow, and Mary Daly, Spillers noted that these works replicated the racism they purported to move beyond. "As we read these texts . . . the living conditions out of which their search comes and the shape it takes speak monolithically across the empire of women . . . [and] reminds me of the period of symbolic oppression we believe we're leaving."[22] Spillers's call for white women to recognize their texts as one "angle of vision," not *the* angle of vision, denied sexuality was the sole mode of identification feminism must address. It also echoed a common theme set out first by Beal and La Rue in 1970 and developed by Lorde, Walker, and Davis in the late 1970s. Spillers concluded by reframing the goal of feminist sex theory. "As I see it, the goal is not an articulation of sexuality so much as it is a global restoration and dispersal of power. In such an act of restoration, sexuality is rendered one of several active predicates. So much depends on it."[23]

Dorothy Allison, a member of the group Lesbian Sex Mafia, also adopted and transformed the language of the antipornography movement in her workshop paper "Public Silence, Private Terror."[24] Self-consciously invoking the concept of "safety" and "silence," Allison articulated a different level of danger women faced within feminists' communities—the danger of speaking openly about the many variations of desire women feel. Like Spillers, Allison articulated the repression of difference within feminism.

> Even within the community of my friends and lovers, I have never felt safe. I have never been safe and that is only partly because everyone else is as fearful as I am. None of us is safe, because we have never made each other safe. . . . We have addressed violence and exploitation and heterosexual assumption without establishing first the understanding that for each of us desire is unique and necessary and simply terrifying.[25]

Citing *This Bridge Called My Back*, Allison argued that such models for thinking frankly about racial difference challenged her to acknowledge other differences feminism was not addressing. "Just as I was terrified of addressing my own racism, so too other women were afraid of stepping into the deep and messy waters of class and sexual desire."[26] Such "private terror" when speaking honestly about sexual desire enforced a profound silence within feminism. For Allison and others, speaking about women's desires was itself radical. Allison described the joy and relief women discovered at meetings of the Lesbian Sex Mafia. "Every forbidden thought that was spoken enriched us. Every terrible desire that we shared suddenly assumed human dimensions, and our meetings were full of warmth and laughter."[27]

Feminists inside the Barnard conference both reasserted and complicated what had been a starting point for feminists in the early 1970s. Radical feminists in the early years of the movement insisted on the political significance of women's sexual self-determination. For feminists at Barnard, twelve years later, the goal of sexual self-determination had gone through at least two waves of conflict between lesbian and straight women and a powerful critique of racist universalism. Such conflict between competing groups of feminists and competing analyses under the banner "feminist" had produced a refashioning of the radical feminist goal of women's sexual self-determination.

Feminists at Barnard offered a new model for understanding the politics of sexual desire. Across the conference, participants agreed that the nature of sexual desire was such that it could not be standardized or policed. No one group—be they cultural feminists, white feminists, or lesbian feminists—could define sexual pleasure and sexual identity for any other group of women. As psychoanalyst and anthropologist Muriel Dimen argued,

> The discovery/creation of sexual pleasure is very much an individual journey. . . . No matter how carefully charted by conscious intentionality, the journey's course is determined finally by a complex mix of conscious and unconscious, rational and irrational currents that represents a swirling together of personal desire and cultural force.[28]

Rather than seeking out a common experience of sexual oppression or of sexual pleasure as a base for feminism, feminists at Barnard reaffirmed sexual self-determination as the only defensible feminist sexual politic.

This model of sexual desire as complex and radically individual emerged out of what Barnard participants saw as narrow feminist standards that sought to govern notions of authentic female desires and properly feminist sexual practices. Anthropologist Esther Newton and journalist Shirley Walton described what the feminist dream of sexual freedom had become under cultural feminism:

> Any form of fetishism or sado-masochism is a male-defined no-no, as is any sex with too much emphasis on orgasm. Sexual interaction should not be genitally focused. More specifically, lesbians should not engage in any form of "hetero" sex. This includes both penetrations, either by fingers or dildoes, and tribadism (rubbing the cunt against the partner's body) which can resemble the heterosexual missionary position. If heterosexual women are not actually urged to refrain from penetration, the insistence that the clitoris is the only center of female sexual response

implies that penetration is a superfluous "male trip." Certainly all acts which could be interpreted as submissive should be eliminated, such as cock-sucking.[29]

Against a view of feminism that dictated sexual practice, feminists like Dimen, Newton, and Walten called for a more complicated view of sexual desire as unruly and utterly individual. In Dimen's view, sexuality retained a kernel of sisterhood when feminists stop policing each other. "Desire," she explained, "always rushes beyond its psychocultural channels. It is what moves us, in our personal uniqueness, towards both intimacy and collectively [*sic*], and back to self, and again towards society." For Dimen and others, "Feminism . . . must be a struggle for sexual emancipation. We must make sure that we desire all we can so that we will be able to create, and therefore get, all we desire."[30]

Joan Nestle, cofounder of the Lesbian Herstory Archives, also addressed the problematic politics of defining standards of feminist sexual desire. She described her rejection of what Barnard participants defined as "politically correct" sex as continuing the true spirit of radical feminism. "One of the most deeply held opinions in feminism is that women should be autonomous and self-directed in defining their sexual desire," Nestle wrote. "Yet when a woman says, 'This is my desire,' feminists rush in to say, 'No, no it is the prick in your head; no women should desire that act.' "[31] Nestle, like Allison, Dimen, and Spillers, argued that open discussions of sexuality by feminists had been prematurely and problematically terminated. "If we close down exploration, we will be forcing some women once again to live their sexual lives in a land of shame and guilt; only this time they will be haunted by the realization that it was not the patriarchal code they have failed, but the creed of their own sisters who said they came in love."[32] Nestle based her particular vantage point on her experience of lesbian butch/femme couples of the 1950s and 1960s. Nestle and other self-identified butch and femme lesbians claimed to have lived long enough to see the "enemy" turn from homophobic gay bashers and Stonewall-era police to lesbian feminists of the seventies.[33] Lesbian feminists had dismissed butch/femme couples as "cheap rip-offs" of heterosexuals and thus not truly woman-identified.[34] As Nestle explained,

> A femme is often seen as a lesbian acting like a straight woman who is not a feminist—a terrible misreading of self-presentation which turns a language of liberated desire into the silence of collaboration. An erotic

conversation between two women is completely unheard, not by men this time but by other women, in the name of lesbian feminism.[35]

The Barnard conference, then, recycled a central insight of radical feminists: the value of women's sexual self-determination as the foundation for feminist politics. They rightly reintroduced insights about pleasure to a moment that had been defined primarily through the dangers posed to women by unregulated male sexuality. These feminists abandoned key elements of the universal categories of men and women, categories that provided cultural feminism with its explanatory power. In their place, they opted for a more complicated view of competing identities within women. Informed by identity politics on the one hand and postmodern theories of subjectivity on the other, Barnard feminists used sexual self-determination as a value that was both specific and universal. The particular and the principle could be reconciled if feminists stopped defining standards of authentic sexuality. This was the new model offered for feminism in the future: coalition based on strategic identifications.

At the same time, feminist sex radicals had to compete with cultural feminists over the legacies of radical feminism. Cultural feminists promoting theories of women's difference from men rightly claimed radical feminism as their own. The dream of, first, radical feminism and, then, cultural feminism was that the category "woman" would be enough to propel feminism into the future. Politicizing women as a category, valuing women's experiences as the basis for theory, and privileging women's connections to other women did historic work for the second wave. In many ways, the culmination of gender universalism with singer-songwriter Helen Ready's feminist ballad "I Am Woman, Hear Me Roar," or in the form of Carol Gilligan's "different voice," constituted feminism's high-water mark of popularity in mainstream American life.

But the radical challenge of gender universalism, which reached its pinnacle in the mid-1970s, imploded along the fault lines of its own contradictions. The value of organizing around one's own oppression built the possibility of radical pluralism into the foundations of feminism, even as the project of feminism was about the importance of women as a unified social identity. As the NOW conference hinted at in 1974 and the Barnard conference in 1982 graphically displayed, even sisters joined in feminism desired revolutions that offended, challenged, and threatened each other. Likewise, as radical feminists of color in the 1980s argued, gender universalism simply could not stand up to the full force of racial and class difference. The revolution they desired involved a more profound assault on racial hierarchies than the promises of sisterhood could deliver.

The blending of sexual freedom, broadly defined, and women's liberation was the characteristic feature of second-wave feminism. Unlike first- and third-wave feminists, second-wave feminists saw the politics of private life as the source of women's oppression. For second-wave feminists, the relationships between men and women constituted the very infrastructure upon which other oppressions relied. Without patriarchy, rooted in the unconscious and enacted sexually, all hierarchies of power were incomplete. Without a feminist theory of patriarchy, defined psychologically and focused on sexuality, women could never be free. Second-wave feminists of all stripes—radical and cultural—argued that the psychology of male domination had sunk its roots deep into women's sense of their sexuality. Such entanglement eradicated traditional accounts of privacy or individuality. It rendered what was "private" social and political. Extricating women's desires from the tangled pathology of male domination became, for the second wave, the very definition of liberation.

The fictional woman of Freudian nightmares who desired more than her vaginal destiny had shed the pathologizing labels experts bequeathed to her. She had also cast off the burdens to be sexually expressive in the ways her liberated boyfriends wanted. Standing on the ground of her own desires, the woman who animated feminist visions of freedom determined her own destiny. For a moment in the late 1960s and the early 1970s, radical feminists' account of the importance of women's sexual self-definition fueled some of the movement's central and enduring insights: that patriarchal power relationships originated in men and women's psychology, that "woman" was as much a political classification as a personal identification, and that heterosexuality was unnaturally constituted to uphold male power over women. Thanks to women claiming the mantle of "expert" from the experts, a mainstream version of feminism came into being that popularly linked women's liberation to their sexual liberation.

Yet the animating vision of womanhood generated in and through key texts of radical and cultural feminist sex theory was flawed in many ways, limited by the terms of American sexual thought of which it formed a part. Radical and cultural feminists relied on psychology, broadly defined, for its theory of women's oppression. Many second-wave feminists unquestionably absorbed psychoanalytic assumptions like the unconscious and the repression of polymorphous authenticity as well as its privileging of theory. Ironically, the vision of womanhood underwriting second-wave feminism was also fragmented by feminists' attempts to give sexuality its rightful place in the political understanding of women. Second-wave feminists, like the Freudians and sexologists whose work they read and refashioned, saw sexuality as the most salient component of women's identity. This assumption, above all, paradoxically gave second-wave feminism much of its radicalism and set the terms for its undoing. The fictional white woman who unconsciously dominated second-wave feminist sex theory could no longer stand in unproblematically for the "feminist," no matter how much she desired revolution.

INTRODUCTION: SEX AND THE FEMINIST, 1970

1. *Personal Politics: The Roots of Women's Liberation in the Civil Rights Movement and the New Left* (New York: Vintage, 1979); Alice Echols, *Daring to Be Bad: Radical Feminism in America, 1967–1975* (Minneapolis: University of Minnesota Press, 1989); Lauri Umansky, *Motherhood Reconceived: Feminism and the Legacies of the Sixties* (New York: New York University Press, 1996); Barbara Ryan, *Feminism and the Women's Movement: Dynamics of Change in Social Movement Ideology and Activism* (New York: Routledge, 1992); Flora Davis, *Moving the Mountain: The Women's Movement in America Since the 1960s* (New York: Simon and Schuster, 1991); Winifred Wandersee, *On the Move: American Women in the 1970s* (Boston: Twyane, 1988); Lillian Faderman, *Odd Girls and Twilight Lovers: A History of Lesbian Life in Twentieth-Century America* (New York: Penguin, 1991); Arlene Stein, *Sex and Sensibility: Stories of a Lesbian Generation* (Berkeley: University of California Press, 1997); Lisa Marie Hogeland, *Feminism and Its Fictions: The Consciousness-Raising Novel and the Women's Liberation Movement* (Philadelphia: Uni-

versity of Pennsylvania Press, 1998); Susan Douglas, *Where the Girls Are: Growing Up Female with the Mass Media* (New York: Times Books, 1994).

2. Cherríe Moraga and Gloria Anzaldúa, *This Bridge Called My Back: Writings by Radical Women of Color* (New York: Kitchen Table, 1981); Gloria Hull, Patricia Bell Scott, and Barbara Smith, eds., *All the Men Are Black, All the Women Are White, But Some of Us Are Brave: Black Women's Studies* (New York: Feminist, 1982); Asian Women United of California, *Making Waves: An Anthology of Writings by and About Asian American Women* (New York: Beacon, 1989).

3. Barbara Findlen, *Listen Up: Voices from the Next Feminist Generation* (Seattle: Seal, 1995); Rebecca Walker, *To Be Real: Telling the Truth and Changing the Face of Feminism* (New York: Anchor, 1995); Leslie Heywood and Jennifer Drake, eds., *Third-Wave Agenda: Being Feminist, Doing Feminism* (Minneapolis: University of Minnesota Press, 1997).

4. Leslie Heywood and Jennifer Drake, "Introduction," *Third-Wave Agenda*, 8.

5. Douglas, *Where the Girls Are*, 163–192.

6. The Boston Women's Health Book Collective, *Our Bodies, Our Selves* (New York: Simon and Schuster, 1971); Kate Millett, *Sexual Politics* (New York: Simon and Schuster, 1970); Robin Morgan, ed., *Sisterhood Is Powerful* (New York: Vintage, 1970); Shulamith Firestone, *The Dialectic of Sex* (New York: Bantam, 1970); Germaine Greer, *The Female Eunuch* (New York: Bantam, 1970).

7. Erica Jong, *Fear of Flying* (New York: Signet, 1973); Rita Mae Brown, *Rubyfruit Jungle* (New York: Bantam, 1973); Barbara Raskin, *Loose Ends* (New York: St. Martin Press, 1973); Alix Kates Schulman, *Memoirs of an Ex-Prom Queen* (New York: Knopf, 1972); Margaret Atwood, *Surfacing* (New York: Popular Library, 1972); Lisa Alther, *Kinflicks* (New York: Signet, 1975); Sara Davidson, *Loose Change* (Garden City, N.J.: Doubleday, 1977); Marilyn French, *The Woman's Room* (New York: Summit, 1977); Alix Kates Shulman, *Burning Questions* (New York: Knopf, 1978); Marge Piercy, *Vida* (New York: Fawcett, 1979).

8. Judith Butler, *Gender Trouble: Feminism and the Subversion of Identity* (New York: Routledge, 1990), 7.

1. MODERN WOMEN AND MODERN MARRIAGE: REINVENTING FEMALE HETEROSEXUALITY

1. Thomas Laqueur, *Making Sex: Body and Gender from the Greeks to Freud* (Cambridge: Harvard University Press, 1990), 11.

2. For histories of psychoanalysis, psychology, and psychiatry see Mari Jo Buhle, *Feminism and Its Discontents: A Century of Struggle with Psychoanalysis* (Cambridge: Harvard University Press, 1998); Nathan G. Hale Jr., *The Rise and Crisis of Psychoanalysis in the United States, 1917–1985* (New York: Oxford University Press, 1995); Ellen Herman, *The Romance of American Psychology: Political Culture in the Age of Experts* (Berkeley: University of California Press, 1995); and

Elizabeth Lundeck, *The Psychiatric Persuasion: Knowledge, Gender, and Power in Modern America* (Princeton: Princeton University Press, 1994).

3. Kevin White, *The First Sexual Revolution: The Emergence of Male Heterosexuality in Modern America* (New York: New York University Press, 1993).

4. Nancy Cott, *The Grounding of Modern Feminism* (New Haven: Yale University Press, 1987), 161.

5. John D'Emilio and Estelle Freedman, *Intimate Matters: A History of Sexuality in America* (New York: Free Press, 1988), 229–235.

6. Estelle Freedman, "Separatism as Strategy: Female Institution Building and American Feminism," in Kathryn Kish Sklar and Thomas Dublin, eds., *Women and Power in American History: A Reader,* vol. 2: *From 1870* (Englewood Cliffs, N.J.: Prentice-Hall, 1991), 10–24; Kathryn Kish Sklar, "Hull House in the 1890s: A Community of Women Reformers," in Sklar and Dublin, *Women and Power in American History*, 2:54–69.

7. For a history of the suffrage movement, see Cott, *The Grounding of Modern Feminism*; and Ellen DuBois, *Feminism and Suffrage: The Emergence of an Independent Women's Movement in America, 1848–1869* (Ithaca: Cornell University Press, 1978). For more on nineteenth-century white women's culture, see Carroll Smith-Rosenberg, *Disorderly Conduct: Visions of Gender in Victorian America* (New York: Oxford University Press, 1985).

8. The Woman's Christian Temperance Union is the best example of the politicization of women's difference from men in turn-of-the-century America. See Ruth Bordin, *Woman and Temperance: The Quest for Power and Liberty, 1873–1900* (Philadelphia: Temple University Press, 1981). See also Paula Baker, "The Domestication of Politics: Women and American Political Society, 1780–1920," *American Historical Review* 89 (June 1984), rpt. Ellen DuBois and Vicki Ruiz, *Unequal Sisters: A Multicultural Reader in U.S. Women's History* (New York: Routledge, 1990), 66–91.

9. Alice Kessler-Harris, *Out to Work* (New York: Oxford University Press, 1982), 167.

10. Kathy Peiss, *Cheap Amusements: Working Women and Leisure in Turn-of-the-Century New York* (Philadelphia: Temple University Press, 1986).

11. Joanne Meyerowitz, *Women Adrift: Independent Wage Earners in Chicago, 1880–1930* (Chicago: University of Chicago Press, 1988).

12. Lewis Erenberg, *Steppin' Out: New York Nightlife and the Transformation of American Culture, 1890–1930* (Chicago: University of Chicago Press, 1981); John Kasson, *Amusing the Millions: Coney Island at the Turn of the Century* (New York: Hill and Wang, 1978).

13. Kathy Peiss, "Charity Girls and City Pleasures," in Sklar and Dublin, *Women and Power in American History,* 91–92.

14. June Sochen, *The New Woman in Greenwich Village: 1910–1920* (New York: Quadrangle, 1972); Ellen Kay Trimberger, "Feminism, Men, and Modern Love:

Greenwich Village, 1900–1925," in Anne Snitow, Christine Stansell, and Sharon Thompson, eds., *The Powers of Desire* (New York: Monthly Review Press, 1983), 131–152.

15. Paula Fass, *The Damned and the Beautiful: American Youth in the 1920s* (New York: Oxford University Press, 1977).

16. Peiss,"Charity Girls and City Pleasures," 91.

17. Horace Coon, *Coquetry for Men* (New York: Amour, 1932). Quoted in Christina Simmons, "Companionate Marriage and the Lesbian Threat," in Sklar and Dublin, *Women and Power in American History*, 185.

18. Julian Carter, "Normality, Whiteness, Authorship: Evolutionary Sexology and the Primitive Pervert," in Vernon A. Rosario, ed., *Science and Homosexualities* (New York: Routledge, 1997), 155–176.

19. Gail Bederman, *Manliness and Civilization: A Cultural History of Gender and Race in the United States, 1880–1917* (Chicago: University of Chicago Press, 1995).

20. Carter, "Normality, Whiteness, Authorship," 173.

21. Hazel Carby, "Policing the Black Woman's Body in an Urban Context," *Critical Inquiry* 18 (Summer 1992), 738–755; and Carby, *Reconstructing Womanhood: The Emergence of the Afro-American Woman Novelist* (New York: Oxford University Press, 1897); Darlene Clark Hine, "Rape and the Inner Lives of Black Women in the Middle West: Preliminary Thoughts on the Culture of Dissemblance," in Ellen Carol DuBois and Vicki Ruiz, eds., *Unequal Sisters: A Multicultural Reader in U.S. Women's History* (New York: Routledge, 1990), 292–297; Deborah McDowell, " 'It's Not Safe. Not Safe at All': Sexuality in Nella Larson's Passing," in Henry Abelove, Michèle Aina Barale, David M. Halperin, *The Lesbian and Gay Studies Reader* (New York: Routledge, 1993), 616–625.

22. Carby, "Policing the Black Woman's Body in an Urban Context"; Carby, *Reconstructing Womanhood*. Scholarship on the Harlem Renaissance is too large to do justice to in a single footnote. See the novels of Nella Larson, Carl Van Vechten, Zora Neale Hurston, Jessie Fauset.

23. Sigmund Freud, *Civilization and Its Discontents* (London, 1938).

24. Carolyn Dean, *Sexuality and Modern Western Culture* (New York: Twayne, 1996), 25.

25. Buhle, *Feminism and Its Discontents*

26. Leonard Wilcox, "Sex Boys in a Balloon: V. F. Calverton and the Abortive Sexual Revolution," *Journal of American Studies* 23 (1989), 7–26.

27. D'Emilio and Freedman, *Intimate Matters*, 224.

28. Carter, "Normality, Whiteness, Authorship," 155.

29. Buhle, *Feminism and Its Discontents*, 43; Laurie Umansky, *Motherhood Reconceived: Feminism and the Legacies of the Sixties* (New York: New York University Press, 1996).

30. Quoted in Buhle, *Feminism and Its Discontents*, 45.

31. Nancy Cott, "Passionlessness: An Interpretation of Victorian Sexual Ideology,

1790–1850," in Nancy Cott and Elizabeth Pleck, eds., *A Heritage of Her Own* (New York: Simon and Schuster, 1979), 162–181.

32. Christina Simmons, "Companionate Marriage and the Lesbian Threat," *Frontiers* 4, no.3 (1979), 54–59.

33. Dean, *Sexuality and Modern Western Culture*, 6.

34. Experts include Lorine Pruette, "The Flapper," in V. F. Calverton and S. D. Schmalhausen, *The New Generation: The Intimate Problems of Modern Parents and Children* (New York: Macaulay, 1930); Maurice A. Biglow, *Sex-Education: A Series of Lectures Concerning Knowledge of Sex in Its Relation to Human Life* (New York: Macmillan, 1916); Floyd Dell, *Love in the Machine Age: A Psychological Study of the Transition from Patriarchal Society* (New York: Farrar, 1930); LeMon Clark, *Emotional Adjustment in Marriage* (St. Louis: Mosby, 1937); Grete Meisel-Hess, *The Sexual Crisis: A Critique of Our Sex Life*, trans. Eden and Cedar Paul (New York: Critic and Guide, 1917); V. F. Calverton, "Sex and Social Struggle," in V. F. Calverton and S. D. Schmalhausen, eds., *Sex in Civilization* (New York: Macauley, 1929); Margaret Sanger, *Happiness in Marriage* (New York: Blue Ribbon, 1926).

35. Dean, *Sexuality and Modern Western Culture*.

36. New scholarship on the clitoris includes Paula Bennett, "Critical Clitoridectomy: Female Sexual Imagery and Feminist Psychoanalytic Theory," *Signs* 18, no. 2 (1993), 235–259; Margaret Gibson, "Clitoral Corruption: Body Metaphors and American Doctors' Constructions of Female Homosexuality, 1870–1900," in Vernon A. Rosario, *Science and Homosexualities* (New York: Routledge, 1997), 108–132; Rachel P. Maines, *The Technology of Orgasm: Hysteria, the Vibrator, and Women's Sexual Satisfaction* (Baltimore: Johns Hopkins University Press, 1999); Lisa Jean Moore and Adele E. Clarke, "Clitoral Conventions and Transgressions: Graphic Representations in Anatomy Texts, 1900–1991," *Feminist Studies* 21, no. 2 (Summer 1995), 255–301.

37. Freudian experts include Karl Abraham, "Manifestations of the Female Castration Complex," in *Selected Papers on Psycho-Analysis* (London: Hogarth, 1920), rpt. *The Selected Papers of Karl Abraham*, trans. Douglas Bryan and Alix Strachey (New York: Basic); Marie Bonaparte, *Female Sexuality* (New York: Grove, 1953); Helene Deutsch, *The Psychology of Women: A Psychoanalytic Interpretation*, vols. 1, 2 (New York: Grune and Stratton, 1944, 1945); Karen Horney, "The Flight from Womanhood: The Masculinity Complex in Women as Viewed by Men and by Women," *International Journal of Psycho-Analysis* 7 (1926), 324–339; and Horney, "The Problem of Feminine Masochism," *Psychoanalytic Review* 12, no. 3 (1935), 241–257; Eduard Hitschmann and Edmund Bergler, *Frigidity in Women: Its Characteristics and Treatment* (New York: Nervous and Mental Disease Monographs, 1936); Clara Thompson, " 'Penis Envy' in Women," *Psychiatry* 6 (1943), 123–125, and "Some Effects of the Derogatory Attitude Toward Female Sexuality," *Psychiatry* 13 (1950), 349–354. Others include Ralph Hay, "Mannish Women

or Old Maids?" *Know Yourself* 1 (July 1938); John Meagher, M.D., "Homosexuality: Its Psychobiological and Psychopatholgical Significance," *Urologic and Cutaneous Review* 33 (1922); Elenor Bertine, M.D., "Health and Morality in the Light of the New Psychology," *Proceedings of the International Conference of Women Physicians*, no. 4 (New York: Woman's Press, 1919); Olga Knoph, *Women on Their Own* (Boston: Little, Brown, 1935).

38. Meagher, "Homosexuality," 510; cited in Simmons, "Companionate Marriage and the Lesbian Threat," 190.

39. Elizabeth Abel, Barbara Christian, Helene Moglen, eds., *Female Subjects in Black and White: Race, Psychoanalysis, Feminism* (Berkeley: University of California Press, 1997).

40. White, *The First Sexual Revolution*.

41. Theodore H. Van Der Velde, *Ideal Marriage: Its Physiology and Technique* (New York: Random House, 1926), 8.

42. Barbara Ehrenreich, Elizabeth Hess, and Gloria Jacobs, *Remaking Love: The Feminization of Sex* (New York: Doubleday, 1986), 47.

43. John Heidenry, *What Wild Ecstasy: The Rise and Fall of the Sexual Revolution* (New York: Simon and Schuster, 1997), 174.

44. Christina Simmons, "Companionate Marriage and the Lesbian Threat," 54–59, and "Modern Sexuality and the Myth of Victorian Repression," 157–177.

45. For a history of romantic heterosexuality, see Steven Seldman, *Romantic Longings: Love in America, 1830–1989* (New York: Routledge, 1992).

46. Van Der Velde, *Ideal Marriage*, 8.

47. Gibson, "Clitoral Corruption," 117.

48. Van Der Velde, *Ideal Marriage*, 242.

49. Ibid., see chapter 8 and 9 for examples.

50. Ibid., 18.

51. My analysis of the romance narrative and the cultural work it does is informed by Janice Radway, *Reading the Romance: Women, Patriarchy, and Popular Literature* (Chapel Hill: University of North Carolina Press, 1984). For more analysis, see Linda K. Christian-Smith, *Becoming a Woman Through Romance* (New York: Routledge, 1990). Much of the literature on romance comes from television studies such as Deborah Rogers, "Daze of Our Lives: The Soap Opera as Feminine Text," *Journal of American Culture* 14, no. 4 (Winter 1990), 29–41; Robert Allen, *Speaking of Soap Operas* (Chapel Hill: University of North Carolina Press, 1985); Sandy Flitterman, "Psychoanalysis, Film, and Television," and E. Ann Kaplin, "Feminist Criticism and Television," in Robert Allen, ed., *Channels of Discourse: Television and Contemporary Criticism* (Chapel Hill: University of North Carolina, 1988). See Amy Kaplan, "Romancing the Empire: The Embodiment of American Masculinity in the Popular Historical Novel of the 1890s," *American Literary History* 3 (December 1990), 659–690, for her analysis of the work romance narratives do for masculinity.

52. Van Der Velde, *Ideal Marriage*, 161.

53. Ibid., 157.

54. Van Der Velde, *Ideal Marriage*, 132.

55. Ibid., 134.

56. Ibid., 131.

57. See Mary Poovey, *Uneven Developments: The Ideological Work of Gender in Mid-Victorian England* (Chicago: University of Chicago Press, 1989), for her discussion of how the vision of women as asexual, or virtuous, competed with an older view of women as overly sexual and dangerous. She states in her introduction that "the contradiction between a sexless, moralized angel and an aggressive, carnal magdalen was . . . written into the domestic ideal as one of its constitutive characteristics" (11). She develops this argument most thoroughly in chapter 2, on the debate over giving chloroform to women in labor. While important differences remain between the period Poovey discusses and America in the 1920s, Poovey's work nonetheless identifies an important and enduring tension in the cultural construction of women over the meaning of female sexuality. Also see Thomas Laqueur, "Bodies, Details, and the Humanitarian Narrative," in Lynn Hunt, ed., *The New Cultural History* (Berkeley: University of California Press, 1989), 176–205.

58. Van Der Velde, *Ideal Marriage*, 253.

59. Ibid., 252–253.

60. Ibid.

61. Ibid.

62. Ibid. Van Der Velde drew from psychoanalysis for this "fact." "It is now universally recognized and accepted by neurologists that the feminine psyche reacts to every repression (conscious or unconscious) of sexual wishes, with neurotic symptoms." See 253, note 4.

63. Ibid., 254.

64. See Barbara Melosh, *Engendering Culture: Manhood and Womanhood in New Deal Public Art and Theater* (Washington, D.C.: Smithsonian Institution Press, 1991), for her analysis of gender during the Depression.

65. Caroline Reynolds Milbank, *New York Fashion: The Evolution of American Style* (New York: Abrams, 1989), 98–129.

66. William Chafe, *The American Woman: Her Changing Social, Economic, and Political Roles, 1920–1970* (New York: Oxford University Press, 1972), 54.

67. Ibid., 64.

68. See Sigmund Freud, "The Dissolution of the Oedipus Complex," in James Strachey, ed., *The Standard Edition of the Complete Psychological Works of Sigmund Freud* (London: Hogarth, 1953–1974), 19:173–179; Freud, "Some Psychical Consequences of the Anatomical Distinction Between the Sexes," *The Standard Edition*, 19:248–258; Freud, "Female Sexuality," *The Standard Edition*, 21:225–243; and Freud, "Femininity," *New Introductory Lectures on Psycho-Analysis*, chapter 33, *The Standard Edition*, 22:112–135.

69. Sigmund Freud, *Three Essays on the Theory of Sexuality* (1905), trans. James Stra-chey (New York: Basic, 1975), 73–109.

70. Ibid., 73.

71. Ibid., 87.

72. Ibid.

73. Nancy Chodorow proposes that this preoedipal moment of psychological and li-bidinal focus on the mother, which both boys and girls experience, is best called "gynesexuality" or "matrisexuality" for its exclusive focus on the mother rather than on a classification of persons. See *The Reproduction of Mothering: Psycho-analysis and the Sociology of Gender* (Berkeley: University of California Press, 1978), 95.

74. Abraham, "Manifestations of the Female Castration Complex"; Bonaparte, *Fe-male Sexuality*; Helene Deutsch, *The Psychology of Women: A Psychoanalytic Inter-pretation, Vol I and II* (New York: Grune and Stratton, 1944 and 1945), Karen Horney, "The Flight from Womanhood: The Masculinity Complex in Women as Viewed by Men and by Women," *International Journal of Psycho-Analysis* 7 (1926), 324–39 and "The Problem of Feminine Masochism," *Psychoanalytic Review* 12, n. 3 (1935), 241–57, Eduard Hitschmann and Edmund Bergler, *Frigidity in Women: Its Characteristics and Treatment* (New York: Nervous and Mental Disease Monographs, 1936), Clara Thompson, " 'Penis Envy' in Women," *Psychiatry* 6 (1943), 123–25 and "Some Effects of the Derogatory Attitude Toward Female Sexuality," *Psychiatry* 13 (1950), 349–54.

75. Deutsch frequently had the feeling that Freud absorbed her ideas without citing her. While she thought this was a compliment, she also felt somewhat eclipsed by Freud's unconsciousness on this point. See Paul Roazen, *Helene Deutsch: A Psy-choanalyst's Life* (New York: Doubleday, 1985), chapter 10.

76. Deutsch, *The Psychology of Women*.

77. Deutsch's early writings on women include Helene Deutsch, *Psychoanalysis of the Sexual Functions of Women* (Vienna, 1925); "The Psychology of Women in Rela-tion to the Functions of Reproduction," *International Journal of Psycho-Analysis* 6 (1926); and "The Significance of Masochism in the Mental Life of Women," *In-ternational Journal of Psycho-Analysis* 11 (1930).

78. See Peter Gay, *Freud: A Life for Our Times* (New York: Norton, 1988) for more on the Freud and Abraham relationship.

79. Some of Karen Horney's most famous articles on women are "On the Genesis of the Castration Complex in Women," *International Journal of Psychoanalysis* 5 (1924), 50–65; "The Flight from Womanhood" (1926); "Inhibited Femininity: Psychoanalytic Contributions to the Problem of Frigidity," (1926–1927), rpt. *Fem-inine Psychology*, 54–70, 71–83; "The Overvaluation of Love: A Study of a Com-mon Present-Day Feminine Type," *Psychoanalytic Quarterly* 3 (1934), 605–638. All of Horney's early writings on women are collected in *Feminine Psychology* (New York: Norton, 1967).

80. Janet Sayers, *Sexual Contradictions: Psychology, Psychoanalysis, and Feminism* (London: Tavistock, 1986), 40.

81. Marcia Westkott, *The Feminist Legacy of Karen Horney* (New Haven: Yale University Press, 1986).

82. Sayers, *Sexual Contradictions*, 38.

83. From her earliest writing in 1922, Horney consistently challenged what she considered to be clinically unsubstantiated claims about the primacy of penis envy in the psychosexual development of women. Horney delivered her first international paper, "On the Genesis of the Castration Complex in Women" (1922) in response to Karl Abraham's widely praised paper, delivered at the Sixth International Psychoanalytic Congress two years earlier, entitled "Manifestations of the Female Castration Complex." See Susan Quinn, *A Mind of Her Own: The Life of Karen Horney* (New York: Summit, 1987), chapter 11.

84. Horney uses this phrase in note 8 of her paper "The Denial of the Vagina," in *Feminine Psychology*, 157.

85. Karen Horney, "The Denial of the Vagina: A Contribution to the Problem of the Genital Anxieties Specific to Women," *International Journal of Psychoanalysis* 14 (1933), 57–70. All citations are to the reprinted essay in *Feminine Psychology*, 147–161.

86. Ibid., 154. Horney is especially dismayed by Freud's view that motherhood is a secondary reaction formation against primary penis envy. "The special point about Freud's viewpoint," she claims, "is that it sees the wish for motherhood not as an innate formation, but as something that can be reduced psychologically to its ontogenetic elements and draws its energy originally from homosexual or phallic instinctual desires," 149.

87. Ibid., 161.

88. By the late 1930s, Horney abandoned Freud's emphasis on drives and her focus on women and turned to an examination of the social, cultural, and psychological origins of neurosis and specific character types. As a result of her change in focus, many studies of Horney have kept her earlier work on women separate from her more culturalist, later work, or have relegated it to a footnote. See D. Ewen Cameron, "Karen Horney: A Pioneer in the Science of Human Relations," *American Journal of Psychoanalysis* 14, no. 3 (1954), 19–29; Jay Greenberg and Stephen Mitchell, *Object Relations in Psychoanalytic Theory* (Cambridge: Harvard University Press, 1983); J. A. C. Brown, *Freud and the Post-Freudians* (Baltimore: Penguin, 1961); Quinn, *A Mind of Her Own*. However, I would argue that the tension in Horney's early work between biological and cultural explanations of femininity and female sexuality cannot, and should not, be explained by seeing it as a product of her transition between two models of subjectivity. The contradictions in her work on women, and specifically in her use of both instinctual and cultural models, I believe, reflect the larger and more pervasive theoretical impasse over the role of social and cultural values in the biologically dominated discourse of

psychoanalysis. Explaining away Horney's early efforts to synthesize social factors with a theory of instincts masks her effort to untangle one of the central professional issues of her day: Could Freud's theory of instincts be made to accommodate women's experience and subjectivity? If women were not biologically castrated men, if their psychology was not to be interpreted solely through the lens of their castrated physiology, what then characterized women? What was essential to femininity? Horney's use of both cultural and essentialist theories to explain femininity, while at times contradictory, helped her recast psychoanalytic theory by using a sense of cultural "values" to displace the hegemony of biology and the drive model.

89. See Brown, *Freud and the Post-Freudians*, chapter 7.

90. All of Horney's biographers show the influences of sociology and anthropology on Horney's thought, especially the sociological work of George Simmel. See Quinn, *A Mind of her Own*; Westkott, *The Feminist Legacy of Karen Horney*; Janet Sayers, *Mothers of Psychoanalysis: Helene Deutsch, Karen Horney, Anna Freud, Melanie Klein* (New York: Norton, 1990).

91. With her emphasis on the body as the primary origin of femininity, Deutsch incorporated the concept of drives into her examination of women's psychology. Freud defined drives in *Three Essays on the Theory of Sexuality* (1905) as "lying on the frontier between the mental and the physical." Sigmund Freud, "Three Essays on the Theory of Sexuality," *The Standard Edition*, 7:168. Freud regarded drives as the determinant of motivation, "the ultimate cause of all activity." Freud's drive theory functioned as the intellectual structure of psychoanalysis and was the model by which early psychoanalysts conceived of the relationship between the body and the mind.

92. Deutsch, *The Psychology of Women*, 1:386.

93. Ibid., 229; emphasis added.

94. Ibid., 319; emphasis added.

95. Ibid., 192.

96. Deutsch, *The Psychology of Women*, 1:190.

97. Ibid., 2:80.

98. Ibid., 80.

99. Ibid., 79–80.

100. Ibid., 81.

101. Ibid., 230.

102. Ibid., 231.

103. Horney found Deutsch's use of the term *rape* difficult to fathom. See Horney, "The Problem of Feminine Masochism," originally published in the *Psychoanalytic Review* in response to Deutsch's first article on masochism in 1930, "The Significance of Masochism in the Mental Life of Women"; see notes 37 and 77, this chapter.

104. Sayers, *Sexual Contradictions*, 39.

105. Horney, "Denial of the Vagina."

106. Sayers, *Sexual Contradictions*, 41.

107. Horney, "Inhibited Femininity," 73–74.

108. Ibid., 83.

109. Ibid.

110. Hitschmann and Bergler, *Frigidity in Women*.

111. Ibid., 20.

112. Edmund Bergler, "Frigidity in the Female—Misconceptions and Facts," *Marriage Hygiene* 1 (August 1947), 16–21.

113. Ibid., 3.

114. Ibid., 5.

115. Hitschmann and Bergler, *Frigidity in Women*, 24.

116. Ibid., 52.

117. These underlining premises about frigidity were common to most psychoanalysts writing in this period. Hitschmann and Bergler, along with Marie Bonaparte and Helene Deutsch, adhered to the dominant paradigm within Freudian theory for understanding female sexuality. The discussion of frigidity remained bound within this Freudian interpretive schema until the late 1950s, when its hegemony within psychoanalysis declined.

118. Ibid., 56–57.

119. Ibid., 51.

120. George Chauncey Jr. argues, in "From Sexual Inversion to Homosexuality: The Changing Medical Conceptualization of 'Female Deviance,' " in Kathy Peiss and Christine Simmons, eds., *Passion and Power: Sexuality in History* (Philadelphia: Temple University Press, 1989), 87–117, that Freud's view of sexuality challenged the nineteenth-century model of sexual inversion but did not completely overturn it. Sexology and medicine continued to rely on inversion as a paradigm for homosexuality beyond the period covered in his research. My examination of frigidity shows that the inversion model also appeared in psychoanalytic discussions of heterosexual women.

121. Susan D. Becker, *The Origins of the Equal Rights Amendment: American Feminism Between the Wars* (Westport, Conn.: Greenwood, 1981), 49.

122. Lila Rupp and Verta Taylor, *Survival in the Doldrums: The American Women's Rights Movement Between the Wars* (Columbus: Ohio State University, 1989), 20.

123. "A Word for Women," *Atlantic Monthly* 148 (November 1931), 545–554.

124. *New York Times*, May 23, 1897, 16:1. Quoted in Jonathan Ned Katz, *The Invention of Heterosexuality* (New York: Dutton, 1995), 89.

125. J. Lionel Taylor, *The Nature of Women* (New York: Dutton, 1913).

126. *New York Times Book Review*, October 19, 1913, 56. Review of Walter Heape's *Sex Antagonism* (New York: Putnam, 1913). Quoted in Katz, *The Invention of Heterosexuality*, 89.

127. Marynia Farnham and Ferdinand Lundberg, *Modern Woman: The Lost Sex* (New York: Harper, 1947).

128. Buhle, *Feminism and Its Discontents*, 179.

129. Arnold W. Green and Eleanor Melnick, "What Has Happened to the Feminist Movement?" in Alvin W. Gouldner, ed., *Studies in Leadership* (New York: Russell and Russell, 1950), 183. Quoted in Rupp and Taylor, *Survival in the Doldrums*, 19.

130. Quoted in Rupp and Taylor, *Survival in the Doldrums,* 19.

131. "Psychosurgery," *Life* 22 (March 3, 1947), 94–95.

132. Buhle, *Feminism and Its Discontents,* 168–169.

133. Farnham and Lundberg, *Modern Woman*, 143.

134. Ibid., 169.

135. Buhle, *Feminism and Its Discontents*, 175.

136. Farnham and Lundberg, *Modern Woman*, 172.

137. Ibid., 173.

138. Ibid., 178.

139. Ibid., 265.

140. Ibid., 237.

141. Ibid., 271.

2. BETWEEN FREUDIANISM AND FEMINISM: SEXOLOGY'S POSTWAR CHALLENGE

1. See Mari Jo Buhle, *Feminism and Its Discontents: A Century of Struggle with Psychoanalysis* (Cambridge: Harvard University Press, 1998), for an account of women analysts' relationship to Freud and his ideas.

2. Ferdinand Lundberg and Marynia Farnham, *Modern Woman: The Lost Sex* (New York: Harper, 1947); Alfred C. Kinsey, Wardell B. Pomeroy, Clyde E. Martin, and Paul H. Gebhard, *Sexual Behavior in the Human Female* (Philadelphia: Saunders, 1953), hereafter *SBHF*.

3. William Masters and Virginia Johnson, *Human Sexual Response* (Boston: Little, Brown, 1966).

4. For histories of sexology, see Janice Irvine, *Disorders of Desire: Sex and Gender in Modern American Sexology* (Philadelphia: Temple University Press, 1990); Edward Brecher, *The Sex Researchers* (Boston: Little, Brown, 1969); Shere Hite, *The Hite Report: A Nationwide Study of Female Sexuality* (New York: Dell, 1976); Paul Robinson, *The Modernization of Sex: Havelock Ellis, Alfred Kinsey, William Masters, and Virginia Johnson* (New York: Harper and Row, 1976); Edwin Schur, *The Americanization of Sex* (Philadelphia: Temple University Press, 1988).

5. For histories of the second wave of feminism, see William Chafe, "Feminism in the 1970s: A Historical Perspective," in *Women and Equality: Changing Patterns in American Culture* (New York: Oxford University Press, 1977), 115–142; Flora Davis, *Moving the Mountain: The Women's Movement in America Since 1960* (New York: Simon and Schuster, 1991); Alice Echols, *Daring to Be Bad: Radical Feminism in America, 1967–1975* (Minneapolis: University of Minnesota Press, 1989); Sara Evans, *Personal Politics: The Roots of the Women's Liberation Move-

ment in the Civil Rights Movement and the New Left (New York: Vintage, 1979);
Judith Grant, *Fundamental Feminism: Contesting the Core Concepts of Feminist
Theory* (New York: Routledge, 1993); Barbara Ryan, *Feminism and the Women's
Movement: Dynamics of Change in Social Movement Ideology and Activism* (New
York: Routledge, 1992); Laura Umansky, *Motherhood Reconceived: Feminism
and the Legacies of the Sixties* (New York: New York University Press, 1996);
and Winifred Wandersee, *On the Move: American Women in the 1970s* (Boston:
Twayne, 1988).

6. For example, see Kate Millett, *Sexual Politics* (Simon and Schuster, 1970); Shu-
lamith Firestone, *The Dialectic of Sex* (New York: Bantam, 1970); Martha Shelley,
"Notes of a Radical Lesbian," in Robin Morgan, ed., *Sisterhood Is Powerful* (New
York: Vintage, 1970), 343–348; Ti-Grace Atkinson, *Amazon Odyssey* (New York:
Link, 1974), and "The Institution of Sexual Intercourse," in Shulamith Firestone
and Anne Koedt, eds., *Notes from the Second Year* (New York: New York Radical
Feminists, April 1970), 42–48; Germaine Greer, *The Female Eunuch* (New York:
Dell, 1970). Anne Koedt, "The Myth of the Vaginal Orgasm," first appeared in
Notes from the First Year (New York, 1968), 2. A longer version appeared in *Notes
from the Second Year*, 37–41. This version was reprinted in the anthology edited
by Koedt, Ellen Levine, Antia Rapone, *Radical Feminism* (New York: Quadrangle Books, 1973), 198–207.

7. May uses "togetherness" as a key trope of family life in her analysis. See Elaine
Tyler May, *Homeward Bound: American Families in the Cold War Era* (New
York: Basic, 1988), chapter 8. Also Joanne Meyerowitz, ed., *Not June Cleaver:
Women and Gender in Postwar America, 1945–1960* (Philadelphia: Temple Uni-
versity Press, 1994); and Betty Friedan, *The Feminine Mystique* (New York:
Dell, 1963).

8. Barbara Ehrenreich, *The Hearts of Men: American Dreams and the Flight from
Commitment* (New York: Anchor, 1983), 14–28.

9. May, *Homeward Bound*, 3–15.

10. E. Franklin Frazier, *The Negro Family in the United States* (Chicago: University
of Chicago Press, 1939), and *The Black Bourgeoisie* (New York: Free Press, 1957);
Jacqueline Jones, *Labor of Love, Labor of Sorrow: Black Women, Work, and the
Family from Slavery to the Present* (New York: Vintage, 1985), 232–322; Janet
Zandy, *Calling Home: Working-Class Women's Writings* (New Brunswick, N.J.:
Rutgers University Press, 1990), 1–19.

11. William H. Chafe, *The American Woman: Her Changing Social, Economic, and Po-
litical Roles, 1920–1970* (New York: Oxford University Press, 1972), chapter 7;
Susan M. Hartman, "Women's Employment and the Domestic Ideal in the Early
Cold War Years" in Meyerowitz, *Not June Cleaver*, 84–102.

12. Talcott Parsons, "The Social Structure of the Family," in Ruth Anshen, ed., *The
Family: Its Functions and Destiny* (New York: Harper and Row, 1949), 241–273.
For more on postwar sociology and its conception of social roles, see Wini

Breines, *Young, White, and Miserable: Growing Up Female in the Fifties* (Boston: Beacon, 1992), chapter 1.

13. As Gail Bederman has noted in *Manliness and Civilization* (Chicago: University of Chicago Press, 1996), "civilization" has a long history of being encoded with racial meanings, predominantly the superiority of whiteness.

14. Nathan G. Hale Jr., *The Rise and Crisis of Psychoanalysis in the United States* (New York: Oxford University Press, 1995), 296.

15. Dorothy Barclay, "Trousered Mothers and Dishwashing Dads," *New York Times Magazine*, April 28, 1957, 48. Quoted in Hale, *The Rise and Crisis of Psychoanalysis*, 296.

16. Quoted in Breines, *Young, White, and Miserable*, 34–35.

17. Ehrenreich, *The Hearts of Men*, 20–21; Janet Walker, *Couching Resistance: Women, Film, and Psychoanalytic Psychiatry* (Minneapolis: University of Minnesota Press, 1993), 1–23.

18. Alfred C. Kinsey, Wardell B. Pomeroy, Clyde E. Martin, and Paul H. Gebhard, *Sexual Behavior in the Human Male* (Philadelphia: Saunders, 1948).

19. Mary Jane Sherfey, M.D., *The Nature and Evolution of Female Sexuality* (New York: Vintage, 1966), 4–6.

20. Brecher, *The Sex Researchers*, 144.

21. Irvine, *Disorders of Desire*, 35–36.

22. Brecher, *The Sex Researchers*, 143.

23. Wardell B. Pomeroy, *Dr. Kinsey and the Institute for Sex Research* (New York: Harper and Row, 1972), 97–137.

24. Breines, *Young, White, and Miserable*, 3.

25. Kinsey mentions religion, location, and age as important factors shaping the research, but not race. See *SBHF*, 31–37.

26. Kinsey, *SBHF*, 380.

27. Ibid., 46.

28. Kinsey explains his seven-point scale measuring the range of behaviors between heterosexuality and homosexuality on 471–472 in *SBHF*. The concept of sexuality as a continuum of behavior was politicized by feminists in the 1970s, most specifically by Adrienne Rich in "Compulsory Heterosexuality and Lesbian Existence," in Ann Snitow, Christine Stansell, and Sharon Thompson, eds., *Powers of Desire: The Politics of Sexuality* (New York: Monthly Review, 1983), 177–205.

29. Kinsey, *SBHF*, 446.

30. Ibid., 450–451. Emphasis added.

31. Ibid., 580.

32. Ibid., 582. Anne Koedt repeated this analysis of the vagina in "The Myth of the Vaginal Orgasm," *Notes from the Second Year*.

33. Kinsey, *SBHF*, 584. Edmund Bergler, M.D. and William Kroger, M.D., *Kinsey's Myth of Female Sexuality* (New York: Grune and Stratton, 1954); Karl Menninger, "What the Girls Told," *Saturday Review*, September 26, 1953.

34. Kinsey, *SBHF*, 592.

35. Ibid., 375.

36. Ibid., 375.

37. Brecher, *The Sex Researchers*, 154.

38. Kinsey, *SBHF*, 371.

39. Ibid., 371.

40. Ibid., 688.

41. Ibid., 652–686.

42. Irvine, *Disorders of Desire*, 59.

43. Freud also arrived at the same conclusion in "New Introductory Lectures" (1933), in *The Standard Edition of the Complete Psychological Works of Sigmund Freud,* ed. and trans. James Strachey (London: Hogarth, 1953–1974), 22:135. "If you want to know more about femininity, inquire from your own experiences, or turn to the poets, or wait until science can give you deeper and more coherent information."

44. Pomeroy, *Dr. Kinsey and the Institute for Sex Research*, 348.

45. Ibid., 359–360.

46. Ibid., 362–364.

47. See Bergler and Kroger, *Kinsey's Myth of Female Sexuality*, introduction and chapter 2: "Kinsey's Misconceptions of the Meaning of Frigidity."

48. Ibid., 78.

49. Pomeroy, *Dr. Kinsey and the Institute for Sex Research*, 365.

50. Ibid., 373–381.

51. Irvine, *Disorders of Desire*, 58.

52. Masters and Johnson, *Human Sexual Response* .

53. For instance, David Reuben, M.D., *Everything You Always Wanted to Know About Sex, But Were Afraid to Ask* (New York: Bantam, 1969); Helen Singer Kaplan, *The New Sex Therapy* (New York: Brunner/Mazel, 1972); Seymour Fisher, *The Female Orgasm: Psychology, Physiology, Fantasy* (New York: Basic, 1973). See also the Committee on Human Sexuality, *Human Sexuality* (American Medical Association, 1972), for an example of the acceptance of *HSR* by mainstream American medicine.

54. This class marker is somewhat questionable. Most likely, the noncollege educated participants were the wives of the doctors and academics from which the bulk of the research population was drawn. Brecher's account of the research population, and his assertion that Masters' population was diverse, seems to be a preemptive move to enhance the credibility of Masters' findings.

55. Brecher, *The Sex Researchers*, 334. According to Brecher, this woman had a vaginoplasty done by Masters and provided useful information about artificial vaginas for *HSR*. Generally, Masters and Johnson found that artificial vaginas were no different from biological vaginas in terms of lubrication. See *HSR*, 101–110.

56. Brecher, *The Sex Researchers*, 334–335.

57. Masters and Johnson, *HSR*, 8.

58. Brecher, *The Sex Researchers*, 337.

59. See Robinson, *The Modernization of Sex*, 129–130; and Irvine, *Disorders of Desire*, 82–86.

60. Irvine, *Disorders of Desire*, 45–48.

61. Ibid., 5–6.

62. Ibid., 285.

63. Ibid., 45.

64. Ibid., 133.

65. Ibid., 65.

66. On the vagina as passive, see Lundberg and Farnham's reference to the vagina as a "log," in *Modern Woman*, chapter 11, "The Failure of Modern Sexuality," 263–297. They draw heavily on Helene Deutsch's work to make this claim. See also Freud's famous metaphor of the clitoris as a "pine shaving" that is used "to set a log of harder wood on fire," in *Three Essays on the Theory of Sexuality* (1905), cited in Thomas Laqueur, *Making Sex: Body and Gender from the Greeks to Freud* (Cambridge: Harvard University Press, 1990), 235. For Masters and Johnson's view of the vagina, see *HSR*, 68–100.

67. Masters and Johnson, *HSR.*, 66–67.

68. Ibid., chapter 5, "The Clitoris," 45–67.

69. "Human Sexual Inadequacy," *Newsweek*, May 4, 1970, 90–94.

70. "The $2,500 Understanding," *Newsweek*, June 10, 1968, 78.

71. *HSR*'s first printing of fifteen thousand sold out the day it went on sale and it lasted six months on the *New York Times* bestseller list. More than three hundred thousand copies of *HSR* sold in hardback and five hundred thousand in paperback. Self-help books popularized their techniques to mainstream readers and helped to extend Masters and Johnson's influence on American understandings of sexuality and sex. See Reuben, *Everything You Always Wanted to Know About Sex*; Kaplan, *The New Sex Therapy*; Fisher, *The Female Orgasm*. See also the Committee on Human Sexuality, *Human Sexuality*, for an example of the acceptance of *HSR* by mainstream American medicine.

72. May, *Homeward Bound*.

73. John D'Emilio and Estelle Freedman, *Intimate Matters: A History of Sexuality in America* (New York: Harper and Row, 1988), 301–326.

74. Irvine, *Disorders of Desire*, part 3. Reuben, *Everything You Wanted to Know About Sex*; J, *The Sensuous Woman* (New York: Dell, 1969); Alex Comfort, *The Joy of Sex: A Gourmet Guide to Love Making* (New York: Simon and Schuster, 1973).

75. Theodore Roszak, *The Making of a Counter Culture* (New York: Anchor, 1969); Brecher, *The Sex Researchers*.

76. Reuben, *Everything You Wanted to Know About Sex*, 1.

77. Ibid., 7.

78. Ibid., 27.

79. Ibid., 33.

80. Ibid., 214.

81. Ibid., 144.

82. Ibid., 154.

83. Ibid., 120–122.

84. Helen Gurley Brown, *Sex and the Single Girl* (New York: Pocket Books, 1962).

85. J, *The Sensuous Woman*, 17.

86. Ibid., 25.

87. Ibid., 181.

88. Ibid., 94.

89. Ibid., 97.

90. Ibid., 98.

91. Ibid., 41.

92. Ibid., 115.

93. Ibid., 113.

94. See Janice Radway, *Reading the Romance: Women, Patriarchy and Popular Literature* (Chapel Hill, N.C.: University of North Carolina Press, 1984, 1992) for her analysis of the lessons women learn from engaging with romance literature.

95. J, *The Sensuous Woman*, 186.

96. Ibid., 189.

97. Ibid., 13.

98. Ibid., 97.

99. Ibid., 98.

100. Ibid., 72.

3. POLITICIZING PLEASURE: RADICAL FEMINIST SEXUAL THEORY, 1968–1975

1. Barbara Ehrenreich, Elizabeth Hess, and Glora Jacobs, *Remaking Love: The Feminization of Sex* (Garden City, N.Y.: Anchor, 1987), 42.

2. The concern with orgasm in the early days of feminism has tended to be ignored or folded into larger histories of feminist thought with little appreciation for its centrality to the feminist project of politicizing sexuality. At the same time, feminists writings on the subject abound, as this chapter details. See Josephine Donovan, *Feminist Theory: The Intellectual Traditions of American Feminism* (New York: Continuum, 1985); Alice Echols, *Daring to Be Bad: Radical Feminism in America, 1967–1975* (Minneapolis: University of Minnesota Press, 1989); Ehrenreich, Hess, and Jacobs, *Remaking Love*; Judith Grant, *Fundamental Feminism: Contesting the Core Concepts of Feminist Theory* (New York: Routledge, 1993); Alix Kates Shulman, "Sex and Power: The Sexual Bases of Radical Feminism," *Signs* 5, no. 4 (Summer 1980), 590–604.

3. Elaine Tyler May, *Homeward Bound: American Families in the Cold War Era* (New York: Basic, 1988); John D'Emilio, "The Homosexual Menace: The Politics of Sexuality in Cold War America," in Kathy Peiss and Christina Simmons, eds.,

Passion and Power: Sexuality in History (Philadelphia: Temple University Press, 1989), 226–240.

4 Herbert Marcuse, *Eros and Civilization: A Philosophical Inquiry Into Freud* (Boston: Beacon, 1955, 1966), xxvii.

5. Norman O. Brown, *Life Against Death: The Psychoanalytical Meaning of History* (Middletown: Wesleyan University Press, 1959).

6. Theodore Roszak, *The Making of a Counter Culture: Reflections on the Technocratic Society and Its Youthful Opposition* (Garden City, N.Y.: Anchor, 1968), 84.

7. Abraham Maslow, *Towards a Psychology of Being* (New York: Van Nostrand, 1968); Carl Rogers, *On Becoming a Person: A Therapist's View of Psychotherapy* (Boston: Houghton Mifflin, 1961). For a history of the human potential movement's place in American psychology, see Ellen Herman, *The Romance of American Psychology: Political Culture in the Age of Experts* (Berkeley: University of California Press, 1995), 264–280. For a history of the new psychology's impact on ideas of masculinity, see Barbara Ehrenreich, *The Hearts of Men: American Dreams and the Flight from Commitment* (New York: Anchor, 1983), 88–99.

8. Quoted in Herman, *The Romance of American Psychology,* 267.

9. Ehrenreich, *The Hearts of Men*, 89–91.

10. Frederick Perls, Ralph Hefferline, and Paul Goodman, *Gestalt Therapy: Excitement and Growth in the Human Personality* (New York: Delta, 1951).

11. George Bach and Herb Goldberg, *Creative Aggression: The Art of Assertive Living* (Garden City, N.Y.: Doubleday, 1974).

12. Ehrenreich, *The Hearts of Men*, 95–96.

13. Ellen Herman, "Being and Doing: Humanistic Psychology and the Spirit of the 1960s," in Barbara Tischler, ed., *Sights on the Sixties* (New Brunswick, N.J.: Rutgers University Press, 1992), 87–101.

14. Abbie Hoffman, *Revolution for the Hell of It* (New York: Dial, 1969), 61. Quoted in Herman, "Being and Doing," 97.

15. Lauri Umansky, *Motherhood Reconceived: Feminism and the Legacies of the Sixties* (New York: New York University Press, 1996), 21–27.

16. Ehrenreich, Hess, and Jacobs, *Remaking Love*, 60.

17. Ibid., 58.

18. Ibid., 61.

19. John D'Emilio and Estelle Freedman, *Intimate Matters: A History of Sexuality in America* (New York: Harper and Row, 1988), 287–288.

20. Dany Lacombe, *Blue Politics: Pornography and the Law in the Age of Feminism* (Toronto: University of Toronto Press, 1994), 28.

21. Linda Williams, *Hard Core: Power, Pleasure, and the "Frenzy of the Visible"* (Berkeley: University of California Press, 1989), 53.

22. John Heidenry, *What Wild Ecstasy: The Rise and Fall of the Sexual Revolution* (New York: Simon and Schuster, 1997), 129–148.

23. The phrase "dildo journalism" comes from Abe Peck, *Uncovering the Sixties:*

The Life and Times of the Underground Press (New York: Pantheon, 1985), 207–221.

24. Friedan, *The Feminine Mystique*, 95.

25. For a different analysis of Friedan's use of "human potential," see Joanne Meyerowitz, "Beyond the Feminine Mystique: A Reassessment of Postwar Mass Culture, 1946–1958," *Journal of American History* 79, no. 4 (March 1993), 1455–1482.

26. Freidan, *The Feminine Mystique*, 249.

27. For more on Friedan's analysis of orgasm, see *The Feminine Mystique*, chapter 13, "The Forfeited Self," 299–325.

28. The literature on the black family is too numerous to cite in total. See, for example, Patrica Hill Collins, *Black Feminist Thought: Knowledge, Consciousness, and the Politics of Empowerment* (Boston: Unwin Hyman, 1990); bell hooks, *Ain't I a Woman: Black Women and Feminism* (Boston: South End, 1981), and *Feminist Theory from Margin to Center* (Boston: South End, 1984); Gloria Hull, Patricia Bell Scott, and Barbara Smith, eds., *All the Women Are White, All the Blacks Are Men, But Some of Us Are Brave: Black Women's Studies* (New York: Feminist, 1982); Paula Giddings, *When and Where I Enter: The Impact of Black Women on Race and Sex in America* (New York: William Morrow, 1984); Jaqueline Jones, *Labor of Love, Labor of Sorrow: Black Women, Work, and the Family from Slavery to the Present* (New York: Vintage, 1985); Barbara Omolade, "Heart of Darkness," in Beverly Guy-Sheftall, ed., *Words of Fire: An Anthology of African-American Feminist Thought* (New York: New, 1995), 362–378.

29. Abraham H. Maslow, *Motivation and Personality* (New York: Harper and Row, 1954). Erik H. Erikson, *Identity: Youth and Crisis* (New York: Norton, 1968).

30. Friedan, *The Feminine Mystique*, 69.

31. Ibid., 115.

32. Ibid., 116.

33. Ibid., 115.

34. Ibid., 178.

35. For example, Freidan examined the popular discourse around consumerism and its weakening effect on the country. She complained that women were expected to provide for the needs of their families, which includes shopping for food and clothing, yet were held responsible for the effects of a consumer-oriented society. See Friedan, *The Feminine Mystique*, chapter 9. For more on momism, see Ruth Feldstein, *Raising Citizens, Black and White* (Ithaca: Cornell University Press, 2000).

36. This tension between petitioning for rights based both on individualism and on collective membership in a group continued to haunt the second wave of feminism as it had the first. For more on how this tension played out in the 1910s and 1920s, see Nancy Cott, *The Grounding of Modern Feminism* (New Haven: Yale University Press, 1989).

37. For more on the sexual revolution, see Ehrenreich, Hess, and Jacobs, *Remaking Love*; Sheila Jeffreys, *Anticlimax: A Feminist Perspective on the Sexual Revolution* (New York: New York University Press, 1990); Kevin White, *The First Sexual Revolution: The Emergence of Male Heterosexuality in Modern America* (New York:New York University Press, 1993); and Susan J. Douglas, *Where the Girls Are: Growing Up Female with the Mass Media* (New York: New York Times, 1994).

38. Daniel Horowitz, *Betty Friedan and the Making of the Feminine Mystique: The American Left, the Cold War and Modern Feminism* (Amherst: University of Massachusetts Press, 1998).

39. Millett, *Sexual Politics*, 178.

40. Friedan, *The Feminine Mystique*, 96.

41. Both authors explain the histories of their projects in their opening pages. See Millett, *Sexual Politics*, ix–xiv, and Friedan, *The Feminine Mystique*, 11–27.

42. For more on the history of NOW, see Wandersee, *On the Move*, 36–55; Flora Davis, *Moving the Mountain: The Women's Movement in America since 1960* (New York: Simon and Schuster, 1991), 51–67; and Judith Hole and Ellen Levine, *Rebirth of Feminism* (New York: Quadrangle, 1971). For a history of women's political activism in the 1960s, see Amy Swerdlow, *Women's Strike for Peace* (Chicago: University of Chicago Press, 1993); and Susan Lynn, "Gender and Post-World War II Progressive Politics: A Bridge to Social Activism in the 1960s U.S.A.," *Gender and History* 4, no. 2 (Summer 1992), 215–239.

43. For more on Kate Millett, see Wandersee, *On the Move*, 66–69; and Hester Eisenstein, *Contemporary Feminist Thought* (Boston: Hall, 1983), 5–10.

44. Eisenstein, in *Contemporary Feminist Thought*, attributes Millett with popularizing the term *patriarchy*. See chapter 1, 5–14.

45. Kate Millett, *Sexual Politics*, 25.

46. Millett's book is divided into three sections, each which examines the centrality of patriarchy to western culture. The first defines what she called "sexual politics." The second set out her history of sexual politics, and the third examined literary representations of sexual politics.

47. Millett, *Sexual Politics*, 178.

48. Ibid., 177.

49. Ibid., 177.

50. Betty Friedan, *The Feminine Mystique*, 96–97.

51. Shulamith Firestone, *The Dialectic of Sex*, 43.

52. Ibid., 47.

53. Ibid., 50–55.

54. Ibid., 205.

55. Ibid., 206

56. Ibid., 209.

57. Anne Koedt, "The Myth of the Vaginal Orgasm," in Anne Koedt and Shulamith Firestone, eds., *Notes from the Second Year* (New York: New York Radical Femi-

nists, April 1970), 38. This article was originally published in *Notes from the First Year*, 1968. She expanded her essay and published it in *Notes from the Second Year*, 1970. It is reprinted in Anne Koedt, Ellen Levine, and Anita Rapone, eds., *Radical Feminism* (New York: Quadrangle, 1973), 198–208.

58. Ti-Grace Atkinson, "The Institution of Sexual Intercourse," in Koedt and Firestone, *Notes from the Second Year*, 42. This article can also be found in Atkinson's collected essays: Ti-Grace Atkinson, *Amazon Odyssey* (New York: Links, 1974).

59. Echols, *Daring to Be Bad,* 158.

60. Roxanne Dunbar, "What Is to Be Done?" *No More Fun and Games: A Journal of Female Liberation*, no. 1 (October 1968). Cited in Echols, *Daring to Be Bad,* 159.

61. The Boston Women's Health Course Collective, *Our Bodies, Our Selves* (New York: Simon and Schuster, 1971), 1.

62. Ibid., 1.

63. Kathie Sarachild, "Consciousness-Raising: A Radical Weapon" (1968), in Redstockings, *Feminist Revolution* (New York: Random House, 1975), 144–149, 145.

64. Ibid., 145.

65. Francis Beal, "Double Jeopardy: To Be Black and Female," in Robin Morgan, ed., *Sisterhood Is Powerful* (New York: Vintage, 1970), 383–396, 394.

66. Linda La Rue, "The Black Movement and Women's Liberation," in Guy-Sheftall, *Words of Fire*, 164–173, 164.

67. Hull, Scott, and Smith, *All the Women Are White*.

68. See, for example, bell hooks, "Feminism: A Movement to End Sexist Oppression" and "Ending Female Sexual Oppression," in hooks, *Feminist Theory*.

69. Koedt, "The Myth of the Vaginal Orgasm"; Atkinson, "Vaginal Orgasm as Mass Hysterical Survival Response," speech delivered to the Medical Committee for Human Rights, Philadelphia, April 5, 1968, and "The Institution of Sexual Intercourse."

70. Echols, *Daring to Be Bad,* 167–169.

71. Koedt, "The Myth of the Vaginal Orgasm," 38.

72. Ibid., 37.

73. Ibid., 38.

74. Atkinson defined "institution" as "any form of activity specified by a system of rules which defines offices, roles, moves, penalties, defenses, and so on, and which gives the activity its structure." See "The Institution of Sexual Intercourse," 42.

75. Koedt, "Myth of the Vaginal Orgasm," 41.

76. Susan Lyndon, "The Politics of Orgasm," in Morgan, *Sisterhood Is Powerful*, 219–228.

77. Ibid., 225.

78. Dr. Mary Jane Sherfey, "A Theory of Female Sexuality," in Morgan, *Sisterhood Is Powerful,* 249. Sherfey published a longer version of this article in 1966, in the *Journal of American Psychoanalytic Association*, titled "The Evolution and Nature of Female Sexuality in Relation to Psychoanalytic Theory." She subse-

quently published it as a book titled *The Nature and Evolution of Female Sexuality* (New York: Vintage, 1972).

79. Sherfey, "A Theory of Female Sexuality," 246.

80. Germaine Greer, *The Female Eunuch* (New York: Bantam, 1970).

81. Quoted in Heidenry, *What Wild Ecstasy*, 143.

82. Greer, *The Female Eunuch,* 327.

83. Heidenry, *What Wild Ecstasy*, 142–143.

84. Greer, *The Female Eunuch*, 37.

85. For feminist critiques of the sexual revolution, see Dana Densmore, "Independence from the Sexual Revolution," *No More Fun and Games: A Journal of Female Liberation* (1971), reprinted in Koedt, Levine, and Rapone, *Radical Feminism*, 107–118; Barbara Seaman, "The Liberated Orgasm," *Ms.* 1, no. 2 (August 1972), 55–59; Anselma Dell'Olio, "The Sexual Revolution Wasn't Our War," *Ms.* 1, no. 1 (Spring 1972), 104–109.

86. Densmore, "Independence from the Sexual Revolution," 110.

87. "Brainwashing and Women," *Radical Therapist* 1, no. 3 (August-September 1970), 5.

88. Ibid.

89. Roxanne Dunbar, " 'Sexual Liberation': More of the Same Thing," *No More Fun and Games: A Journal of Female Liberation*, no. 3 (November 1969), 49–56, quote on 49.

90. Ibid., 49, 56.

91. Barbara Leon, "The Male Supremacist Attack on Monogamy" (1971), reprinted in Redstockings, *Feminist Revolution*, 128.

92. Ibid.

93. Beal, "Double Jeopardy," 385.

94. Mary Ann Weathers, "An Argument for Black Women's Liberation as a Revolutionary Force," in Guy-Sheftall, *Words of Fire,* 158–161, 158.

95. Densmore, "Independence from the Sexual Revolution," 114.

96. Atkinson, "The Institution of Sexual Intercourse," 46.

97. Ibid., 42–48. See also Atkinson, "Vaginal Orgasm as Mass Hysterical Survival Response."

98. Sidney Abbott and Barbara Love, *Sappho Was a Right-On Woman: A Liberated View of Lesbianism* (New York: Stein and Day, 1972), 129. Quoted in Wandersee, *On the Move*, 67.

99. See Phyllis Chesler, *Women and Madness* (New York: Avon, 1972); Martin Duberman, Martha Vicinus, and George Chauncey Jr., *Hidden from History: Reclaiming the Gay and Lesbian Past* (New York: Signet, 1989).

100. The group later changed their name to Radicalesbians. Radicalesbians, "The Woman-Identified Woman," (1969), reprinted in Koedt, Levine, and Rapone, *Radical Feminism*, 243. See Echols, *Daring to Be Bad*, 214–215.

101. Radicalesbians, "The Woman-Identified Woman," 245.

102. Quoted in Echols, *Daring to Be Bad*, 217–218.

103. Ibid., 218.

4. DESIRES AND THEIR DISCONTENTS: FEMINIST FICTION OF THE 1970S

1. John D'Emilio and Estelle Freedman, *Intimate Matters: A History of Sexuality in America* (New York: Harper and Row, 1988), 301–326; Linda Grant, *Sexing the Millennium: Women and the Sexual Revolution* (New York: Grove, 1994); John Heidenry, *What Wild Ecstasy: The Rise and Fall of the Sexual Revolution* (New York: Simon and Schuster, 1997), 129–166.

2. Betty Friedan, *The Feminine Mystique* (New York: Dell, 1963); Kate Millett, *Sexual Politics* (New York: Simon and Schuster, 1969); Shulamith Firestone, *The Dialectic of Sex* (New York: Bantam, 1970); Robin Morgan, ed., *Sisterhood Is Powerful* (New York: Random House, 1970).

3. Erica Jong, *Fear of Flying* (New York: Signet, 1973); Rita Mae Brown, *Rubyfruit Jungle* (New York: Bantam, 1973); Barbara Raskin, *Loose Ends* (New York: St. Martin's, 1973); Alix Kates Shulman, *Memoirs of an Ex-Prom Queen* (New York: Knopf, 1972); Margaret Atwood, *Surfacing* (New York: Popular Library, 1972); Lisa Alther, *Kinflicks* (New York: Signet, 1975); Sara Davidson, *Loose Change* (Garden City, N.J.: Doubleday, 1977); Marilyn French, *The Woman's Room* (New York: Summit, 1977); Alix Kates Shulman, *Burning Questions* (New York: Knopf, 1978); Marge Piercy, *Vida* (New York: Fawcett Crest, 1979).

4. Rosalind Coward, "Are Women's Novels Feminist Novels?" in Elaine Showalter, ed., *New Feminist Criticism* (New York: Pantheon, 1985), 225–239.

5. Lisa Maria Hogeland, *Feminism and Its Fictions: The Consciousness-Raising Novel and the Women's Liberation Movement* (Philadelphia: University of Pennsylvania Press, 1998).

6. Peter Prescott, "Pipe Dreams," *Newsweek*, October 4, 1976, 62. Cited in Hogeland, *Feminism and Its Fictions*, 83.

7. See Hogeland, *Feminism and Its Fictions*; Maria Lauret, *Feminist Fiction in America* (New York: Routledge, 1994); and Judi M. Roller, *The Politics of the Feminist Novel* (Westport, Conn.: Greenwood, 1986).

8. Hogeland examines the picaresque narrative and Coward, the romance as structures used by feminist fiction writers.

9. Jong, *Fear of Flying*, 154.

10. For example, the 1973 tennis match between Billie Jean King and Bobby Riggs, television shows like *Maude* and *One Day at a Time*, films like *Alice Doesn't Live Here Anymore* and *An Unmarried Woman*. *Life*, *Time*, *Newsweek* and *Playboy* regularly covered feminism in the 1970s. See Hogeland, *Feminism and Its Fictions*, 1–2, for her interpretation of a "feminist public sphere."

11. See Hogeland for her wonderful account of how feminist novels participated in teaching nonactivist women a feminist worldview, or, in her words, "a reading

strategy," we label feminism: "Rather than seeing allegiance to the Women's Liberation Movement in terms of activity, we should see it in terms of a set of reading and interpretive strategies." *Feminism and Its Fictions*, 4.

12. See chapter 5.

13. Audre Lorde, *Zami: A New Spelling of My Name* (Persephone, 1982); Alice Walker, *Meridian* (New York: Washington Square, 1976), and *The Color Purple* (New York: Washington Square, 1982).

14. Philip Roth, *Portnoy's Complaint* (New York: Random House, 1969), 103.

15. Jaqueline Susann, *Valley of the Dolls* (New York: Random House, 1966), 9.

16. D'Emilio and Freedman, *Intimate Matters*, 275–300.

17. Lauret, *Feminist Fiction in America*, 75–78.

18. "View from the Catacombs," *Time*, April 26, 1968, 68–69.

19. Cited in "View from the Catacombs," 66.

20. Norman Mailer, "An Impolite Interview: An Interview with Paul Krassner," in Norman Mailer, *Pieces and Pontifications* (Boston: Little, Brown, 1982), 6–16, 12.

21. Roth, *Portnoy's Complaint*, 127.

22. Mailer, "An Impolite Interview," 12.

23. Roth, *Portnoy's Complaint,* 101–102.

24. Ibid., 104.

25. John Updike, *Couples* (New York: Fawcett Crest, 1968), 113–114.

26. Ibid., 158.

27. Jose Yglesias, "Coupling and Uncoupling," *Nation*, May 13, 1968, 637.

28. Diana Trilling, "Prisoner of Sex," *We Must March My Darlings: A Critical Decade* (New York: Harcourt, Brace, Jovanovich, 1977), 199–210.

29. For example, see Jane Tompkins, *Sensational Designs: The Cultural Work of American Fiction, 1790–1860* (New York: Oxford University Press, 1985), for her analysis of the marginalization of women's writing.

30. Lillian Faderman, *Odd Girls and Twilight Lovers: A History of Lesbian Life in Twentieth-Century America* (New York: Penguin, 1991), 146.

31. Barbara Ehrenreich, Elizabeth Hess, and Gloria Jacobs, *Remaking Love: The Feminization of Sex* (Garden City, N.J.: Anchor, 1987), 42.

32. Jane Howard, "Happiness Is Being Number One," *Life*, August 19, 1966, 69–78, 69.

33. Ibid., 70.

34. See Janice Radway, *Reading the Romance: Women, Patriarchy, and Popular Literature* (Chapel Hill: Duke University Press, 1984).

35. Hogeland, *Feminism and Its Fictions*, 4.

36. Shulman, *Memoirs of an Ex-Prom Queen*, 22.

37. Alther, *Kinflicks*, 31–32.

38. Shulman, *Memoirs of an Ex-Prom Queen*, 56–57.

39. Jong, *Fear of Flying,* 9

40. Shulman, *Memoirs of an Ex-Prom Queen*, 61–62.

41. Ibid., 63.

42. Ibid., 67.

43. Ibid., 130.

44. Ibid., 301.

45. Ibid., 239.

46. Ibid., 157.

47. Shulman, *Memoirs of an Ex-Prom Queen,* 46.

48. Jong, *Fear of Flying*, 195.

49. Shulman, *Memoirs of an Ex-Prom Queen*, 130.

50. Ibid., 135.

51. Alther, *Kinflicks*, 195.

52. Ibid., 186.

53. Alther, *Kinflicks*, 242.

54. Jong, *Fear of Flying*, 94.

55. Ibid., 89.

56. Ibid., 147.

57. Shulman, *Memoirs of an Ex-Prom Queen*, 259.

58. Ibid., 195.

59. Jong, *Fear of Flying,* 17.

60. For a critique of "experience" within feminism, see Judith Grant, *Fundamental Feminism: Contesting the Core Concepts of Feminist Theory* (New York: Routledge, 1993); and Kimberly Christensen, " 'With Whom Do You Believe Your Lot Is Cast?' White Feminism and Racism," *Signs* 22, no. 3 (Spring 1997), 617–648.

61. Hogeland, *Feminism and Its Fictions*, 48.

62. Brown, *Rubyfruit Jungle*, 39.

63. Ibid., 70.

64. Ibid., 71.

65. Adrienne Rich, "Compulsory Heterosexuality and the Lesbian Continuum," *Signs* 5, no. 3 (Summer 1980), 631–659.

66. Brown, *Rubyfruit Jungle*, 70.

67. Ibid., 44.

68. Ibid., 49–50.

69. Ellen Herman, "Being and Doing: Humanistic Psychology and the Spirit of the 1960s," in Barbara Tischler, ed., *Sights on the Sixties* (New Brunswick, N.J.: Rutgers University Press, 1992), 87–101.

70. Firestone, *The Dialectic of Sex*; Germaine Greer, *The Female Eunuch* (New York: Bantam, 1970). See chapter 3.

71. Faderman, *Odd Girls and Twilight Lovers*, 204–246; Arlene Stein, *Sex and Sensibility: Stories of a Lesbian Generation* (Berkeley: University of California Press, 1997), 23–46.

72. Brown, *Rubyfruit Jungle*, 108.

73. Ibid., 246.

74. Jong, *Fear of Flying*, 11.
75. Ibid., 14.
76. Ibid., 9.
77. Ibid., 10.
78. Ibid. 127.
79. Ibid., 122.
80. Ibid., 90.
81. Ibid., 250.
82. Ibid., 277.
83. Ibid., 299.

5. CULTURAL FEMINISM: REIMAGINING SEXUAL FREEDOM, 1975–1982

1. Diane Gosier, L. N. Gardel, Alice Aldrich, "Now or Never," *Off Our Backs* 4, no. 11 (November 1974).
2. Ibid.
3. Vickie Leonard, "On the Other Hand," *Off Our Backs* 4, no. 11 (November 1974).
4. Ann Snitow, "Retrenchment Versus Transformation: The Politics of the Anti-Pornography Movement," in Varda Burstyn, ed., *Women Against Censorship* (Toronto: Douglas and McIntyre, 1985), 107–120, 108.
5. Flora Davis, *Moving the Mountain: The Women's Movement in America Since 1960* (New York: Simon and Schuster, 1991), 385.
6. Arlene Stein, *Sex and Sensibility: Stories of a Lesbian Generation* (Berkeley: University of California Press, 1997), 44.
7. For accounts of lesbian bar life, see the novels of Ann Bannon, collected as *The Beebo Binker Chronicles* (1957, 1959, 1959, 1962; New York: Naiad, 1995); Elizabeth Lapovsky Kennedy and Madeline D. Davis, *Boots of Leather, Slippers of Gold: The History of a Lesbian Community* (New York: Routledge, 1994); Joan Nestle, *A Restricted Country* (Ithaca, N.Y.: Firebrand, 1987); and Stein, *Sex and Sensibility*.
8. Jill Johnston, *Lesbian Nation: The Feminist Solution* (New York: Simon and Schuster, 1973); Lillian Faderman, *Odd Girls and Twilight Lovers: A History of Lesbian Life in Twentieth-Century America* (New York: Penguin, 1991), 215–245.
9. The beginning of lesbian separatism is often traced to the founding of the Furies in 1971. Stein, *Sex and Sensibility*, 113.
10. Charlotte Bunch, "Lesbians in Revolt" (1972), in Charlotte Bunch and Nancy Myron, eds., *Lesbianism and the Women's Movement* (Baltimore: Diana, 1975), 29–36, 30.
11. Ibid., 36.
12. Ibid., 34.
13. Barbara Solomon, "Taking the Bullshit by the Horns," in Bunch and Myron, *Lesbianism and the Women's Movement*, 46.
14. Ibid., 44.

15. Linda La Rue, "The Black Movement and Women's Liberation" (1970), in Beverly Guy-Sheftall, ed., *Words of Fire: An Anthology of African-American Feminist Thought* (New York: New Press, 1995), 164–173, 165.

16. Mary Ann Weathers, "Civil Rights and Women's Liberation," (1970), in Guy-Sheftall, *Words of Fire*, 158–161, 161.

17. Kimberly Christensen, " 'With Whom Do You Believe Your Lot Is Cast?' White Feminism and Racism," *Signs* 22, no. 3 (Spring 1997), 617–648; Judith Grant, *Fundamental Feminism: Contesting the Core Concepts of Feminist Theory* (New York: Routledge, 1993).

18. Combahee River Collective, "A Black Feminist Statement" (1977), in Gloria Hull, Patricia Bell Scott, and Barbara Smith, eds., *All the Women Are White, All the Men Are Black, But Some of Us Are Brave: Black Women's Studies* (New York: Feminist, 1982), 13–22.

19. Audre Lorde, *Zami: A New Spelling of My Name* (Watertown, Mass: Persephone, 1982), and *Sister Outsider: Essays and Speeches* (Trumansburg, N.Y.: Crossing, 1984); bell hooks, *Ain't I a Woman: Black Women and Feminism* (Boston: South End, 1981), and *Feminist Theory from Marigin to Center* (Boston, South End, 1984); Barbara Smith, "Racism and Women's Studies," and "Toward a Black Feminist Criticism," in Hull, Scott, and Smith, *All the Women Are White*, 48–51, 157–176.

20. Combahee River Collective, "A Black Feminist Statement," 17.

21. Faderman, *Odd Girls and Twilight Lovers*, 272.

22. Stein, *Sex and Sensibility*, 109.

23. Mary Daly, Kathllen Barry, Adrienne Rich, and Joan Hoff Wilson, "An Open Letter to the Women's Movement," *Big Mama Rag* 3, no. 2 (August 1974). Cited in Alice Echols, *Daring to Be Bad: Radical Feminism in America, 1967–1975* (Minneapolis: University of Minnesota Press, 1989), 274.

24. Susan Rennie and Kirsten Grimstad, eds., *The New Woman's Survival Sourcebook* (New York: Knopf, 1975), 236. Cited in Echols, *Daring to Be Bad*, 271.

25. Davis, *Moving the Mountain*, 271.

26. Quoted in Stein, *Sex and Sensibility*, 110.

27. Ibid., 111.

28. Ibid., 111.

29. Mary Daly, *Beyond God the Father: Toward a Philosophy of Women's Liberation* (Boston: Beacon, 1973), and *Gyn/Ecology: The Metaethics of Radical Feminism* (Boston: Beacon, 1978); Jane Alport, "Mother Right: A New Feminist Theory," *Ms.* 2, no. 2 (August 1973), 52–55, 88–94.

30. Adrienne Rich, *Of Woman Born: Motherhood as an Experience and Institution* (New York: Norton, 1976).

31. Shulamith Firestone, *The Dialectic of Sex* (New York: Bantam, 1970).

32. Rich, *Of Woman Born*, 39

33. Ibid., 56.

34. Ibid., 71.

35. Ibid., 73.

36. Betty Friedan, *The Feminine Mystique* (New York: Dell, 1963); Kate Millett, *Sexual Politics* (New York: Simon and Schuster, 1970).

37. Ibid., 80–81.

38. Anne Koedt, "The Myth of the Vaginal Orgasm," in Anne Koedt and Shulamith Firestone, eds., *Notes from the Second Year* (New York: New York Radical Feminists, April 1970), 37–41.

39. Ibid., 285–286.

40. Audre Lorde, "Uses of the Erotic: The Erotic as Power," in Laura Lederer, ed., *Take Back the Night: Women on Pornography* (New York: William Morrow, 1980), 295–300.

41. Ibid., 296.

42. Ibid., 295.

43. Ibid., 297.

44. Lorde, *Zami.*

45. Idid., 249.

46. Audre Lorde, "Uses of the Erotic," 300.

47. Ibid., 300.

48. Audre Lorde, "An Open Letter to Mary Daly," in Cherríe Moraga and Gloria Anzaldúa, eds., *This Bridge Called My Back: Writings by Radical Women of Color* (New York: Kitchen Table, 1981), 95.

49. Ibid., 96.

50. See also Audre Lorde, "Age, Race, Class, and Sex: Women Redefining Difference," *Sister Outsider: Essays and Speeches* (Trumansburg, N.Y.: Crossing, 1984).

51. Lorde, "An Open Letter to Mary Daly," 97.

52. Alice Walker, "One Child of One's Own: A Meaningful Digression Within the Work(s)—An Excerpt," in Hull, Scott, and Smith, *All the Women are White*, 43.

53. Ibid., 43.

54. Alport, "Mother Right," 52–55, 88–94; Faderman, *Odd Girls and Twilight Lovers*, 249.

55. Lauri Umansky, *Motherhood Reconceived: Feminism and the Legacies of the Sixties* (New York: New York University Press, 1996), 132–158.

56. Ibid., 127.

57. Ibid., 77–102.

58. Mari Jo Buhle, *Feminism and Its Discontents: A Century of Struggle with Psychoanalysis* (Cambridge: Harvard University Press, 1998), 241.

59. Ibid., 242.

60. Jean Baker Miller, *Towards a New Psychology of Women* (Boston: Beacon, 1976), 6–8.

61. Ibid., 7.

62. Ibid., 10.

63. Ibid., 23.

64. Ibid., 32.

65. Dorothy Dinnerstein, *The Mermaid and the Minotaur: Sexual Arrangements and Human Malaise* (New York: Harper and Row, 1976). Dinnerstein defined sexual arrangements as "the division of responsibility, opportunity, and privilege that prevails between male and female humans, and the patterns of psychological interdependence that are implicit in this division." See 4.

66. Janet Sayers, *Sexual Contradictions: Psychology, Psychoanalysis, and Feminism* (London: Tavistock, 1986), 57.

67. Dinnerstein, *The Mermaid and the Minotaur*, 111.

68. Nancy Chodorow, *The Reproduction of Mothering* (Berkeley: University of California Press, 1978).

69. Ibid., 65.

70. Ibid., 207.

71. Carol Gilligan and John M. Murphy, "Development from Adolescence to Adulthood: The Philosopher and the 'Dilemma of the Fact,' " in D. Kuhn, ed., *Intellectual Development Beyond Childhood,* New Directions for Child Development no. 5 (San Francisco: Jossey-Bass, 1979); Carol Gilligan and Mary F. Belenky, "A Naturalistic Study of Abortion Decisions," in R. Selman and R. Yando, eds., *Clinical Developmental Psychology*, New Directions for Child Development no. 7 (San Francisco: Jossey-Bass, 1980); Carol Gilligan, "Moral Development in the College Years," in A Chickering. ed., *The Modern American College* (San Francisco: Jossey-Bass, 1981); Carol Gilligan, *In a Different Voice: Psychological Theory and Women's Development* (Cambridge: Harvard University Press, 1982).

72. Gilligan, *In a Different Voice,* 170–171.

73. For example, the antipornography legislation written by MacKinnon and Dworkin for Indianapolis and Minneapolis. See Danny Lacombe, *Blue Politics: Pornography and the Law in the Age of Feminism* (Toronto: University of Toronto Press, 1994), 26–29.

74. Nan D. Hunter, "Contextualizing the Sexuality Debate: A Chronology," in Lisa Duggan and Nan Hunter, *Sex Wars: Sexual Dissent and Political Culture* (New York: Routledge, 1995), 16–29, 23.

75. Friedan, *The Feminine Mystique*; Millett, *Sexual Politics*; Firestone, *The Dialectic of Sex*; Koedt, "The Myth of the Vaginal Orgasm"; Ti-Grace Atkinson, "The Institution of Sexual Intercourse," in Koedt and Firestone, *Notes from the Second Year*, 42–47.

76. Echols, *Daring to Be Bad*, 243–287, and "The Taming of the Id: Feminist Sexual Politics, 1968–1983," in Carole Vance, ed., *Pleasure and Danger: Exploring Female Sexuality* (London: Pandora, 1989), 50–72.

77. Susan Brownmiller, *Against Our Will: Men, Women, and Rape* (New York: Simon and Schuster, 1975), 15.

78. Millett, *Sexual Politics*; Koedt, "The Myth of the Vaginal Orgasm"; Germaine Greer, *The Female Eunuch* (New York: Bantam, 1970).

79. Angela Davis, "Rape, Racism, and the Myth of the Black Rapist," in *Women, Race, and Class* (New York: Vintage, 1981), 172–201, 179.

80. Ibid., 201.

81. Susan Griffin, *Rape: The Politics of Consciousness* (New York: Harper and Row, 1979).

82. Andrea Dworkin, "Pornography and Grief," Lederer, *Take Back the Night*, 286–291.

83. Ibid., 287–288.

84. Andrea Dworkin, "For Men, Freedom of Speech; for Women, Silence Please" (1979), Lederer, *Take Back the Night*, 256–258.

85. Ibid., 256–257.

86. Ibid., 257.

87. Dworkin, "Pornography and Grief," 289.

88. Ibid., 288.

89. Dworkin and MacKinnon wrote city ordinances for Minneapolis and Indianapolis in 1983 and 1984, neither of which become law. See Catherine MacKinnon, *Feminism Unmodified: Discourses on Life and Law* (Cambridge: Harvard University Press, 1987); Duggan and Hunter, *Sex Wars*, 24–25. For a historical account, see Lisa Duggan, "Feminist Historians and Anti-Pornography Campaigns: An Overview," in *Sex Wars*, 68–73; and Lynne Segal and Mary MccIntosh, eds., *Sex Exposed: Sexuality and the Pornography Debate* (New Brunswick, N.J.: Rutgers University Press, 1993).

90. Dworkin, "Pornography and Grief," 289.

91. Susan Brownmiller, "Let's Put Pornography Back in the Closet," Lederer, *Take Back the Night*, 252–255.

92. Brownmiller cited the 1970 report of the Presidential Commission on Obscenity and Pornography to support her claim that women found pornography "disgusting." According to the report, 77 percent of men found pornography or visual images arousing, while 68 percent of the women respondents reported "disgust" and "offense." The commission drew these statistics from Alfred Kinsey's *Sexual Behavior of the Human Female*, a telling, if ironic, moment of how the empirical slippages of Kinsey's research on female sexuality functioned in the service of many divergent agendas. See Brownmiller, *Against Our Will*, 392.

93. Ibid., 254.

94. Echols, "The Taming of the Id," 60.

95. Adrienne Rich, "Compulsory Heterosexuality and Lesbian Existence," *Signs* 5, no. 3 (Summer 1980), 631–659.

96. Ibid., 637.

97. Ibid., 641.

98. Ibid., 650.

99. Ibid., 650.

CONCLUSION: NEGOTIATING LEGACIES IN THE FEMINIST SEX WARS, 1982

1. Nan D. Hunter, "Contextualizing the Sexuality Debate: A Chronology," in Lisa Duggan and Nan Hunter, *Sex Wars: Sexual Dissent and Political Culture* (New York: Routledge, 1995), 16–29.

2. Carole S. Vance, "Pleasure and Danger: Towards a Politics of Sexuality," in Carole S. Vance, ed., *Pleasure and Danger: Exploring Female Sexuality* (London: Pandora, 1983), 3.

3. Ibid., 24.

4. Gayle Rubin, "The Leather Menace: Comments on Politics and S/M," in Samois, *Coming to Power: Writings and Graphics on Lesbian S/M* (Boston: Alyson, 1981), 194–229, 217.

5. Lillian Faderman, *Odd Girls and Twilight Lovers: A History of Lesbian Life in Twentieth-Century America* (New York: Penguin, 1991), 250–251.

6. Barbara Lipschutz, "Nobody Needs to Get Fucked," in *Lesbian Voices* (September 1975), 57. Cited in Faderman, *Odd Girls and Twilight Lovers*, 231–232.

7. Alice Echols, *Daring to Be Bad: Radical Feminism in America, 1967–1975* (Minneapolis: University of Minnesota Press, 1989), 213.

8. Faderman, *Odd Girls and Twilight Lovers*, 252.

9. Gayle Rubin, "Talking Sex: A Conversation on Sexuality and Feminism," *Socialist Review* 11 (July-August 1981), 43–62.

10. Faderman, *Odd Girls and Twilight Lovers*, 257.

11. See, for example, Samois, *Coming to Power*; Pat Califia's critique of repression of sexual minorities in feminism, "Among Us, Against Us—The New Puritans," in *The Advocate*" (San Francisco, 1980); *Heresies: The Sex Issue*, 12 (1981); and Varda Burstyn, ed., *Women Against Censorship* (Toronto: Douglas and McIntyre, 1985).

12. Carole S. Vance, "Epilogue," Vance, *Pleasure and Danger*, 431.

13. Carole S. Vance, "Concept Paper," Vance, *Pleasure and Danger*, 443.

14. Coalition for a Feminist Sexuality and Against Sadomasochism, "Notes and Letters," *Feminist Studies* 9, no. 1 (Spring 1983), 180.

15. Ibid., 182.

16. Elizabeth Wilson, "The Context of 'Between Pleasure and Danger': The Barnard Conference on Sexuality," *Feminist Review* 13 (Spring 1983), 35–52.

17. Many of these can be found in Vance, *Pleasure and Danger*.

18. Carla Freccero, "Notes of a Post-Sex Wars Theorizer," in Marianne Hirsch and Evelyn Fox Keller, eds., *Conflicts in Feminism* (New York: Routledge, 1990), 311.

19. Hortense Spillers, "Interstices: A Small Drama of Words," Vance, *Pleasure and Danger*, 74.

20. Ibid., 76.

21. Ibid., 79.

22. Ibid., 81.

23. Ibid., 96.

24. Dorothy Allison, "Public Silence, Private Terror," Vance, ed., *Pleasure and Danger*, 107.

25. Ibid., 108.

26. Ibid., 110.

27. Ibid., 113.

28. Muriel Dimen, "Politically Correct? Politically Incorrect?" Vance, *Pleasure and Danger*, 141.

29. Ester Newton and Shirley Walton, "The Misunderstanding," Vance, *Pleasure and Danger*, 250.

30. Ibid., 148.

31. Joan Nestle, "The Fem Question," Vance, *Pleasure and Danger*, 234.

32. Ibid., 234.

33. Joan Nestle, *A Restricted Country* (Ithaca, N.Y.: Firebrand, 1987); Joan Nestle, ed., *The Persistent Desire: A Femme-Butch Reader* (Boston: Alyson, 1992); Elizabeth L. Kennedy and Madeline Davis, *Boots of Leather, Slippers of Gold: The History of a Lesbian Community* (New York: Penguin, 1993).

34. Faderman, *Odd Girls and Twilight Lovers*, 231–232.

35. Nestle, "The Fem Question," 236.